CONTEMPORARY PERSONALITIES

THE RIGHT HON.
THE EARL OF BIRKENHEAD

CONTEMPORARY PERSONALITIES

By

The Right Hon.

THE EARL OF BIRKENHEAD

P.C., D.L., D.C.L., LL.D.

*High Steward of Oxford University, Lord Rector of
Glasgow University, Treasurer of Gray's Inn*

*With Frontispiece and Photographs and
30 Half-tone Plates from Cartoons by Matt*

Essay Index Reprint Series

BOOKS FOR LIBRARIES PRESS
FREEPORT, NEW YORK

First Published 1924
Reprinted 1969

LIBRARY OF CONGRESS CATALOG CARD NUMBER:
69-17562

PRINTED IN THE UNITED STATES OF AMERICA

To the Memory of
MY BROTHER HAROLD
Upon whose judgment of men and affairs
I almost always relied;
and whose fidelity and devotion
never failed me in
the anxieties of my life
I dedicate this book.

B.

PREFACE

To write a series of contemporary sketches must always be a matter of delicacy and of difficulty. I can hardly expect to have surmounted all the difficulties, or to have avoided all the indelicacies of this task.

But I have made an honest attempt in dealing with men nearly all of whom have been well known to me to give a sincere and unprejudiced view of their special qualities and of the part which they have played in the pregnant years from which I hope, without being confident, that we are about to emerge. I have attempted to discharge my pen from excessive eulogy; and it has not I believe incurred the charge of malice.

BIRKENHEAD

CHARLTON,
   NORTHANTS,
      September, 1924

CONTENTS

The Right Hon.
Andrew Bonar Law

Photo: Elliott & Fry.

CONTEMPORARY PERSONALITIES

The Right Hon. Andrew Bonar Law

MR. ANDREW BONAR LAW was born in New Brunswick in the year 1858, so that he is now sixty-four years old.[1] He was educated at the Gilbert Field School, Hamilton, New Brunswick, and at the High School, Glasgow. He obtained employment in the office of a firm of iron merchants in the City of Glasgow, and was so successful that in 1900 he was able to withdraw with a sufficient competence. And in his case such a withdrawal meant a comfortable competence, for there never lived a Scotsman who was more indifferent to money for its own sake; or more generous for himself, or his friends in his own expenditure.

Business activities did not consume all the young man's time. He was reckoned a good player, according to the standard of those days, at the local lawn tennis club; and in those societies which devoted themselves to literature and debate he was a regular and extremely promising recruit. Carlyle was his early hero, as he has been to so many men who have afterwards become prominent in the State. At this period indeed Carlyle was the guiding star of most aspiring young men. While recognising his remarkable qualities I have myself always been

[1] This article was written some months before Mr. Bonar Law's death.

definitely repelled by his screaming and rather bully-
ing style. But from him Bonar Law imbibed early
the stimulus of an honourable ambition which never
deserted him in later life. And I do not doubt that
the young merchant whose intellectual advancement marched side by side with his business progress
cherished political hopes of the highest order from the
days of his earliest youth. Mr. Asquith is said—I
know not with what truth—to have described him once
as "meekly ambitious." But I can detect no moment
in a distinguished career at which he has shown any
undue meekness, or faltered before any legitimate
occasion of forwarding a legitimate purpose.

His success in business proved so rapid that in
the year 1900 he found himself in a position to
contest the Blackfriars Division of Glasgow, a constituency which he represented until his defeat in
1906. The House of Commons which he so entered
was a very remarkable one. Elected upon the
khaki issue, and pledged to enter upon no controversial topics, it immediately proceeded to deal
in the most controversial manner with the vexed
subjects of Licensing and Education. Soon most
of its abler and younger members became disaffected.
Even Lord Hugh Cecil joined a cave, though he
was never prepared, as Mr. Winston Churchill and
his friends were, to join the Liberal Party.

In a Parliamentary situation already charged
with disillusionment and discontent, Mr. Chamberlain suddenly launched his proposals for Tariff
Reform. This is not the place to discuss in detail
the merits of those proposals, or the manner in
which they were put forward. But it is sufficient
to note that there was hardly anyone upon the

Conservative front bench, with the exception of Mr. Balfour and Mr. Chamberlain, capable of giving an explanation at once intellectual and economic of the new policy. Mr. Akers Douglas was Home Secretary and deputy leader of the House. When left in charge of an economic debate, his tactics were those of reticence. Almost all the young men, tired of seeing promotion given, as the Conservative party has almost always given it, to middle-aged dullards, had ranged themselves, more or less definitely, against the Government. The Opposition, now apparently united, had become very powerful. Debate after debate was raised upon fiscal subjects. The difference of outlook, such as it was, between Mr. Balfour and Mr. Chamberlain was mercilessly exploited. It was seldom that the Government had the better of the argumentative exchange. Upon one of these disagreeable occasions, when matters were going specially badly and there was much need for help and no one to give it, a member known to few by sight, and quite undistinguished in appearance, arose on the Government side to address the House. He used no notes, but with the most complete self-possession, and in a quiet, lucid, and unassuming manner showed that he had a mastery of the business and economic problems involved. An agreeable Glasgow accent contributed an impression of competence. Protection might be right or might be wrong, but it became at once evident that a new controversialist of exceptional attainments believed in and was capable of defending its tenets in relation to the principles of business and economics.

Mr. Bonar Law, indeed, dropped like the gentle

rain from heaven upon the harassed Whips, and had the good fortune of being complimented by Mr. Balfour and Mr. Chamberlain upon so important a Parliamentary intervention. Promotion did not lag behind either merit or expectation, and in 1902, a vacancy occurring, Mr. Bonar Law became Parliamentary Under-Secretary for the Board of Trade. The Tory Party has never really been lacking in humour, and it is interesting to note that the Head of the Board of Trade at that time was the Marquess of Salisbury, who was, and I believe still is, a Free Trader. From 1902 to 1906 the Unionist Government indeed sagged on to discredit and ruin. But the reputation of the new Under-Secretary (except in his own constituency) steadily grew, and had it not been that so many Ministers of higher rank perished in that unhappy Sedan, more attention would have been given to his defeat in the Blackfriars Division.

The set-back was not of long duration. Tariff Reform was still nailed to the mast of the Unionist Party. The strength and health of Mr. Chamberlain were visibly flagging ; the Conservative minority in the House was contemptible in numbers, and a judicious consideration (more judicious perhaps than that to which we have become recently accustomed) of the claims and value of those for whom vacancies might be created, led to the selection of him who had now become recognised second and successor of Mr. Chamberlain in his campaign. Accordingly, he became member for the Dulwich Division of Camberwell a few months after the new Parliament met. In the fierce controversies that followed he played a useful, but not a specially conspicuous, and never a dominating, part. It was at this time that the Unionist Party, under the influence of the Die-hards of the day, committed the incredible folly (playing into Mr. Lloyd George's hands) of rejecting the notorious Budget. I cannot recall that Mr. Bonar Law's influence was strongly exerted on one side or the other of this controversy. I am, however, glad to remember that I spent two hours attempting to convince one of the chief Die-hards of the folly of the step which he was supporting. Our argument took place upon the deck of a yacht upon a delightful summer evening, as we cruised up the Channel. I produced no impression upon Sir Frederick Banbury. I never, in fact, have produced any impression upon those who think as he does. But I am human enough to recall with satisfaction that he has since generously admitted to me that he was wrong and that I was right. He has of course always been wrong; a kind of conversed Cassandra. However, foolish and Die-hard counsels prevailed. The Tory ship once again drifted (as from extreme influence it always has done, and always will do) on to the rocks, and the first General Election of 1910 returned a majority adequate to bring disaster to every cause for which an intelligent Unionist Party would have stood. If wiser counsels had prevailed the faked popularity of the ludicrous land-taxers would soon have exhausted itself. Once again, reaction would have set in; and in six months the Unionist Party would have been where it was before the Budget was introduced. But the rash and foolish challenge made by the Peers carried in its womb the Parliament Act, and the historians of the future will truthfully record that Die-hardism—not through malignity, but through inherent stupidity—destroyed the House of Lords, which, under wise guidance, could have been maintained for generations as a bulwark against Communism and anarchy.

I have said that, in my recollection, Mr. Bonar Law was neutral in this controversy. But in another, and an equally grave one, which succeeded he took an active part. Were the Peers to acquiesce in their own destruction, or, having challenged an issue so terrible, were they, founding themselves upon principle, to carry their quarrel to an end, whatever end that might be ? Many of us who had opposed the original decision took the view that it was impossible for the Peers *propter vitam vivendi perdere causas.* Lord Curzon took that view at first, but afterwards (and rather quickly) abandoned it. Mr. Bonar Law agreed with him. So did Mr. Balfour and Lord Lansdowne. Against these were Mr. Austen Chamberlain, Sir Edward Carson, Lord Milner, Lord Salisbury, Lord Halsbury and Lord Selborne. On this occasion the party of concession prevailed, and the vital power of the House of Lords was surrendered for ever. The Die-hards, having compelled Mr. Balfour to throw out the Budget, characteristically began to place on his shoulders the blame for the consequences. " B.M.G." (Balfour Must Go) became the motto of these loyal men.

The corrosive effect of intrigue within the Party grew and grew, until early in 1911 Mr. Balfour, deeply wounded, it may be supposed, at the ingratitude of a Party in whose service he had lavished his shining intellectual gifts, resigned his position as Leader. For the vacancy thus created there were two aspirants, with claims by no means unequally balanced. Walter Long brought his distinguished lineage, his remarkable commonsense, and his great administrative experience to the lists. Austen Chamberlain was the son of an illustrious father ; had himself held high office, and was continually giving evidence that his mastery of Parliamentary efficiency was strengthening and deepening. No one thought of any other possible candidate, and the partisans of the two rival leaders became more and more active.

It was at this juncture in the career of Mr. Bonar Law that the present Lord Beaverbrook, then Sir Max Aitken, first gave evidence of the intuitive political " flair " which he possesses. With as much boldness, subtlety, and friendship as Lucien Bonaparte showed on the 18th Brumaire, he realised that a supreme opportunity lay in front of a third candidate whose intervention might avoid the disruptive consequences of a contested election at the Carlton Club. Lord Beaverbrook is a vivid and arresting personality, capable of great friendships, not unwilling to sustain powerful antagonisms, and possessing immense driving power. He persuaded Mr. Bonar Law to allow his name to be put forward. Both the other candidates with great public spirit withdrew in favour of one whose claims—if only anyone had thought of them—were not in themselves inconsiderable ; and Mr. Bonar Law became Leader of the Unionist Party in the House of Commons.

This is not the place to examine the history of that Leadership from 1911--1914. It was direct and courageous, if occasionally a little naïve and inexperienced. All the time the simplicity and

7

sincerity of his character endeared him to those with whom he fought side by side in a desperate struggle. And he was, on the whole, aided rather than hindered by the ludicrous intellectual contempt which critics as acute as Mr. Asquith and Mr. Winston Churchill genuinely felt for him.

All the time the Ulster crisis raged. His nerve did not fail him during the anxious days when, with Sir Edward Carson, he raised the flag of resistance to a policy which the whole world now admits to have been criminal and impossible of attainment.

Then came 1914, and with it the beginning of Mr. Bonar Law's admirable war services. He wrote, with Lord Lansdowne, a spontaneous letter to Mr. Asquith assuring the Government of the support of the Conservative Party in the long and bloody task which confronted the nation. Nor did he ever fail to carry out this pledge until the responsibility became more direct when the first Coalition Government was formed in May, 1915. Of that Government it is sufficient to say that, although Mr. Bonar Law's gifts and position were never fairly recognised by Mr. Asquith, he none the less supported it until it became apparent to all that its doom was sealed. The emergence of Mr. Lloyd George as a powerful and brilliant war leader had impressed the whole world. But the King was in the first place advised to send for Mr. Bonar Law. It is typical of the relationship between the two men—a relationship which only ended with Mr. Bonar Law's health—that the Conservative leader utterly refused to place himself in competition with the demoniac energy of Mr. Asquith's successor. He agreed to serve under him, and with that agreement the first Coalition Government tottered in irretrievable collapse.

The events of the intervening years until the time of Mr. Bonar Law's illness may be treated for this purpose shortly. Under the agony of a double bereavement he discharged the duties of Leader of the House of Commons, Chancellor of the Exchequer, and member of the War Cabinet, with admired efficiency. In the actual conduct of the war, as in the details of the Treaty of Peace, he leaned constantly and even heavily upon Mr. Lloyd George. To the very moment when his health failed he was an earnest supporter of the necessity of coalition. No one, in fact, can doubt that, if his health had not failed, he would have declined, as Mr. Chamberlain declined, to haul down the colours in which he believed at the bidding of a minority of the party, whom it is certain that intellectually he despised. But his health did fail him, and he parted, the Coalition still intact, from Mr. Lloyd George, with friendship and even with emotion.

Nor, when his health was happily, if only for a period, restored, did any difference of principle cloud the old relationship. The more foolish section of the party besought him to curse the Irish Treaty. On the contrary, in a remarkable speech he went out of his way to bless and approve it.

The irony of the situation was that Lord Salisbury and his friends, who derived their principal driving power against the Coalition from the Irish settlement, should have taken office under a Prime Minister who not only declared that it must be carried out, but who had voted and spoken for it before it was binding upon Parliament.

I approach now the meeting at the Carlton Club. Whatever else is doubtful, it is, I think, certain that had Mr. Bonar Law's health remained good he would have found himself in precisely the position of Mr. Chamberlain. The situation therefore required careful handling. Nobody but Mr. Bonar Law (if he knows) can be sure with what intention he went to the Carlton Club meeting. I myself suspect that he did not himself clearly know, and that the loud cheers given to him, in marked contrast with Mr. Chamberlain's tepid welcome, decided his action at the last moment. It is claimed that his action saved the Tory Party. Is it saved? How much will be left of it when this Government has finished with it? Are we approaching another 1906 débâcle? Is this Government alone the most efficient instrument available for the purpose of combating Socialism? Was it wise to extrude with contempt from co-operation in this task many men highly qualified, both from experience and combative quality, to render stout help? The answer to these questions, when time has revealed it, will render the task of the historian easier than ours.

Another interesting question presents itself. What would have happened if Mr. Bonar Law had flung his persuasive powers on the same side as Mr. Chamberlain and Lord Balfour? Few will doubt that the result would have been different. The responsibility, then, is principally his, and the credit, if credit emerge, will be his, too. And both the responsibility and the credit (if there be credit) will prove to be very great.

The Right Hon.
The Earl of Balfour, K.G., O.M.

The Right Hon. the Earl of Balfour, K.G., O.M.

I T requires some audacity to attempt to write of Lord Balfour's career or to portray his character in a brief space. It is indeed like sketching a chameleon upon a postage stamp. He was already a Prime Minister seventeen years ago. Yet, while other ex-Premiers, like Lord John Russell and Lord Rosebery, long survived or survive their retirement from that eminence, they adopted a detached attitude until they reached the Nirvana of complete political quiescence.

Lord Balfour, on the contrary, remains an active force to this day. He has led an Opposition. He has occupied high Government office almost up to the present time—so that his actual political life, which began with his return to Parliament in 1874, covers almost exactly half a century. And the quantity as expressed in time is balanced by the quality of the intellect devoted to what must often have appeared to it fleeting things, and by the practical achievement wrested out of the conflict. So that in the end he remains, now that Morley, too, has gone, a great and solitary figure, a member who voted with Disraeli, a Secretary of State who was the right hand of his uncle, Lord Salisbury, a tactician who had fought Parnell in Ireland, a debater who had crossed no inefficient sword with Gladstone at Westminster.

And his youth stands out against the years as his experience ripens with them. That lean, active frame seems to have found in exercise some method of averting the physical fate which time brings with it, just as some other cause, possibly the study of metaphysics and science, has evolved some charm which prevents that decay, or, at least, arrestment, of the intellect, which is the usual penalty of age. If age could, if youth knew—the proverb has been falsified by the mere existence of Arthur Balfour.

And yet this brilliant figure—a man whose name was as familiar to our fathers as to ourselves—was excluded a year ago from taking his share in the direction of the State at one of the most critical moments of its destiny. Had he assisted with counsel the Government then formed, the history alike of the Conservative and Socialist parties would have been written with a different pen. His view of the election policy was not concealed. Had it prevailed, the Conservatives would have been in office to-day; the Socialists perhaps not for ten years. And Tariff Reform would not be dead. *Dis aliter !*

But I am anticipating the story of Lord Balfour's career. He began almost as a dilettante in an age I was not privileged to see. It was a wonderful period when one section of the Victorians grew tired of accumulating wealth in the towns and another emerged from the rather stuffy country-house atmosphere of the Whig and Tory nobility. The combination turned to intellect as a new kind of diversion. It broke out in various forms at a time when I was still at school—into Decadence, New Art, the forcible cult of Henley and Kipling,

the almost all-inclusive embrace of the " Souls "—
or into a renewed interest in social problems and the
life of the poor.

Through all this Arthur Balfour moved like a
wonderful dream, of which he, too, was a part. But
it may be noted that this new development coincided
not entirely by accident with a revulsion against
the claim of Liberalism to possess the monopoly
of intellect. The ex-Premier, cradled in Hatfield,
was thus born of Toryism out of Scepticism. Behind all this art or fun, or popular concerts, there
lurked a steely nature just as a rapier might, by a
chance, be concealed in a parasol. Despite his
affectations Mr. Balfour was becoming a fierce party
controversialist educated in the school of Randolph
Churchill; but never for a moment dominated by
that school, or by the personality of Randolph. Mr.
Churchill, in his biography of his father, has recorded
the early stages of this development, and has recalled
how Lord Balfour's adhesion to the Fourth Party
was regarded as socially important, but politically
negligible, until, speaking with unexpected vehemence and power, he denounced the Kilmainham
Treaty as " an infamy." Mr. Churchill has put
his own construction on the relation of the Fourth
Party to their recruit. He suggests, in a perfectly
courteous manner, that Arthur Balfour's objection
to the Old Gang was limited to the idea of discredit-
ing Sir Stafford Northcote in the Commons in order
to clear the way for Lord Salisbury, the leader in
the Lords; and that he abandoned Randolph the
moment this object was achieved. His Tory-Demo-
cracy, according to this view, had a " limited ob-
jective." It would be fair to retort that the bio-

grapher has, on this particular subject, a " limited "
outlook.

Lord Balfour was, no doubt, bored in common
with the great bulk of the Conservative Party of
the period with the futile opposition of the " Goats."
Like Lord Randolph, he had no great respect for
" holy men." But then, neither had Lord Salisbury. The Marquis and Randolph, as their correspondence proves, had an equal contempt for the
fat bourgeois mediocrity of the Front Bench. On
this point the three men were agreed. But when
it came to a real death-grapple, and final intellectual
choice, Mr. Arthur Balfour sided with his uncle
and not with his friend. Why not ? Allowing
for differences of age, and, consequently, of environment, his ingrained convictions were not so very
different from those of the older man—also a Tory,
a scientist, and a political sceptic. Against all this
Randolph could offer nothing except temperament,
genius, a sympathy with the masses—but of constructive intellectual scheme, or conviction, not a
shred. One may search the Randolph Churchill
biography without picking up the very element
of an idea, except a few tags stolen from Disraeli
about the essential unity of People, Throne, and
Altar.

It was intellect, and not interest, which drew
A. J. Balfour to Lord Salisbury's side. The Marquis
had a creed ; he believed in executive government
by highly trained people, and he disbelieved in almost
everything else, except in science. His nephew was
more susceptible to the democratic conditions which
the age imposed. He would not have denied the
inevitability of a more popular form of government

than that sustained by the Tories up to 1832, or imposed by the Liberals between 1832 and 1867. He would be far less certain than Lord Salisbury that Property was in danger from Democracy, and, while believing in individual talent and leadership, he would not in the least agree with his senior that all social legislation was necessarily a change for the worse. Yet when all this has been said, it may be doubted whether there were any great differences in view or temperament between the political general at Hatfield and his successor—except that the first dealt in most cases in certainties, and the second was quite content with probabilities.

What Arthur Balfour may have felt with conviction, as the advance guard and leader of a group of distinguished young men like Alfred Lyttelton, George Wyndham, and Harry Cust, was the absurdity of the Liberal Victorian claim to an undisputed possession of the field of intellectual predominance. The political philosophy of Bentham, Mill and Cobden was so easy to riddle—and has to-day been left by modern thought little better than a sieve. Yet in the 'eighties and 'nineties there was still an extant belief that no man could be intelligent unless he was a Liberal. Against this notion Lord Balfour's mere existence was a standing protest. And he shatters other cherished beliefs too—the idea that no scientist can be a philosopher, no philosopher a scientist, and that a scientist cannot have, and a metaphysician will prove not to have, a religion.

Ultimately the fact remains that the greatest political and philosophic intelligence of our age is a Conservative, while the Liberalism even of men so able as Mr. Asquith or Sir John Simon has about it a smack of the incarnation of Beta-Plus—just sufficient philosophic intelligence not to fly with unpinioned wings.

Of this brilliant little Tory group Lord Balfour, though the senior, is the only survivor. Its members came from both Universities. One of Lord Balfour's most striking attributes is that no one first meeting him would be absolutely certain at a glance whether he hailed from Oxford or Cambridge—a thing which can be said of few men. Yet Cambridge undoubtedly gave the bias to his thought. Had he been at Christ Church he would conceivably have devoted himself to metaphysics and theology; Cambridge guided him to philosophy and science.

Some of the political " Souls " allowed their social attractions to interfere with their Parliamentary efficiency. But Lord Balfour resisted this temptation. In his celebrated phrase about Mrs. Asquith " he was thinking of having a career of his own." And in a sense he did live for himself, think for himself, and fight for himself. The sweetness of his manner gave no indication of the steel-like strength of his resolve.

So when he was made Irish Secretary in the stormy 'eighties most people thought the appointment a job. The new Secretary instantly justified his promotion. His subtle, and hitherto concealed, debating batteries were unmasked with crushing effect. Unflinchingly firm in supporting his cause and his officials, he was, perhaps, for this very reason, far more popular in Ireland among the ranks of his opponents than many Home Rule Secretaries have been. His variety in debate did not lag behind his strength of purpose. " You may be right," he cried, "in calling my Government odious; but I will not suffer you to make it also ridiculous!"

Later, when he had become Premier, he was severely censured for his treatment of George Wyndham and of the latter's Irish policy. The charge, crudely put, is that of the betrayal of an intimate, with whose views he agreed, for the purpose of placating Ulster bigotry. The evidence on which any opinion on this vexed question could be based is by no means fully published; but certain general considerations certainly govern the case. In the first place, the average Conservative regarded the Land Act policy as one thing and the Devolution policy as something quite distinct. The first was obviously on principle a Conservative idea because it aimed at creating order by improving social and material conditions. Even so, carrying the Land Act was a desperate battle which strained all the Premier's influence with certain sections of his party. On one occasion Lord Carson broke out practically into open revolt, saying that he had ninety followers who would vote against the Bill.

However, the great task was accomplished, and the prophets of failure and evil put out of countenance by the working of the Act. But the second scheme, that of Devolution, was by no means an essential Conservative ideal. It might have been, and, indeed, on one occasion was, introduced as a Liberal measure of Home Rule. Looking backwards, I have no doubt that it would have been a wise measure to pass in the opening years of the century. But the practical point is that it was by no means an easy measure, with its semi-Liberal flavour, for a Conservative Premier to recommend

in any event. To press it when a heavy, even if
lucrative, blow had just been struck at the party
of Ascendency in Ireland might easily have proved
fatal to Conservatism.

George Wyndham did not see matters in this
light. To him Land Act and Devolution were twin
constituents of one common progressive Irish policy.
Then in his generous enthusiasm he made one or
two bad tactical slips; and so it happened that he
fell with his policy. But was the Prime Minister
very much, or at all, to blame for all this ? He was
being asked to do what was probably the impossible
—at least, he was being invited to take part in a
crusade. Crusades do not appeal to Lord Balfour's
temperament.

In some ways Lord Balfour's political good
fortune culminated when he attained the Premiership. For many years he enjoyed both in the country
and in Parliament, the friendship, alliance, and
assistance of Mr. Joseph Chamberlain—a priceless
asset. For each party to the combination supplied
exactly the qualities the other lacked, and yet there
was no breach of sympathy between them. This
close union was most unhappily destined to reach
an end.

Lord Salisbury, on his retirement in 1902, left
his nephew something of a *damnosa hereditas :* the
league-long wave of Unionist and Imperialist sentiment which had swept Conservatism along ever since
1884 was beginning to lose its vital force. Other
voices talking Social Reform were to be heard with
an ever-rising clamour in the country. The physical
and financial effort of the South African War, puny
as it appears to this generation, was beginning to

react. Trade was bad, and a 2s. income-tax appeared staggering to our happy forefathers. Mr. Chamberlain, indeed, had provided the Premier with an ample majority by the snap election of 1900, and several wise and moderate measures of Reform which, like the Education Act, the Licensing Act, and the Irish Land Act, have proved of enduring social value, had been placed on the Statute Book. Yet the Khaki Election had in reality been a mistake. It would have been better to let the Liberal forces assert their claim to power in a moderate form and with a majority of a reasonable size. But the Conservative Party when accustomed to power cannot get rid of the idea that it is theirs for ever by vested right. This is particularly the nightmare of the Dieharder. It was clear that the horse was flagging, but a new stimulus could be applied in Mr. Chamberlain's enthusiastic championship of the idea of National Protection and Imperial Tariff Reform. But while one section, and the most democratic and popular, responded magnificently to the spur, there was great discord among the older men. What was gained on the swings of vigour was lost on the roundabouts of internal dissension, and the party went to its doom in the crash of 1906.

It has often appeared to me strange that Lord Balfour, with an interest so soundly established in abstruse subjects like bimetallism, takes so little real interest in the economics of the fiscal problem. That an intellect like his could accept the dreary dogmas of Free Trade, based on a philosophic conception of life and fact long since exploded, would be, of course, impossible. But I should have imagined that he might have found a fascination in exploring the more recent European theories of the Protectionist creed. In the event, however, he seems to have applied an almost equal scepticism to both contentions, to have left the controversy in the far less able hands of his lieutenants, and to have concentrated his immense dialectic resources upon the task of preserving the Parliamentary unity of his party. This he did with incredible ingenuity and resource, though at the cost of parting with some old friends.

After 1906, and in what appeared to be a hopeless opposition, he displayed all the inexhaustible courage, tireless energy, and dialectic skill which he had shown as Irish Secretary. In a single session he had dominated a hostile House of Commons. But the final cards, under pressure of men with more enthusiasm than insight, were badly played by forcing the decisive battle on the Budget issue just when Liberalism was failing under the weight of its own ineptitude. This decision, I am able to say with knowledge, received an impetus, which in the event proved decisive, from Mr. Joseph Chamberlain at a moment when the opinion of that great man no longer retained its earlier value.

After a time even Lord Balfour's patience was exhausted by the continual attacks of extreme partisanship among his own followers, and he retired from the leadership as the result of a blunder which was not in essence his. He was no doubt recalling his own career when he said at the famous Carlton Club meeting : " It has never been a Conservative principle to abandon a leader : though I concede that it has sometimes been a Conservative practice." He might have added, with historical truth, that it has been an almost invariable Conservative practice.

Right Hon. the Earl of Balfour, K.G.

His career seemed to be definitely ended, whereas strangely enough it was just about to start anew. The breaking and fusing of parties which sprang out of the war called him again to positions of high authority and decisive influence. One is apt to forget how intimately Lord Balfour has been associated with the foreign policy of the last forty, or nearly fifty, years. He went to Berlin with Beaconsfield and Salisbury in 1878. The latter, both by early intellectual interest and by later official life, possessed a consummate first-hand knowledge of European affairs dating from the early 'sixties. By all this experience Lord Balfour profited even when he was holding quite other posts in successive Ministries. During his Premiership, therefore, he was able to assume, to a large extent, the direction of our foreign policy, and to inaugurate, in conjunction with Lord Lansdowne, the new system which, when accepted by Lord Grey, brought France, and finally Russia, into clear accord with Great Britain. As Foreign Secretary and President of the Council, both during and after the war, he was able to devote to his country the immense fruits of this garnered experience.

And this the man, luminous in judgment, unrivalled in knowledge, unquestioned in integrity, whose charm dissolves all personal enmity, an ex-Premier, an ex-Foreign Secretary, an ex-leader of the Conservative Party, tracing a direct descent from the most glorious and successful days of that party's leadership, is happily once again restored to the councils of a historic party. I do not insist here (it would be inopportune) upon the disasters which his party sustained by rejecting his advice at the Carlton Club. "This was the noblest Roman of them all," but an inexperienced generation preferred the medicine of younger counsellors. I hope they like it now that they have got it.

Upon the personal side it is not easy to write, for there is too much to say. He brings to life in all its aspects a freshness which age cannot quench; and a curiosity and charm which time and knowledge have failed to dim. He is in thought and interest as modern as modernity itself; and yet retains an exquisite courtliness of manner which belonged to a polished few in a vanished age. The English language in his hands is a supple and beautiful instrument, fit to express the various purposes of a very various mind. No living philosopher, except, perhaps, F. H. Bradley, in his cloistered Merton study, has written upon impalpable subjects with such beauty, ease, and limpidity.

His qualities are such and so manifold that no short or superficial survey of the political history of England will provide an Elder Brother so radiant, so youthful, so sophisticated, so learned.

The Right Hon.
H. H. Asquith, M.P.

The Right Hon. H. H. Asquith, M.P.

MR. ASQUITH stands in that half-light which falls on statesmen who have held the Premiership once, and of whom it is uncertain whether time or opportunity will allow them another term. The full glare has passed on. Will the orb of Party revolve again to disperse a twilight which already begins to take on a tinge of the night of history?

The war has so foreshortened events that much of the ex-Premier's career already belongs to the historian. He is the last of the Gladstonian age—which seems after the storm-blast of this century remote even to one who was an undergraduate at the time of the second Home Rule Bill. And he is a typical Gladstonian-Liberal in a sense in which Lord Balfour could never be described as a typical Salisburian-Conservative. He seems to breathe the quintessence of the years which stretch from the glories of Midlothian to the bleak wastes of the Newcastle Programme.

When I spoke on the occasion of the unveiling of his bust in the Debating Hall of the Oxford Union, I had a fanciful idea that the sculptor had of intent given an almost monolithic appearance to the statue —quite dwarfing the naturally more ponderous frame of the late Lord Salisbury. It was to remind us that here we had a living relic of the political Ice Age. Already a large part of Mr. Asquith's career had passed the test of history and been judged by time as something of permanent excellence.

23

Mr. Asquith sprang of the class which rallied to Mr. Gladstone's " Radicalism " when the influences of birth and property which had long sustained the Whig cause passed definitely to the other side. His circumstances gave him the chance of a good education if no opportunity were let slip. As a result he was almost the first Balliol Scholar to come from outside the circle of the great schools. His entrance to the stage of Oxford was therefore almost revolutionary, and the authorities pricked up their ears when they heard that the City of London School had obtained the blue ribbon of scholarship. Yet that scholarship, though remarkably sound, never rose to the level attained by Raymond. The father had to be content with " Proxime Accessit," where the son helped himself with consummate ease to Irelands and Cravens. Mr. Asquith lacks temperament—and therefore both its blessings and its curses.

He was no mean star in the constellation of the Milners and the Curzons which shone forth in the golden age of Jowett at Balliol. " Cæsarian," apparently, was the epithet applied to Asquith by young Oxford. The comparison with the youthful Julius would be absurd, and yet one can see a certain meaning in the epithet. Clarity of judgment—a colourlessness of style which is the essence of Classicism, a form of detachment slightly inhuman—all qualities which make personality hard to grasp for subsequent generations—are Asquithian and also Cæsarian.

And so Mr. Asquith came to the Bar with his firsts and his Union honours. It was the obvious career for him—as natural as for Lord Morley to stray into the hallowed places of political literature and journalism.

It is said that Asquith received his chance at the Bar by a series of flukes, such as the absence of a leader on a critical occasion in the Parnell case.

I do not believe that a mind like his could, in the circumstances, have failed of success, but I feel sure that the volume of his practice was limited by his mental endowments. In the ordinary course of events the luminosity and impartiality of his mind would have predestined him to the Bench.

And it is certain that if he had devoted himself to the scientific study of law he would have become one of the Empire's great judges. Balanced, impressive, patient, courteous, scholarly, and learned, he would have been an ornament to the Final Court of Appeal. To speculate upon what might have happened with different decisions is a fascinating if a futile performance. But I have, none the less, often wished that it had been possible for the change from the Asquith to the Lloyd George Administration to have been effected rather by substitutions than by resignations. How different would have been the development of our politics ; how different the fate of the Liberal Party, if Mr. Asquith had passed from No. 10, Downing Street, to the Woolsack ; leaving behind him the memory of great services greatly rendered ; and carrying to his new office so much weight and so much character !

But his absorbed interest in politics made the question academic. Here he never doubts where he stands. He is a Liberal of the older dispensation, just touched with the new version of Whiggism Lord Rosebery called Liberal Imperialism. His self-consistency is almost terrible. He could ' defend all his policies by logic, which makes one doubt whether he could defend them all in reality. The world cannot be shaped to suit a logical system.

His appointment to the Home Secretaryship in 1892 came almost as a surprise. Yet, next to Lord Morley, he was undoubtedly Mr. Gladstone's favourite disciple and narrowly resembled his past chief in his powers of fence.

After this the Liberal Party was in Opposition till 1906. They were troublous times. No one was quite certain on whom the mantle of Elijah had descended, except the people who were sure that it had fallen on them. In these circumstances, an Opposition knows that its duty is to oppose—its own leaders. The veil of the temple had been rent in twain only to reveal two separate tabernacles. One belonged to the pro-Boer section of Sir Henry Campbell-Bannerman and the other to Lord Rosebery. The Liberal Imperialists thus became a definite group distinguished in their Party by their intellect rather than by their numbers.

It has always appeared to me a little strange that Mr. Asquith should have been one of the planets in this tiny, if brilliant, solar system. One would not have expected the Radical element in his mentality to have been so completely submerged. But in some ways the chance was fortunate for Liberalism in 1906 and for England in 1914. It was the Radical extremists who won the election of 1906, but the spoils of office did not, upon a close analysis, go to the victors. Sir Henry Campbell-Bannerman came to an accommodation with the Vice-Presidents of the Liberal League by which the Exchequer, the Foreign Office, and the War Office passed into the hands of men whom Radical enemies dubbed as Whigs.

These appointments proved to be of intense significance. The foreign policy of the Empire was vitally affected, and when the final clash with Germany came it was the heads of the great departments who enabled Mr. Asquith as Premier to carry the Cabinet and the Liberal Party with him, and so avoid the terrible, perhaps ruinous, calamity of a powerful pro-German opposition.

Mr. Asquith played no small part in effecting the reconciliation between the sundered wings of Liberalism. Of all the Liberal Leaguers he was the least suspect of heresy. Even quite stupid people recognised his adherence to the doctrines of the older Radicalism. The issue of Fiscal Reform raised by Mr. Joseph Chamberlain in 1903 came as a godsend to him, by which he might re-establish his claim to orthodoxy. Watching in those days with all the keenness of a Parliamentary candidate the swaying of fortune in this battle of giants, one could not help admiring the immense resources of learning, eloquence, and logic which the Free Trade spokesman rallied to his assistance. He does not revel in trade statistics, as did Mr. Bonar Law, but he has the capacity for getting up the intricate details of a brief entirely in harmony with his own convictions. That these convictions may be profoundly erroneous does not alter the fact. All this found its reward in the Chancellorship of the Exchequer and finally in the Premiership.

We are no sooner born than we begin to die, and the tragedy of Mr. Asquith's loss of office may be said to begin to date from the day when he became Premier. He has a mind at once too rigid on principle and too accommodating in detail. The two qualities may very easily blend into a whole not advantageous to a statesman. Rigidity in fixed political principle easily leads to an utter disregard of external reality—a force unconditioned by party. Again perpetual accommodations over detail, particularly of a more or less personal description, tend to sap the vitality of principle. Mr. Asquith, unfortunately for himself, had to deal with at least two grave menaces not coming within the ordinary category of British politics—problems for the solution of which his temperament was by nature suited. He also always held office by a majority which was in essence composite, and demanded a continual practice of the arts of compromise. His original Cabinet was not over-representative of the rank and file, and he had to consider the Labour Party and —after 1910—the Nationalists. The quality demanded from the leader was a dialectic sufficient to defend these accommodations in the House of Commons without derogating from the dignity of his position in the country or from his authority over his own party. All this I admit was done in a masterly manner. It is my main impression of Mr. Asquith in the pre-war Parliament.

He was, indeed, a very remarkable Parliamentary debater. He was, without notes and without preparation, able to produce in endless succession a long series of Ciceronian sentences which recalled to an audience, which had hardly known it, the classical period of Parliamentary oratory. He never lacked the just word ; he never failed to improvise that subtle cadence of the sentence which is pure gold to him who has studied the qualities of spoken rhetoric. The form, indeed, was matchless. If at times the spirit was less mighty than the expression, it may be replied that it is not given to every age to produce an orator armed with every gift. Disraeli was brilliant and mordant in form, but wholly lacking in the gifts of a natural orator. Gladstone was inspired in the gift of spoken eloquence, but turgid to such a degree that it is now impossible to read any long speeches of his without impatience.

And it must be remembered of Mr. Asquith that the speech at the very beginning of the war, in which he defined the conditions under which, and under which alone, we should sheathe the sword was one of the noblest, as it was one of the most courageous, of the war.

But could he have succeeded if his very nature had not become attuned to the nightly task of reconciling the irreconcilable, and keeping up with portentous solemnity what was often little better than a farce? And then wave after wave of actuality broke on this man, who was at once rigid, subtle and unactual. The dependence on the Nationalist vote raised an Ulster issue which no Parliamentary adroitness could avoid, and then, like some long Atlantic roller, topping all its predecessors, came down the shattering deluge of the war.

Mr. Asquith, indeed, met the onset with the courage and endurance of a stoic, and the nation should never forgo their gratitude to the Premier of 1914, who kept the straight course in the crucial moment of our destiny. But the long years of compromise had left their mark on the intellect; the edge of executive keenness had been blunted, the principles of Gladstonian or even Roseberian Liberalism were hardly adequate guides with which to meet a whole world at war.

From Mr. Asquith, as the head of the Government, I never received anything but great courtesy, consideration, and loyalty to a subordinate colleague. Loyalty to the Members of his Government and Party has always been his distinguishing characteristic. He will support them even when they are manifestly in the wrong. But every virtue may degenerate into a vice, and such a tendency may easily produce a clique. And a clique, however well intentioned, is a thing which stands between a man and the opinion of the world—particularly if that opinion be harsh and therefore dangerous. It was under the influence of those who surrounded him that, in 1916, Mr. Asquith went blindly to his doom.

Yet in the early days of the struggle his calmness, his refusal to be hustled into measures which would have broken the united front of the nation, were a priceless asset. His judgment was the main influence which enabled Conscription, in the teeth of his special protégé Sir John Simon, to be carried by public acclaim. Had he failed the Empire must have perished. And when the trend of events marched past him, and ultimately over him, the conflict reached an intensity almost unknown to history. The nation was thoroughly broken to all the works of war. Sacrifice had already reached such a point that all that the people demanded was action, action, action, and victory at any cost.

The Whig side of Mr. Asquith's temperament could not acclimatise itself to this hectic and feverish atmosphere. He had been steeped too long in caution and compromise to fling a life-habit away like a garment. The phrase " Wait and see " was, no doubt, used against him unfairly, in the sense that it had originally been applied to a perfectly legitimate, if very irritating, refusal to expose in advance a weak hand to a pertinacious Parliamentary adversary. Yet, when the Press pinned this label to the Premier's coat tails, the people inferred, however unreasonably, that it described accurately the weakness of Asquith's war mentality. He was too stiff in his joints to sprint at the finish. "*Non tali auxilio non defensoribus istis,*" it was said by many, was Great Britain to be saved. Mr. Lloyd George was designated as the instrument of salvation, and proved to be so.

Of course, if Mr. Asquith had fully understood the urgent necessities of the war or the temper of the people, there would have been no crisis in 1916, for there would have been no need of one. But it was precisely because he did not appreciate these factors correctly that, tragically misled by his friends, he failed to realise the extent of the forces his successor had at his disposal. They were very powerful—the greater part of the Conservative rank and file—a Press which under war conditions had usurped the functions of the Opposition—and behind all a driving public opinion. In those days the darkness surrounding No. 10, Downing Street, was like that of Ancient Egypt, and the tactics inspired by ignorance and flattery resulted in overwhelming defeat. And the stroke which broke Mr. Asquith shattered Liberal unity.

What of the future ? Prophecy is always a fruitful method of imperilling one's reputation. One can only point out the probabilities which attend any given course of action. Mr. Asquith still adheres to the strictest sect of the older Liberalism. He seems to regard the war as a storm in the night which has passed away, leaving the electoral to-morrow exactly like the political yesterday. Liberal-ism somehow can be continued in direct continuity with the doctrines laid down by Mr. Gladstone. Of the younger men, only the born pedants agree with this conception. The rest of those whom the war caught at a more impressionable age see ac-curately enough that Liberalism can never be quite the same again, however difficult it may be to decide on the precise form which the new creed must take.

But Mr. Asquith would not be Mr. Asquith if he saw this. His danger has always been fixity of conviction carried to an extreme. The character has been more fluid than the intellect. It has not resisted the mellowing influences of time. Glancing from the early photographs to the later develop-ment of the face, one can trace the change from the youthful clear-cut features of the Cæsarian youth to the kindly countenance of the older statesman, which yet still preserves the sardonic curve of the mouth.

And Mr. Asquith's character is a national asset. He fights cleanly, wins without insolence and loses without rancour. In the rotund form of his oratory and the absolute integrity of motive and conduct he recalls to a perverse generation all that was best of a bygone age. And it will be said of him, when the last criticism is weighed, that here was a statesman, honourable, generous, and sagacious, who rendered great service to his country at a time when no other living Englishman could have done that which he did ; and without which the State might have tottered to ruin.

The Right Hon.
David Lloyd George, M.P., O.M.

The Right Hon. David Lloyd George, M.P., O.M.

THE MS. of the following article was already written for inclusion in this volume some months before the recent election took place. The prediction of its results may perhaps be referred to. I have preferred to leave the article as it was originally written; for its substance is unimpaired by anything which has happened since, and the forecasts attempted then are not, I think, without interest to-day.

Mr. Lloyd George was born in Manchester in the year 1863. His father was the late Mr. William George, schoolmaster, of the Hope Street Unitarian Schools, Liverpool. Early bereavement left him dependent upon the affectionate upbringing of a comparatively humble Welsh uncle. It was his good fortune to have inherited strength, ability, and ambition. But he has always extolled with moving gratitude the debt which he owes to the remarkable man who adopted him in extreme youth; who cherished him as a son; who made sacrifices for his education; who formed a just estimate of his nascent ability, and who, because his estimate was just, conceived ambitions for the boy, who had still every obstacle in life to cross, which to his simple neighbours must have seemed extravagant and even ridiculous. But he lived to see them justified. And Fate, which is too often unkind to Romance, beneficently permitted Mr. Lloyd George's relative, in a green old age, to visit his nephew, now a powerful Cabinet Minister, in Downing Street.

To give even a faint impression of this daring and energetic figure within the compass of 2,500 words is rather like exhibiting an elephant in one of those parlourless cottages which were recently offered by the legatees of Disraeli to the working classes. For in Mr. Lloyd George there are so many facets that a new study at a fresh angle inevitably and always suggests a new conclusion. I should like to have known him in the days when, a restless little Welsh school lad, he roamed about the mountains to which he has dedicated so many of his perorations. I suspect that, more than most of us, he has carried through life qualities which even then were in embryonic development. I have his own word for it that he was a Radical from childhood. It is certain that his tender, instinctive, genuine sympathy with unhappy folk is nurtured by the memory of many a cottage tragedy. This sentiment in him, which at its best touches nobility, and at its worst declines into that which is merely maudlin, is one of his strongest characteristics. No affectation was ever needed when it suited him for political purposes to depict the wrongs and sufferings of the poorer classes ; on the contrary, he felt for them with compassionate warmth, so that he was in his early days in the happy position of being able to combine political business with the denunciation of wrongs which he sincerely felt to be intolerable.

I think that the next quality in this complex

personality which I should myself single out for note would be that eerie intuition, subtlety, divination—call it what you will—which enables him with equal clarity of vision to peer into the minds of men and multitudes. I have never known anyone who discovered as quickly as Mr. Lloyd George what was in the minds of those who spoke with him; and I do not believe there ever has been a man who discerned more swiftly and certainly the moods of an assembly—Cabinet, Parliament, or public meeting—with whose mental or emotional processes he was concerned.

This same power, exercised on a larger field, has been of incalculable value to him in his greater political enterprises. He, and he alone, saved the Asquith Government, in whose throat the death rattle was already audible, by the Land Taxes of his notorious and most unscrupulous Budget. I am concerned in this place neither with their economic nor their fiscal quality; still less with their morality. I note only the political genius inspired by which almost alone among his colleagues, he discerned how, with the aid of a stupid Opposition, the whole field of politics could be swiftly and magically transformed. The faculty to which I am drawing attention makes him an uncanny man to do battle with. The man who enters into real and fierce controversy with Mr. Lloyd George must think clearly, think deeply, and think ahead. Otherwise he will think too late. He is incomparably the most profound and subtle political strategist in this country; and the claim is very likely to be further established in the years which lie in front of us.

The qualities which come next into my mind

when I think of Mr. Lloyd George are coolness and moral courage. He is never so happy, so resourceful, or so dangerous as when he is in the middle of a hurricane and whirlwind. " Am I no a bonnie fechter ? " he might have cried with Alan Breck. Here two memories are very vivid in the mind of one who has known him in enmity and in friendship. At the darkest moment of the submarine menace, when competent and calculating Germans so fully believed in its success that they flung America into the scale against them without a qualm ; when each week the tale of stricken merchantmen and drowning crews grew to horrible and ominous dimensions I remember Mr. Lloyd George saying : " I will never haul down the flag of this country as long as one British steamer sails the seas."

What in those dark days this quality of flaming courage meant to the nation can only be known by those who worked with him. I never saw him dismayed ; I never saw him hurried or frightened or rattled by a crisis ; he always exhibited an undaunted imperturbability. No moment was terrible enough to frighten him ; none was too terrible for him to overlook any fugitive humour which the situation could afford.

The second occasion which I have vividly in my mind came on a dark day when, on the whole, the opinion of the Cabinet was that alike in Egypt, India, and Ireland, simultaneous insurrections were to be apprehended. All the fighting services were consulted ; the necessary decisions were taken ; the appropriate orders given. And I can still see Mr. Lloyd George rising from his seat at that fateful moment with the calm observation : " So once again this old Empire must fight for its very life."

It is fashionable now, among those who no longer require him, to dismiss Mr. Lloyd George with the observation that " he certainly rendered great services during the war." This almost contemptuous summary does little justice to the poignant anxieties amid which he pursued an unruffled and a valiant path. Those who stood by his side in that struggle and marked his penetration and his steely resolution will recall the letter written to him by the late Field-Marshal Sir Henry Wilson on the day of the Armistice : " You have done more than any one man in the world to win this war."

Next in order among his more striking qualities I place his fierce, restless energy and his dogged industry. When I speak of dogged industry I do not mean that he would attend with enthusiasm to the details of running a small fishing-smack. But in command of a Dreadnought fleet he would work all day and all night with enthusiasm and even with relish. I have known him almost as a matter of habit begin business at 9 o'clock one morning and carry it on till 2 o'clock the next, and each business, each conference, each document, often carried in it the seeds of crises amid which, clumsily handled, an Empire might have tottered to ruin. The faculty under consideration is, of course, mainly a matter of mental temperament, involving, it may be, even some degree of natural insensibility ; but his superb physical constitution has made no mean contribution thereto. No man cursed with a susceptible nervous system, or affected by a very sensitive mental organism, could have supported the anxieties amid which he walked with a heart serene, confident, unshakable.

He has been much helped in his public career by a certain infectious and merry charm, which few of those thrown into his company have ever found it possible to resist. No one is better company. It is not so much that he ever says anything extra-ordinarily witty in company; it is that he creates an atmosphere of easy and pleasant bonhomie, amid which all his guests seem [to think and talk with spontaneity and enjoyment. Perhaps Lord Northcliffe, before the two men quarrelled, had this quality in his mind when he spoke of the " little Welsh wizard." It has guided him successfully along the doubtful and puzzling mazes of many conferences, national and international. With its aid he has rounded many a difficult political corner and compassed many a menacing crisis.

I should suppose that history, in all its changing pages, can hardly exhibit a more amazing develop-ment than that from the careless Welsh peasant boy to the statesman who flung Emperors from their thrones, and re-drew the map of Europe with an almost Bolshevist pen. Nor does it matter that in the process he sometimes confused a province with a river. No man can know everything. I am not concerned here to discuss the merits or demerits of the Treaty of Versailles; still less to examine, like Mr. Henderson, how far that Treaty can or will survive. But, for good or bad, the in-fluence and the ascendancy which he established in Paris were among the most remarkable achievements of a remarkable life. There is about him a certain almost indefinable trait; suppleness, subtlety, cajolery, plausibility—call it which you will—which surely makes him the most persuasive negotiator in the world. Few who across a table have put a case which he desired to compromise, in the give and take of friendly discussion, have come away with their contentions scathless. He is, like Odysseus, " a man of many devices." Again, he is like a Greek wrestler whose supple body has been anointed with oil. He is not very easy to grip.

This article purports to be neither a history of him, nor a history of the last few years. It is, therefore, sufficient to say here that the country does not even now realise what it owed, in the four terrible years which followed the Armistice, to the demoniacal energy and uncanny intuition of this man. I have not as a colleague always found myself in complete agreement with his views. No one ever did agree with everyone else in all these crises. But in order to reach a valuation you must take the man as a whole, and the crises as a whole. And where there has been failure you must attempt to re-create the atmosphere, and the conditions, amid which decision was imperatively required. If such a process be applied to Mr. Lloyd George, it will still leave him incomparably the greatest living English statesman, and no less certainly one of the greatest who ever lived in this country.

With all the knowledge that I have of him; with all the knowledge that I think I have of existing political conditions in this country, I am unable to judge with any clearness the lines of his political future. That, in one form or another, it will be dominating I cannot doubt. And I think certain inferences may be clearly and confidently drawn. His life, and still more his speeches, have exhibited many strange and glaring inconsistencies. But he has not failed to observe a certain major consistency. He was opposed to the Boer War, not because he wished, even then, to hamper the progress, or diminish the greatness, of Britain, but because to him there was and is something sacrosanct about all small nations, and something irresistible about small nations consisting of farmers; and furthermore, he never believed that the Transvaal situation presented the slightest peril to the security of this Empire. I differed from him then, and I differ from him now; but the point that requires to be made is that a man who opposed the earlier and minor war might quite reasonably determine as a protagonist the fortunes of the second.

It may therefore be quite certainly predicted of Mr. Lloyd George that no quarrel in which the honour of Great Britain is assailed will find him an idle spectator. In the second place, I am still persuaded that the great struggle, and the only struggle, which awaits us in political life, that between the existing system and Socialism, will find him in the end the most eloquent and the most powerful enemy of the Red cause. In every fibre of his being he believes in individualism. Tactical interludes indeed there may be. High authority assures us that the leopard cannot ever change his spots; still less have I heard of one who much altered either his temper or his temperament. I therefore conceive of Mr. Lloyd George as still with us. His incomparable power of platform rhetoric; the prestige which, even in the moment of political defeat, his name retains at home and abroad ; his resources in Parliamentary debate, will inevitably make him an irreplaceable champion of our economic system in the struggle which awaits the nation.

It does not seem to me, on the whole, probable that Mr. Lloyd George's political future lies exclusively with a Liberal Party, whether divided or reunited. Of actual Liberal reunion, indeed, at the moment, I discern little real prospect ; for however much the rank and file of the party may desire it, the antagonisms which Mr. Lloyd George has excited among the leaders of the Independent Liberals are at once too recent and too bitter to admit of real appeasement. But even if reunion should come, it seems to me not reasonable to expect, in competition with Labour and Conservatism, a larger number than 150 Liberals in the new House of Commons. A Party of such dimensions must combine with somebody. The Conservative Party will, in my judgment, be larger, if its affairs are more intelligently managed, than its old opponents ; but it will not, unless strange changes happen, be very much larger.[1]

So that if both these parties retain, on principle, their hostility to Socialism, co-operation will, in the end, prove to be indispensable. It therefore seemed to me and to my friends quite certain that no single Party could hold the pass for more than a very short period ; to-day hardly anyone disputes it. Who is so sanguine as not to agree that after the next General Election there must be a combination of those who oppose the socialisation of industry ? In these circumstances—and apart from all considerations of loyalty

---

[1] I take some satisfaction from the accuracy of this prediction.

and decency—it appeared to some of us to be sound policy to retain association with a man of surpassing power who shared our views upon the gravest issues of all. The meeting which was held at the Carlton Club took a different view. They drove Mr. Lloyd George out. Many grave consequences are already traceable to that decision. And many are still to come.

The Right Hon.
Ramsay MacDonald, M.P.

The Right Hon. Ramsay MacDonald, M.P.

MR. RAMSAY MACDONALD'S personality is little known to the general public, considering the importance of his position. The leader of His Majesty's Opposition has generally battled his way to the forefront of his own party through a series of great public controversies in which he has been a protagonist. His picture and even his peculiarities are known to all. So it was with Gladstone and Disraeli in the 'sixties or 'seventies, or with Mr. Asquith and Lord Balfour. But up till 1922 the Labour Party had never risen to the full dignity of one of the great political parties. Its first great increase in numbers in 1906 was dwarfed by the immense size of the purely Liberal majority. And from thence onward it played an important but still a subsidiary part in the drama of parties and governments. The ordinary man would have known more about Mr. John Redmond than about Mr. Arthur Henderson. Therefore, although Ramsay MacDonald has been in public life for at least a quarter of a century, entered Parliament first in 1906, and has fought as stark a battle for the leadership of his party as any of the giants of old, these things were largely hidden. A figh between the intellectuals of Socialism and the stalwarts of Trade Unionism—Keir Hardie, Ramsay MacDonald, or Snowden, against Barnes, or Burt, or Clynes, was looked upon as a struggle between pigmies and storks—an unimportant encounter fought out on a mimic stage in the world of vestry politics. Leader-writers or caricaturists would not follow the duel as they did the grapple between Mr. Joseph Chamberlain and Lord Balfour in 1903.

Now we must prepare to alter all this. Labour has ceased to be a group ; is swiftly becoming a party, and will on Tuesday form a Government.[1] It is true that, being only one of three Oppositions, it owes its technical supremacy to the divisions of the other two. Indeed, when the prospects of Liberal reunion seemed sufficiently rosy to threaten Mr. Ramsay MacDonald with ejectment from his proud post, he very astutely, if somewhat audaciously, suggested that the left wing of the Asquithites should secede to Labour and so redress the balance. But when all has been 'said, Labour-Socialism as a solid political force of great—it may be of unknown—strength has come to stay, and we have to try and be interested in their leaders, for the same reason that our fathers were anxious to understand the mentality of the great party leaders of past years.

Some may find this rather difficult. They may not be able to detect in the leadership of the I.L.P. the germs of a Pitt, a Palmerston, or a Salisbury, to find in rows of trade union secretaries elected to Parliament almost automatically for doing their own specialised tasks honestly and well, a fount of genius ; or to find in twentieth-century Labour any sign of personalities likely to be remembered in history. They will say that a nation may vote

---

[1] This article was written before the Labour Government was formed, and at a moment when its formation could easily have been avoided.

people into power, but that it cannot make them intelligent or great—or even interesting.

In all this criticism there is some truth—even if it smacks too much of the *Laudator temporis acti*— but by no means the whole truth. It is true that a pledge-bound party largely representing any sectional interest—a class, a church, a race—is no more a favourable breeding-ground for genius and independent thought than a regular army in peacetime. Genius does not emerge by toeing a line. But parties must be given time to develop the atmosphere out of which they can produce great men, and the men themselves that experience which alone can cure them from the narrowness of parochialism or the vagueness of internationalism. As to the charge that respectable nonentities sit at Westminster representing certain classes, Toryism is hardly in a position to cast the first stone. That is why Labour and Toryism understand each other so well. Both can only be induced to accept intellect by progressive, and very tiny, doses. Labour personalities ought to be given time to make themselves interesting or even important to the public. Some have already done so—notably Mr. Keir Hardie and John Burns. In other cases a certain retirement partly due to excessive virtue; partly to excessive shyness; and partly to a fear of jealousy tends to keep the Labour leaders in the social background. Have they not recently been forbidden by resolution to dine with ordinary mortals ?

Having put the case for and against, it seems to me that Mr. Ramsay MacDonald passes the tests as successfully as any man. Beginning life as a school-teacher and secretary, he has risen against odds even more formidable than those which handicapped Mr. Lloyd George. His published works, without being brilliant, possess the sound presentation of an experienced and skilled controversialist. Eleven years of the secretaryship to his party taught him to understand the machine, and four years of the L.C.C. gave him a grip of local government. But it is his capacity as a competent party chief, eloquent on the platform, skilled in Parliamentary tactics and debate, which has given him a leadership many of his followers would have preferred to place elsewhere—could they have found an equally capable rival candidate. Mr. Clynes is the very embodiment of that sane trade unionism whence most of the voting power and all the money comes to Parliamentary Labour. But though capable and respected, it was felt, during his term of leadership, that he could not speak quite on equal terms in the gate with the chosen of Conservatism and Liberalism. He is, in fact, to be quite plain, extremely ineffective. Mr. Thomas is probably by far the ablest politician among the Labour members. But he is too much of a statesman for one section of his party, and too much of a pugilist in outside industrial disputes for another. It is Ramsay MacDonald's sheer debating supremacy over all his rivals which brought him the seat of honour—even though it be studded with thorns.

He was returned to Parliament in the same year that I was, and no man ever set himself more assiduously to understand the procedure and grasp the atmosphere of the House. He was training himself in debate and knowledge against future opportunity It is said now that he is becoming a trifle too loud in method and in voice. But, after all, did not such a mild-mannered individual as Sir Henry Campbell-Bannerman, flushed with the sense of a big poll at a recent General Election, thump the box and exclaim, " Enough of this foolery ! " An extra-assertiveness of manner may make up in the eyes of some of his followers for the fact that their leader is hardly prepared to make the streets of Glasgow run with blood.

In 1914 disaster overtook him. After war was declared he spoke in Parliament seldom, but always in a pacifist or defeatist sense, and his record in the contest was such a black one that he lost his seat at Leicester in 1918 by an overwhelming majority. Anyone who had not studied the record of the democracies in dealing with the opponents of great wars might have imagined that politically he was ruined. He ought to have been. He was a pro-German, according to his adversaries, one habitually referred to with approval in the enemy Press under the confused title of Ramsay and MacDonald. Should such a man ever again lead a Labour party which both in words and action had repudiated the taint of anti-patriotism ? It did not seem very likely.

But the prophets forgot the reaction which follows swiftly after great national efforts. When the excitement has subsided, when last night's champagne is flat, nations forget the glory and the necessity, and are only conscious of the sacrifice and the consequences. The oysters have been eaten and the bill still remains to be paid. In these circumstances the Pacifist acquires a kind of immunity compounded of exhaustion and forgetfulness. Nay more, he has proved to be a man buying a good stock at the very bottom of the market, feeling sure that it must rise. He can always declare that he is not responsible for a 5s. income-tax. It is like the eclipse which awaits the great man of letters in the period which follows his death before posterity returns to an ultimate judgment. History has damned Fox for his factious opposition to the Governments which preserved us from Napoleonic domination, and history will equally condemn Ramsay MacDonald for the far lesser evil he had the power to do to a Britain which was fighting for its life against the Kaiser. But in the meantime the issue is dead, and is only springing into life at the moment when the Labour Party is likely to have a decisive word in the direction of national foreign policy.

I should say that the real objection that the writer of the future will take to Mr. Ramsay MacDonald's attitude on the war is that he was not sufficiently fanatical to be deemed a completely honest fanatic. To use a homely phrase he rather weakly flopped. Unlike Mr. Snowden, he did not fight absolutely blindly for peace and internationalism at any price. Like Mr. Gladstone, he continually rested under the suspicion of trimming his sails to catch a veering of the wind of popular opinion. On the responsibility for the war, on the duty of aiding recruiting, and finally on conscription he was one who would go to the very limit of Pacifism; and then shrink back as though frightened by the hostility which his spoken and written words aroused. The result was a series of not very edifying complaints about " misreporting " or " misrepresentation."

There are those who imagine that because the Leader of the Opposition has given his more extreme or noisy followers a hint or two on Parliamentary decorum, he would prove, if ever he became Premier, a kind of Labour Whig, seeking nothing but to curb the radical excesses of his more rabid followers. This is a mistake due to a confusion between manners (or methods) on one side and principles on the other. Mr. Ramsay MacDonald is a Socialist of the Chair —as much of a doctrinaire as Robespierre or Cobden, both men ready to apply cast-iron doctrines of existence to humanity without any immediate regard for questions of life and happiness. That his own Socialism is growing a trifle démodé is nothing but a new proof of the invariable fate which has always overtaken the gentlemen of the Left since the Devil, as the first Radical, discovered that " in the lowest depth a lower deep still gaping to devour me opens wide." It has certainly been a thirty years' march from Sidney Webb to Trotsky ; and Mr. MacDonald has not galloped the whole course swiftly enough. But what he would of his own volition like to do to the suffering people of this country would, I imagine, be quite sufficiently startling in itself. Those who think the Leader of the Opposition a moderate, mistake the temperament of their man. His very appointment was the triumph of the intellectual extremism of the I.L.P. over the plodding moderation of trades unionism.

But he has declared himself a Constitutionalist. Those who see in this fact a reassurance against the violence of the language used on the Clyde appear to be easily comforted. It is precisely the Socialism of Violence which is most likely to defeat itself. And this is especially the case in England. Only once in the last thousand years has England been subjected to armed revolution and to the government of a violent minority. The Reign of the Saints, however different its ideals, was constitutionally the exact counterpart of the Red Army, and fell in 1660 amid universal rejoicing after a short and bitter experiment.

Mr. Ramsay MacDonald's method of peaceful penetration would be far more insidious, and far more likely to achieve initial success than any doctrine based on violence. The British Constitution has so developed as to give little formal protection against the spoliation of property. Its makers proceeded on the principle that the conception of property would always, at all times, with all parties, be sacred to Parliament. Admitting this, there were manifest political advantages in giving the House of Commons almost absolute powers over finance as a means of promoting the popular control of the Executive.

All this is altered. A definite challenge, which cannot be disregarded, has been issued to the very existence of property. The largest Opposition group in the House, notoriously aiming at government, has supported its destruction, as such, in a formal motion, in the House of Commons, and in four days a Socialist Government will be in office. Yet we are absolutely without the safeguards against hasty action in a matter of vital importance to the community which the more rigid type of written Constitution affords to the citizens of the United States. Our more flexible instrument might permit what was in effect a social revolution, like the Reformation, or the putting down of England to grass and pasturage by a simple majority or even an actual minority of the people in a single session. Private property could practically be wiped out in a Finance Bill—if a tax of 100 per cent. on such property were certified as a purely financial measure. Yet this revolution would be purely "constitutional" in the sense of Mr. Ramsay MacDonald.

The danger lies in that public apathy and scepticism, in face of the Socialist menace, which alone prevents the union of political and Parliamentary forces sufficiently strong in combination to ward it off. The comfortable sort exclaim, "Oh, these resolutions are but formal and pious opinions. The Socialists do not mean what they say. The trade unions themselves own property, and Socialists themselves have six different policies—and could agree on none. The British working man would never consent to a policy of pure spoliation."

This last contention might be true if the British working-man had only more insight than the middle-class quietist as to what would be the consequence of casting a Parliamentary vote for his most respectable trade union secretary. But in fact the political situation has not worked out in this way at all. The existing Government becomes unpopular for some quite different reason; or perhaps a terrible error of judgment is committed. There is a wave of reaction in the country, and before anyone quite knows what has happened Mr. Ramsay MacDonald, as a type of convinced intellectual Socialist with a tame Labour Party, is in power with an instrument to hand, in the Budget, more effective than any method of exactions which could be wielded by the mediæval kings.

That is why the character of the Labour Socialist is as well worth studying by those who believe in the principle of private property as that of Cromwell would have been, when he sat in Parliament as an unknown man, by the supporters of the Crown. And I read the mind of Mr. Ramsay MacDonald as possessing all the rigidity of the school of Mr. Sidney Webb with a slightly sophisticated re-echo of the passion that seems bred on the Clyde. Flexible as a Parliamentarian, he is dogmatic as a schoolmaster. And if the forces which are opposed to Socialism do not forget their other differences and band themselves together in time, this schoolmaster and secretary may be the new, if paler, Cromwell, who will yet give modern England a taste of what the kingdom of the latter-day saints means to life, property and happiness.

* * * *

For now, as unexpectedly as superfluously, the errors of others have antedated by ten—perhaps by twenty—years the moment in which these grave issues are to be tried out. So incredible has been the succession of these mistakes that Mr. MacDonald may fairly retort to criticism that his own policy, however unfortunate, can involve little further failure, and no further discredit. And indeed the distinction is, after all, only between those who make a conclusion achievable and those who achieve it.

But the sceptre has been forfeited by one; and grasped by another. By the manner in which he wields it—be the time long or short—Mr. MacDonald may perhaps show that he is either smaller or greater than the man indicated in the estimate—not intended to be unfriendly—which I have attempted in the foregoing paragraphs.

His Grace
The Archbishop of Canterbury

His Grace the Archbishop of Canterbury

THE Right Honourable and Most Reverend Randall Thomas Davidson, now in his seventy-seventh year, was enthroned some twenty-one years ago as Archbishop of Canterbury. He has sometimes been regarded as the typical Scotsman of capacity, a theological Finlay or Haldane, who descends upon English institutions and, in the manner which Dr. Johnson so much resented, carries all before him.

It is certainly true that the present Primate of All England was born in Edinburgh on April 7, 1848. The traditions, therefore, of this cautious race are undoubtedly inherent in his mental equipment. But environment long ago made of him a representative Englishman.

It is not a figure of speech to say of Lambeth Palace that it is a clearing-house both of ideas and of movements. The purpose of this article is to examine some features of a high ecclesiastic ; but it is necessary, once for all, to insist that behind the ecclesiastic there exists, and ought to exist, one who is alike a politician and a statesman.

It would be misleading and unreasonable to attempt to place any political label upon the lawn-clothed shoulders of the Primate. It is neither necessary nor fair to analyse his politics. He is a very practical man who has attained to the highest position in the Established Church of England.

Beyond this point in dealing with an Archbishop some decent scope must be afforded to reticence.

This practical turn of mind has been an enormous asset to one called upon to deal with affairs dependent on principles which are not of universal acceptance. There are in this connection causes which the vigilance of an active and ingenious mind has kept from death. My own opinion has not been concealed—that some of these causes were hardly worth preserving.

The Archbishop, for instance, has always found himself in an extremely difficult dialectical situation whenever he has been called upon to define his position upon the present law of divorce. He has, indeed, even against episcopal opposition, veered more than once in his finely-balanced way towards reason, mercy, and justice. He has, again, in his own insinuating fashion, attempted to surmount formidable difficulties. He has hazarded ideas which involved compromise and suggested risk. But in this field he still has far to go. Yet no fair critic can blame him for not going farther. And the reason has been already indicated.

The Archbishop of Canterbury cannot discharge his functions efficiently if he be merely a great moralist and a great priest. He can, indeed, if he be also a man of imagination, exercise a far-reaching influence over that cosmopolitan body of theological thought which men call the Church of England. But he cannot govern, without destroying, his historic trust unless he has a genius for compromise.

On the whole, I am of opinion, attempting to measure the history of the Church of England and of its hierarchy in the last half-century, that the

present Archbishop of Canterbury has gathered new
power in recent years. In his tenure of office the
world has immensely multiplied its problems, its
divisions, and its sorrows ; and with the growth of
all these he himself, too, has risen in stature.

Christianity is a remedial religion. There exists,
then, a remedy. And such a remedy, in a world
in which direct Divine interposition is no longer
plainly observable, must be expounded by a man.
" Understanding is a well-spring of life unto him
that hath it." And so we may observe in the
career of the Archbishop how the faith and the
fervour of an apostle, however urbane, have been
developed (perhaps with some slight increase in
sophistication) into the fibre of a statesman. And
I like to think that this development had its source
in the work of energetic youth. And here, even in
this brief commentary, I look back for a moment
to days now very remote.

It is nearly fifty years since Randall Davidson
received his first Office in the Church. His youthful education was not committed to Scotch instructors.
He was, so to speak, caught young. Trinity College,
Oxford, following upon Harrow, gave him his training, as far as I can learn, without either special
effort from the teachers or startling response from
the taught. And since, in dealing with ancient
institutions, we cannot ignore either sentiment or
association, it is worth while recalling that, whilst
Davidson was little more than a boy, Harrow gave,
in the person of Charles Longley, a former head-
master to the Primatial See.

Archbishop Longley was followed at Canterbury
by Archibald Campbell Tait. Within three years

of Davidson's ordination to the curacy of Dartford, in Kent, Longley's successor cast a favourable glance in his direction. The smiles of Archbishops are very pleasant to young curates.

Archbishop Tait formed the view of Davidson that he was both sagacious and sensible—an opinion which the world has since confirmed. And so in 1877 the young curate left Dartford for Lambeth Palace.

The Secretary of 1877 soon became familiar (though vicariously) with every fold of that mantle which he now so decently becomes. He had indeed many a mile to go before he was actually to wear it. And at many stages of his career the prospect must have seemed extremely remote. But his destiny was none the less preordained. And the mantle of the Archbishop of Canterbury is, after all, more than a symbol.

Heredity of any type—normal or abnormal— is of interest, even to the domestic observer. This is a small thing. But there is, after all, a larger thing—a heredity which some few men acquire. These few may live greatly because of it. Any work plainly having its roots in our national history involves a broader conception springing from national, not family, heredity. If officers of the State are conscious of this view, whose terms of office are liable to be determined by sudden chance, still more must another feel it whose tenure lasts for life.

Only with life, as a rule, have our Archbishops been content to surrender the charges committed to them.

In endeavouring, then, to adjudge the achievement of an individual, length of tenure may prove to be an outstanding factor. Archbishop Davidson's time at Canterbury has lasted longer than that of his two predecessors combined. It exceeds now already by seven years that of his father-in-law and preceptor. Thus he embodies the methods and aspirations of three very different men—Tait, Benson, and Temple.

It is evident, of course, that such recent associations do not exhaust the acquired heredity upon which I have already dwelt. The Archbishop of Canterbury lives in a lordly palace. He is still a great prince of the Church. The resonant records of centuries long past surround him under Laud's roof-tree and beneath the Crown of Becket. He reaches out to Anselm, to Cranmer, to Whitgift, to Sancroft, and to many other names revered in the history of the English Church. He is familiar with vicissitudes and with glories. And he must live familiarly, too, with dissensions, ruptures, and cleavages.

There is no sign that the perplexities to which the Archbishop of Canterbury is constantly exposed have diminished in recent years ; but I have great confidence in his ability to surmount them. He learned his work in a great school. Without the appearance of agility, he is very agile ; and with the appearance of adroitness, he is very adroit. He has sometimes, when in a series of parliamentary difficulties, reminded me of a very dignified chamois leaping with precision from crag to crag.

The service which he gave to the Church as Dean of Windsor, as Bishop of Rochester, and afterwards of Winchester all equipped a many-sided character ; and so he went to Canterbury armed with an unusual knowledge of all sorts and conditions of men.

A constant but manly and independent association with the Court has, perhaps, added a little to the mundanity without in the slightest degree sapping the spirituality of his mind. Indeed, a very real simplicity has been the ruling feature of his life ; and this same quality has strongly marked his public utterances. His sermons are packed with sober sense. Their embellishments are drawn from the least recondite of poets and philosophers. And yet, unpretentious as he is, he has produced a *magnum opus*. For the long series of Reports on the Lambeth Conferences shows the impress of his hand throughout, bearing witness to an outlook upon Church affairs at once sane, spiritual, and coherent.

From Lambeth to Westminster is a short journey. No figure is more familiar in the House of Lords than the Archbishop's. The attendance of Bishops in the Chamber has, on the whole, diminished. But the Archbishop is seldom missing from his place when any of those subjects falls under discussion—social, moral, or religious—in which the Church of England is interested. He himself would be the last man in the world to claim the gift of oratory. But he is always lucid. He is always master of his facts. He is always careful to injure in his canny presentation no single cause of which he is trustee. And he is more influential in the House of Lords than some of his predecessors who have been equipped with more showy gifts.

I have already laid stress upon the practical shrewdness by which he is marked. Many matters, indeed, in relation to the Church must in his tenure of office have caused him grave anxiety. " There are things which are shaken." If I did not know this for myself, I could learn it at any time from the Bishop of Durham, or the Dean of St. Paul's, to say nothing of his Holiness the Pope.

It would take a theological treatise to explain exactly what has been shaken ; and an analytical examination of the British Sabbath to illustrate even one local effect of the shock. And, after all, the point of real importance is, what has been done for stabilisation and for the arrest of decay by him who to-day carries so much responsibility ? The phrase is hackneyed enough in which Disraeli spoke of himself as being " on the side of the angels." Writing at a time of almost unrelieved gloom, I nevertheless record my conviction that, whatever may happen to this nation, its fundamental instinct is on this very side. Therefore the ground has always been prepared for a great Primate with vision and dexterity. In these qualities the Archbishop exceeds his contemporaries. Confidently assuming that there exists a general agreement with the aims of the Church, he has made it his special care to strengthen the system by which the presence of that Church is guaranteed in every hamlet in the land.

He has never shut his eyes to abuses, though he would point out that many of them are insepar- able from a body still largely governed by the dead hand. He has done much to cleanse Augean stables. He has welcomed every movement which travelled the right road as he saw it. He has known when to steady, when to spur on, a tendency or a mood.

As for the old controversies which disturbed the peace of Tait, he helped to settle them all.

And now he is faced with recrudescences not wholly dissimilar. Conspicuously composed, he is bewildered neither by agitation over Kikiyu nor by the worries of Malines. All comes to him as part of an ever-shifting challenge. And everywhere, all the time, the work of the pastorate goes on. The home episcopate in both provinces has received, almost to a man, evidence of his fatherly solicitude. As for the Church overseas, hardly a day passes without a missionary and a handbag making their way under Lollards' Tower. His weekly postbag is probably the largest in England.

The Archbishop's recent conference upon the subject of Re-union, fruitless as, in my judgment, it will prove, calls attention to still another far-flung discordance, and throws an interesting light upon the mentality of this very sagacious priest. He is, of course, alive—none better—to the supreme pretensions, or, if you will, the supreme claim of the Latin Church. He never forgets that his own status in Christendom is itself a challenge.

But the Keeper of those Gates of Lambeth, which are never closed, softens the challenge in its modern expression by flinging them wider open than ever. He works for a larger Re-union. He sees that the real enemies are not those of the Churches, however wide the drifts of separation may seem to gape. The gesture is doomed to fail, but it was generous, bold, and spiritual.

And how, it will certainly be asked, has the Church of England prospered during this long and busy reign ? We are told that Churches are failing everywhere ; their jurisdictions derided ; their sanctions despised. And it is freely alleged that the Church of England has deteriorated with the rest. Its comprehensiveness makes it suspect in one quarter ; its unrepresentative character is attacked in another. It is assailed from within and from without.

We have, indeed, to reckon to-day with a disbelief that any or all of the Churches are effectual for the betterment of mankind. We grope in matters sacred or secular through a maze of doubts. What says, what does the Archbishop ? With Kingsley, he commends the doing of the thing that is nearest. He passed through the storms of a great war " with unflurried vision." He recognises in life itself a trial, and he acts, and expects others to act, as though men should endure being tried. If ever he came near to coining a phrase it was when he said of our English Collects that they were " struck from the souls of earnest men as fire from flint."

As we take leave of this kindly, wise, courteous, and conscientious Scotsman, we may, perhaps, recall a sentence of John Morley's :—

" The test of the health of a people is to be found in the utterances of those who are its spokesmen, and in the actions of those whom it chooses to be its chiefs."

This aphorism may be applied to the Church of England with equal honour to Randall Davidson and to the august foundation of which he is at once guide and custodian.

The Right Hon.
Austen Chamberlain, M.P.

The Right Hon. Austen Chamberlain, M.P.

THE history of English politics teems with instances of hereditary succession. But cases where any exceptional political capacity has been transmitted from father to son are rare—very rare, when it is remembered how restricted until recently was the charmed circle of the governing families, and how pronounced the advantage of an early entrance to the political arena. Countless Russells, countless Cecils, countless Stanleys have grasped the Treasury Bench to their respective satisfaction; but there is a long gap between the first Earl and the third Marquis of Salisbury; and, broadly speaking, the hereditary principle has found its justification more often in furnishing the basis on which Cabinets may be built than in providing either vision or leadership. Three very conspicuous pairs of examples to the contrary will occur to everyone—Henry and Charles James Fox, Chatham and the younger Pitt, Randolph and Winston Churchill. And each of these cases provides, in analysis, curious parallels and curious contrasts with another remarkable father and son of our generation—Joseph Chamberlain and Austen Chamberlain.

Both Henry Fox and William Pitt the elder had to fight their ways against an oligarchy which regarded the spoils as the main attraction of political life and as appertaining to a defined group of alternate officeholders. Each of them centred his hopes on the success of an adored boy, designed from his cradle for political life. Between each of these men and his son there existed a tender affection and an unusual intimacy. Both boys, by the most amazing coincidence in history, attained a place in the world and in the hearts of their countrymen as high as the most ardent paternal hope could desire.

And in each case, as in that of the Chamberlains, the characteristic of the success of the son was in marked contrast with that which might have been looked for from the father's pupil. Charles James Fox, indeed, suffered all his life from the disorder and profusion which his father thought appropriate to the education of the young; and in this respect at least he was his father's authentic son. But his genius for friendship, his extraordinary power of attraction, were strange attributes in the heir of Henry Fox, self-seeking, *mauvais coucheur*, mistrusted. And William Pitt, the precise if pedantic financier, sane, persistent, patient, the pilot who weathered the storm, seemed a strange product of that terrible Earl of Chatham, who rode isolated, genius swept, upon the whirlwind.

Similar contrasts might be made between the characters and careers of the father and son with whom we are concerned; and there are similar likenesses. Between Joseph and Austen Chamberlain there existed the same ties of affection and confidence which give a human touch to the lonely majesty of Chatham, and enable the ordinary man to feel sympathy with the cold and unattractive personality of the first Lord Holland.

Austen Chamberlain was born in 1863, and

after an orthodox education at Rugby and Trinity, Cambridge, entered the House of Commons in 1892 as member for East Worcestershire. The general election of that year had placed Mr. Gladstone in office with a precarious and embarrassed majority. It also made it clear that the Conservative Party must seek a more formal alliance with those Conservative elements in the country which still shrank from assuming a purely Conservative label. In 1768, when Charles James Fox was first returned, Lord Holland was already out of politics ; he had retired to the North Foreland, where he " smuggled a few years and strove to mend a ruined character and constitution."

The sun of Chatham had set in gloomy cloud three years before the younger Pitt entered Parliament. But Austen Chamberlain took his seat on the benches on which his father still sat, with the most fruitful days of that father's career still to come. The elder Chamberlain was exulting in the plenitude of his vigour and involved in the full bitterness of personal strife. Perhaps this fact was a disadvantage to the younger man. He sat, almost literally, under the shadow of a greater name ; and the very close physical resemblance between the two suggested that the son was merely the echo or reflection of the father.

In due course, Austen Chamberlain delivered his maiden speech. Its ability, both in form and matter, was at once admitted. But that which chiefly marked the event, both within and without Parliament, was the evident delight of the father and the exquisite compliment paid by Mr. Gladstone both to father and to son. In 1895, as seemed inevitable, Chamberlain the younger entered on office as Civil Lord of the Admiralty, and, by transitions which seemed equally inevitable, he passed thence to the Financial Secretaryship of the Treasury, and thence, in 1902, to the Post Office. Up to this time it might have been lightly said : "*patrissat homo.*"

But then came the fresh disruption. Joseph Chamberlain left the Government in one direction, "to promote the cause which I have at heart from outside." Mr. Ritchie left in another ; and Austen Chamberlain succeeded to the Exchequer. It was perhaps not an advantage that, in unusual circumstances, and while still so young, he should have reached an office so high. The taunt was obvious, if baseless, that Austen was prematurely promoted in order to keep Joseph within bounds. The problems and difficulties which faced the Governments and Oppositions of the first decade of the century seem now absurdly light. They seemed then more than statesmen could solve. Indeed, the task of the Chancellor of the Exchequer in Mr. Balfour's Government—now declining to its fall—was not one which was likely to increase the reputation of the holder of that office. Nor, as I have hinted, was the fact that that holder was Joseph Chamberlain's son a help to him. Yet, when the catastrophe came, Austen Chamberlain on his own merits had none the less become one of three possible competitors for the leadership of the Unionist Party, if any accident should leave that position vacant.

Whence came his strength ? The permanent officials with whom he was associated declared that, if the gods had afforded him opportunities less restricted than were open to his father's son, he would, on merit alone, have become the best Permanent Secretary to the Treasury in history. That genial and sagacious swashbuckler, Sir William Harcourt, once said that if you had a Cabinet of permanent Civil Servants England would be governed admirably, but at the end of a fortnight the whole Government would be hanging from the lamp-posts in Whitehall. Still, the permanent officials applied a strictly intellectual test, and paid, from their point of view, a high compliment. In mental quality Austen Chamberlain came up to the standard of that exacting school, and in a kind of moral quality also. With a very fine courtesy of manner and considerable power of sympathy he united, and unites, just the necessary rigidity of view. Perhaps, indeed, sometimes the rigidity has almost verged upon pedantry. It was not his way to storm through obstacles, or to blast by irony. Indeed, his critics have often called him wooden. No such legends are likely to gather round his name as round those of Sir Michael Hicks-Beach or of Robert Lowe. But he certainly had learnt how to say " No "— a lesson which was to stand him in good stead in days to come. He had acquired, if he did not possess it naturally, a passion for the public service.

I do not think that, as a young man, Austen Chamberlain saw visions, or that, as an old man, he will dream dreams. He would, I think, be a little more formidable if he did. But he saw then, as he sees now, his duty very clearly before him; and towards it he presses without deviation. It has not always been revealed in a flash; nor has the path been chosen without pain or (twice at least) without a vivid sense of sacrifice. But once undertaken the path has been trodden without either heroic gesture or self-pitying moans.

It helped him, I think, that he was not wholly absorbed by the influence of London and the political cabals of London, that most provincial of all English cities. Dependence for support on a great town, which thinks nothing of the gossip of clubs in Pall Mall, or of drawing rooms in Mayfair, or of organisations in Westminster, is a very healthy alternative for a leader of English democracy. Antæus-like, when he revisits his constituency, he breathes in a new strength and a new sanity from his native earth and air.

And with all this, he obtained an authority in speech and a hold on the House of Commons which went far beyond the promise of his first appearance. He seemed to lose a certain fear of "letting himself go" which rested upon him while he appeared before the Commons and the country as his father's son. As that beloved father visibly decreased, and there came over even his keen wit and vehement personality that obliterating eclipse which is fated to us all, so the son increased, stood openly on his own feet, and was endued with, rather than assumed, the mantle of the leader.

Then came his first chance, and his characteristic use of it. The Tory Party, in one of its recurrent fits of forgetfulness of faithful service, determined to sacrifice its leader in a moment of failure. And the choice of a successor must fall on Mr. Walter Long or on Mr. Austen Chamberlain. I say nothing of the respective merits of either of the two candidates, or of the third who was to receive the palm. But in the self-abnegation of the subject of this paper, who, but for his own scruple, must have grasped the prize, there were prefigured the years of self-surrender which were to follow.

He was not lacking in courage. If that was not clearly realised then, a long series of subsequent events have proved it. But he was not willing for the sake of his own ambition to run the risk of internecine strife within the party. He was, and always has been, a party man, believing that in the association together of men with common aims lies the only chance of stable government. He saw that in the unity of the Unionist Party was the best hope of a return to sound administration and of the avoidance of class warfare. And he gave up without a murmur the immediate prize of the leadership of the party, and, as it then seemed, the ultimate crown of the Premiership of England.

Thus when, after the long sojourn in the wilderness, the Unionist Party returned to share with the Liberals in the responsibility of office and government in war-time, Mr. Austen Chamberlain came back not, as he should have done, the chief of the new recruits, but as Secretary of State for India, a thankless post, offering in the circumstances of the time no outlet for ambition, and grave risk of personal discredit. The risk matured. It is not unusual for Ministers to be thrown overboard to lighten the ship, less usual for the victims to assure the crew that they enjoy the process, but very unusual indeed for a Minister to jump overboard on what Mr. George Meredith would have called "a dam punctilio." This was the course pursued

F

by Mr. Chamberlain on the report of the Mesopotamia Commission in July, 1917.

The merits of the issues raised cannot be discussed here. What concerns us is Mr. Chamberlain's own attitude in the circumstances as he saw them. Resignation of office to a man whose life resides in politics is always bitter ; it means, gloss it as you may, separation from the best work a man can do, and the renunciation, at least for a time, of an honourable ambition. But in war-time, to a sensitive and patriotic man, it is doubly bitter. It is a public acknowledgment of failure, where a man can least bear to fail ; it throws a man on himself, when he most longs to serve his country. Mr. Chamberlain was obeying a double loyalty, to his colleagues who, as he thought, would be hampered by his continuance in office; to his subordinates, who, he thought, had been censured unfairly; for his speech was a defence of others rather than of himself. But the fulfilment of this duty and the manner of this fulfilment had an effect widely different from his anticipations. The House of Commons and the country saw in Mr. Chamberlain not only the courteous gentleman and the accomplished public servant whom they had always recognised; but a man of distinguished courage with an unflinching instinct for the right course. They were not mistaken.

Abilities so distinguished, and a character thus displayed, could not, while the war raged, be left unemployed for long. In April, 1918, Mr. Chamberlain returned to office as a member of the War Cabinet. In January, 1919, he was again at the Exchequer, grappling, not always happily, with the insoluble problems of after-war finance. Then in 1921 came that bolt from the sky—(I cannot say the blue, the skies of 1921-1922 were never blue)—the sudden illness of Mr. Bonar Law; and Mr. Chamberlain was the only possible successor.

The events of the months which followed are too fresh in memory to bear description. For Mr. Chamberlain in particular they were marked by incessant toil in the most laborious of all positions. No relationship can be more delicate and more difficult than that of the leader of the House of Commons as an understudy of the Prime Minister, when the latter is also a member of the House. But when, to add a complication, the two men are the leaders of two parties acting in coalition, and the noisy section of one of those parties spends its energy in urging the second in command to betray his chief, the situation demands exceptional moral (or immoral) qualities. Yet through all those long months of strain, when " powers from home and discontents at home " met " in one line," Mr. Chamberlain, " cloak and cincture," held out the tempest.

Of the later story it is my purpose to say little, for it is a moment to forget rather than to recall old quarrels. And still a word must be written, or this study would be incomplete. Mr. Chamberlain believed, as Mr. Bonar Law had believed before him, that the dangers in which this country found itself after the Armistice were almost equal to those of the war ; that their solution urgently required a strong and stable Government over a period of years ; and that no single party afforded the pros-pect of such a Government. He vehemently be-lieved, too, as Mr. Bonar Law had believed before him, that it was by co-operation between the older parties, and by this means alone, that the dangers of a Socialist Government could, for any long period, be averted. Holding these views, he repelled every proposal made to him that he should withdraw from the Coalition and attempt to form a Conservative Government. For he believed, and publicly stated, that such a Government must be short-lived, and that its successors would probably be Socialists. Self-interest and personal ambition would have deflected a less balanced man from a decision neither taken with levity nor formed without reflection. For of a Conservative Government so formed there could at that time have been no Prime Minister but Chamberlain.

It was sometimes superficially said of him that he counted his loyalty to a Liberal leader higher than his loyalty to his own party. As, indeed, he saw the situation, no inconsistency ever arose between the two obligations. And in his clear vision a higher duty, transcending even these obligations, was binding upon his conscience—that of loyalty to those principles which the Conservative Party exists to protect, and of which, in a grave moment, he was the responsible trustee. Time only can prove how great was the breach made eighteen months ago in the only real defence against the forces of social and economic disruption.

A short word may be added about the man himself. He has a warm heart, but it is by no means carried upon his sleeve. He is naturally urbane; but that urbanity hardly reaps the full value in contemporary esteem, for it is masked by some curious quality of *gêne*. In superficial *bonhomie* he is lacking, wherein he is unfortunate, for that currency is one with which great statesmen can easily finance large political business. A more frequent resort to the smokeroom ; a more general revelation of his personal charm would have helped him much. Of his single-mindedness and integrity nothing need be said (even by himself) for neither has ever been assailed.

Twenty-three years ago Joseph Chamberlain applied to the then Prime Minister lines which, though well known, may be recalled here in relation to Joseph Chamberlain's son :—

> " Statesman, yet friend to truth ! Of soul sincere,
> In action faithful, and in honour clear ;
> Who broke no promise, served no private end,
> Who gained no title and who lost no friend."

The Right Hon.
The Viscount Haldane of Cloan, K.T., O.M.

The Right Hon. the Viscount Haldane of Cloan, K.T., O.M.

VISCOUNT HALDANE OF CLOAN was born in the year 1856, of a Scotch family which has produced many citizens of distinction and public service. His youth was greatly occupied with metaphysical studies—a circumstance which I shall presently show was the principal cause of the wanton abuse heaped upon him at a later date by an ungrateful section of his countrymen. But at the time everything seemed for the best; and the friends of the young man who gained a First Class in Philosophy at Edinburgh University and the Gray and Ferguson Scholarships in Philosophy of four Scottish Universities, might well think, and did think, that a man had been born in Cloanden.

And so he brought his metaphysical garlands with him to the English Chancery Bar to humanise this somewhat arid field of humane research. Ultimately, and indeed, as these things go, rapidly, he became successful. He never, indeed, added to the conciseness of the various subject matters to which he applied himself; but he made it plain that an intellect which had enjoyed the Absolute in intimate cohabitation was no unequal antagonist of those who struggled for briefs in Lincoln's Inn. His reputation spread over a circle always growing wider, and soon there came, as there always does come to the elect and daring of the Bar, an oppor-

tunity alike of entering Parliament and of taking
silk. He was elected member for Haddingtonshire
in 1885 ; and continued to represent that faithful
constituency until his elevation to the Woolsack
in 1911.

In the early days of his membership he made
many wise and thoughtful speeches—all of adequate
length—and soon became generally known in the
Liberal Party as a man of character, earnestness,
and intellectual quality. But he hardly became
known to a really wide circle of his countrymen
until the outbreak of the Boer War, when he ranged
himself without fear or hesitation by the side of
those who, like Rosebery and Asquith, believed the
war to be just and necessary. Those who were not
ashamed to vilify him in a later and greater war were
of the same opinion, but they chose to ignore the
fact that Haldane had risked everything in a patriotic
cause which commanded his assent.

To the war succeeded the Khaki Election ; to
the Khaki Election a distracted Liberal Party :
and to that distraction the Tariff Reform Campaign
which was to end it. During the years which preceded 1906 Conservatism grew ever weaker and its
opponents stronger ; so that before long it became
evident that Sir Henry Campbell-Bannerman was to
lead the victorious locusts into the promised land.
Immediately Sir Edward Grey and Mr. Asquith
bent all their energies to obtain the Woolsack for
their ally and friend. But the new leader had
other views and other loyalties, and after crises and
debate the blue riband of the Bench went to a very
courteous and attractive man, who was, however,
far less erudite and less philosophical as a lawyer.

Right Hon. the Viscount Haldane, K.T.

It was in these circumstances that Haldane went to the War Office. The position was one of extreme difficulty. The Parliament of 1906 was, of course, mad, criminally neglectful of, and indifferent to, all matters of national defence. Its members believed with the late Sir John Brunner that international law was a surer safeguard of Great Britain than the Fleet; that sloppy international tea-parties were as valuable as military prevision : in a word, that everything should be abolished except the Radical majority. Haldane had no such delusions. He did not, it is true, believe that Germany would run the incalculable risk of disturbing the peace of Europe ; but he never forgot that she might. He soon realised that the whole Army system needed reform from top to bottom ; that our military strength, actual and potential, must be immensely increased ; and that these measures must be taken in the teeth of a Parliamentary majority which disparaged him as a Jingo ; and derided apprehension as a chimera.

Lord Haldane has all his life been the most industrious man in England. He now flung all his industry, all his address, all his subtlety, and all his eloquence into this gigantic task. He made speeches in the House of Commons of unimaginable length. It must indeed be admitted that his allocutions were sometimes what certain critics have alleged against the Science of Law, a little incognoscible. He deluged his critics with orations which lasted for three or four hours, until they withdrew before him bewildered, dismayed, and numbed by words which fell from him like the snowflakes of Greenland. And soon it became evident that behind all these words there was a brain, a scheme, and a system. Out of chaos came order, until it became generally recognised by everyone who worked under him at the War Office that here was the greatest Secretary of State since Cardwell. Lord French and Lord Haig, differing, it may be supposed, upon many other subjects, have united in their tribute to his admirable exertions; and each has independently and with high authority laid it down that Haldane and Haldane alone, by his co-ordinative reforms, made it possible for this country to play the military part with which she was confronted at the outbreak of the Great War. This tribute has carried weight everywhere except, perhaps, in the columns of the *Morning Post*, an organ which upon every other point has never ceased to place our generals upon an intellectual pinnacle. But when Wilson praises Lloyd George; or Haig Haldane; foolish Mr. Gwynne turns on the Die-hard tom toms; and his bellicose, but I think undecorated, leader writer produces another unfair and malicious article.

Only a brief summary of Lord Haldane's work at the War Office can be undertaken here. He conceived and perfected our Expeditionary Force until it became, in relation to its numbers, the finest military instrument in Europe; he re-organised, if he did not wholly create, the General Staff; he brought into being those Officers' Training Corps without which the war could not have been won; he called into existence that indomitable Territorial Force which ought to have been the framework of our new armies, and which, though never given its proper chance, made a superb contribution to the strength of British arms in France.

Right Hon. the Viscount Haldane, K.T.

Against this amazing record of achievement his critics have only found two things to say : first, that he ought to have supported Lord Roberts in his splendid exertions on behalf of National Service ; second, that he guaranteed to his countrymen the pacific intentions of Germany, and even described that country as his spiritual home. The answer to the first charge is that the men with whom Haldane had to work would never have tolerated Roberts' proposals ; nor indeed did they tolerate them even at the outbreak of war. Had he insisted from 1906 to 1911 on compulsory service in any form, his resignation must have followed, and this calamity would have extinguished the promise of his own courageous and indispensable reforms.

The answer to the second charge is more elaborate. He undoubtedly believed during all these years that the Kaiser did not intend war, and would not undertake the ghastly risk of forcing it on. I did not share his view, and wrote and said so at the time ; but many men of great sagacity and patriotism were of his opinion. It is now even difficult to say with complete certainty at what dreadful moment that decision, fraught with so much tragic doom, shaped itself in the psychology of those in Germany who had the power to precipitate the conflict. One thing at least is certain, that Haldane, in preparing his scheme for a Territorial Army, bore two things constantly in mind : first, that the force should admit of limitless expansion, and, in the second place, that it should lend itself swiftly and conveniently to compulsion if the needs of the nation required compulsion.

As to the statement that Germany was his

spiritual home, this is the kind of thing that philosophers are always saying. I do not happen myself to be a philosopher; and think the observation (if he ever made it) rather a foolish one. I suppose it meant to convey, if anything, that the metaphysical ruminations with which Lord Haldane refreshes his lighter moments are to be affiliated upon the long-winded thinkers who wrote so many large books upon similar topics in the German language. But to read into the saying a vestige of malignity or disloyalty is to play the part of a very stupid man. I am aware (he has been good enough to inform me of the fact), that he disputes ever having used the exact expression. But having examined the evidence I conclude that he did say something very like it. And, at any rate, it is just the kind of thing he would say ; and surely that is good enough for the kind of critics by whom he was assailed.

On a well-known occasion Lord Haldane was sent to Germany to discuss the possibility of making an arrangement to arrest the growing naval competition between the two countries. In the discharge of this duty he has fallen between two schools of criticism. By his English critics he has been freely assailed as one who betrayed the interests of this country. By the Kaiser in his recent book he has been described as a traitor to his German hosts. On the whole perhaps one imbecile may be allowed to answer another.

The truth, of course, as every sane man knows, is that he went to Germany to do, if it were possible, what every sane man desired, namely, to reach an agreement which would diminish our expenditure upon armaments. He failed : knew that he had failed ; and reported his failure to his Government. While he was there he naturally used the opportunities which the Germans afforded him in the interests of his countrymen, and in doing so he betrayed none of the duties of a guest ; for he was entitled to infer, and did infer, that the Germans would only afford such facilities as they did afford to an English Minister with the knowledge that his first duty was to his own country.

By the year 1912 Haldane's work at the War Office was complete. The failing health of Lord Loreburn rendered the burdens of his great office too heavy for him, and Haldane attained his ambition by becoming Lord High Chancellor of Great Britain. He held this office until the formation of the first Coalition Government in 1915.

Of Lord Haldane's qualities as a Judge it becomes a colleague to write with extreme delicacy ; nor indeed should I think it proper to write at all if there were not so much which ought to be said, and has not been said, in his favour. Ever since he left the Woolsack he has laboured during every day of the legal session exactly like any other Judge who is under a legal compulsion to do so. He is immensely courteous, very patient, very learned, and very conscientious. And if he is occasionally somewhat reminiscent, his colleagues at the Bar and on the Bench who know his great qualities hope without being sanguine that nothing worse will be said of them when their obituaries come to be written. In particular his work on the Judicial Committee has been beyond all praise, so that no name throughout the British Empire among all its judges is more respected than that of Lord Haldane.

Such was the man who as a condition of Conservative co-operation was expelled from the first Coalition Government. He was praised almost as a hero by Lord French and Lord Haig. He was denounced almost as a traitor by the Die-hards of 1915. It is certain that the iron entered into the soul of a proud, sensitive and accomplished mind, conscious of a long life spent in the public service. But he may well be sustained by the affection of his friends and by the knowledge that more and more the world is realising how despicable and how maniacal was the assault before which he succumbed.

And now once again the wheel has gone full circle. Time the Avenger has in its ironic vicissitude flung from office the enemies of Lord Haldane. To-day he is Lord High Chancellor of Great Britain, Chairman both of the Committee of Home Affairs, and of the Cabinet Committee on Imperial Defence. Those who once assailed him so bitterly are now looking to him with frankly expressed relief as to one able to contribute caution and moderation to an experiment produced by their own incredible errors.

Of Lord Haldane himself it may be most truly said : that just as adversity never soured him, so advancement has never elated him.

The Right Hon.
Marquess Curzon, K.G.

The Right Hon. Marquess Curzon, K.G.

GEORGE NATHANIEL CURZON, K.G.,,G.C.S.I., G.C.I.E., M.A., P.C., F.R.S., D.C.L., LL.D., J.P., D.L., Marquess Curzon, Baron Scarsdale, Baron Ravensdale, Viscount Scarsdale, Earl Curzon of Kedleston, and Earl of Kedleston (I am indebted to " Who's Who " for these details), was born on January 11, 1859. He has had a life of the utmost possible distinction. The briefest summary of his activities and of the offices which he has held will make this abundantly plain. Soon after he left Oxford he became assistant private secretary to the late Lord Salisbury. He contested South Derbyshire in the year 1885. From 1891-1892 he discharged the duties of Under-Secretary of State for India. The years 1895 to 1898 beheld him Under-Secretary of State for Foreign Affairs.

But more dazzling careers awaited him, and at a very early age he became Viceroy of India. I postpone for a moment the tribute which his illustrious tenure of that office requires, in order that I may complete the summary upon which I have embarked, and which will afford, when complete, a useful text for the general observations I have to offer. On his return from India he became one of the leaders of the Unionist Opposition, and so continued until the war. On the formation of the first Coalition Government he became Lord Privy Seal, adding to that office in 1916 the duties of President of the Air Board. In 1916 he became Lord President of the Council, holding this post until 1919. In that year he became Secretary of State for Foreign Affairs, and held this high and onerous position for four years. He is, therefore, a pilot who has weathered many storms; for he was an important member of the first Coalition Government, of the second Coalition Government, and of the post-war Government; and is now one of the principal and most dignified buttresses of the present Administration.[1] And it should be specially remembered that in the darkest days of the war he was a member of the War Cabinet, upon the shoulders of whose members the principal responsibilities of the war fell.

Lest I omit anything which is helpful to the present survey, let me borrow from the same invaluable book of reference the facts (vividly, even conscientiously, stated) that Lord Curzon has travelled extensively in Central Asia, Persia, Afghanistan, the Pamirs, Siam, Indo-China and Korea, and that he received the gold medal of the Royal Geographical Society in 1895.

This brief record makes it plain that we are called upon to deal with the career of a public servant of the greatest possible distinction. He has laboured unceasingly all his life in the service of the State. Always he has been animated by an honourable public ambition. In the discharge of arduous and manifold tasks he has displayed unimaginable industry; and he has supported the constant pressure of ill-health with composure and fortitude. It is reported of him that he once confided to a friend

[1] Written in 1923.

that he cherished three ambitions in life : first, to be
Viceroy of India ; second, to be Secretary of State for
Foreign Affairs ; and, third, to be Prime Minister.[1]
We may still live to greet him with the recognition,

> Thou hast it now, King, Cawdor, Glamis, all,
> As the weird women promised.

But these speculations, though full of interest,
belong to the impenetrable future, and my business
is rather with the past. I should suppose, though I
had not the honour of knowing him when he was
young, that few men have ever altered less from
boyhood onwards. We do not lack some contemporary light upon our hero when he was an Eton
boy, for Mrs. Lyttelton, in the charming biography
which she recently published of her most distinguished husband, has made known a letter which
Alfred wrote from Cambridge to Lord Curzon, still
at Eton, but destined shortly for the intellectual
society of Balliol. The letter is dated August, 1878.
" I can fancy myself " (writes Lyttelton) " talking
with you over a too-sumptuous tea in the most
comfortable of Eton rooms. . . . I was quite taken
out of (*i.e.*, upset) at seeing the traces which much
dejection had left on you, my shapely boy. . . .
One thing I want you to do before going to Oxford
is to take stock carefully of your present opinions and
aims, and after a year's life there compare the realisation of your aims with your intention. It may possibly
be mortifying, but it is quite sure to be wholesome."
One must not give way overmuch to sentiment ;
but I like to think of the shapely boy sitting over
a too-sumptuous tea in the most comfortable of

[1] Written in 1923.

Eton rooms. And I cannot for a moment doubt that Mr. Curzon, with precocious sagacity, appreciated the supreme wisdom of the advice that he should take stock carefully of his present opinions and aims ; and after a year strike a balance between realisation and intention. Nor, to be just, and having regard to the record of positive achievement which I have already briefly summarised, can the result often have proved mortifying. Certainly his career at Oxford was one of almost unbroken successes. The Lothian and the Arnold Prizes rewarded his efforts as an essayist, and a Fellowship of All Souls College crowned a series of academic successes, which was only marred by his failure to obtain a first-class in Greats. Nor have I the slightest doubt that in this respect his examiners made one of those ludicrous mistakes which from the dawn of history examiners always have made, and which till the last Honours List of all is published it is certain that they will continue to make. Herbert Bradley, after all, the first of living English philosophers, was awarded a second-class in the School of Literæ Humaniores by men who were not intellectually qualified to tie his boot-laces.

Lord Curzon's official career before he became Viceroy was generally recognised as one of great, even of spectacular, success. It was a common amusement in the early 'nineties among political writers in the Press to make comparison between Mr. Curzon and Sir Edward Grey, both of whom were so long to be associated with the conduct of Foreign Affairs in this country. The only criticism which was ever heard, so far as I can remember, of Mr. Curzon at this time was that the manner in which he expressed the results of deep reflection, in sonorous phrases, was a trifle superior. The same judgment had been fashionable at Oxford, and was duly recorded in a well-known quatrain, which placed undue stress upon the frequency of his visits to Blenheim. I have myself always thought that the criticism, though I understand it, is unjust. I do not think that Lord Curzon consciously intends to assume any superiority whatsoever over those whom he addresses; for he is far too clever a man to imagine that such an assumption, if deliberate, would be either politic or tolerable. I choose rather to believe that, year by year, as the revolving seasons pass, Lord Curzon has been following Lyttelton's advice by comparing the realisation of his aims with his intentions. And so far from finding the result mortifying, he has been fortunate enough, like the Almighty after creating the world, to find the result altogether good. Why, then, in the name of common sense, should his attitude be anything but superior? We have the highest authority for believing that the meek shall inherit the Earth; though I have never found any particular corroboration of this aphorism in the records of Somerset House. Lord Curzon is not meek; nor do I know of any particular reason why he should be. But personally I dislike meek men.

I have myself always been an admirer of Lord Curzon's oratory, both upon the platform and in Parliament. In its weight, dignity, and elocution it recalls a classical period unhappily passing away. I recall particularly in this connection his fine peroration when closing the Dyer debate in the House of Lords. He did not, unhappily, succeed in changing the opinion of their lordships; but he produced a

fine illustration of the highest Parliamentary eloquence. His speeches are well conceived, well argued,
and well delivered. The manner is perhaps a little
pontifical, almost pedagogic, so that the less reverent
among the younger peers commonly refer to him
as " The All-Highest " ; and, indeed, in great controversies he does speak a little with the air of Zeus,
the Cloud-Compeller. But, if an indulgent criticism
be permitted, on occasions of a special kind, even
Zeus must have left his thunderbolts behind him.

Lord Curzon's Vice-Royalty was one of extreme
distinction. Here his insatiable industry found
ample scope, and his statecraft has been ultimately
vindicated in many a debatable controversy. Mr.
Lovat Fraser paid a monumental, and, on the whole,
not an excessive, tribute to that achievement in
his work, " Lord Curzon's Vice-Royalty." The
weight of this evidence is not diminished by the
circumstance that recent events have apparently
somewhat lessened Mr. Fraser's enthusiasm for his
hero. Nor is it probable that the splendid pageantry
of this dazzling office was in every way uncongenial
to him. He not only (in a homely phrase) did the
business, but he looked and liked the part. Only
one failure marred the serene record of unbroken
success. The clash of wills between Lord Kitchener,
then Commander-in-Chief in India, and Lord Curzon
ended in Lord Curzon's discomfiture. It is reported, and I believe truly, that it was long before
he forgave Lord Balfour, the Prime Minister, and
Lord Midleton, the Secretary of State for India,
for withholding their support from the Viceroy in a
quarrel which for a time convulsed the official world
of our Indian Empire.

Right Hon. Marquess Curzon, K.G.

Lord Curzon's attitude upon the original Die-
hard controversy of 1910 does not perhaps fill one
of the most shining pages in his biography. The
Lords were threatened, it will be recalled, with a
creation of Peers in numbers adequate to overcome
the majority as displayed in the division lobby.
The proposal was a constitutional indecency ; it
was—and is now known to have been—a bluff. And
at the outset Lord Curzon thundered against it in
his most sonorous and elegant manner. " Let them
create their peers," he cried ; " we are not to be
driven from our duty by threats." The gesture was
sublime ; the courage admirable, and many recruits
flocked to the standard thus manfully unfurled.
But when the battle was deployed, and search was
made for the leader in shining armour :

> The Earl of Chatham, with his sword drawn,
> Stood waiting for Sir Richard Strachan.
> Sir Richard, longing to be at 'em,
> Stood waiting for the Earl of Chatham.

And thereafter Lord Curzon, who had quite evidently been acting in the interim upon the Lyttelton
formula, became the leader of the party of surrender.
Speeches, letters to *The Times*, articles followed like
snowflakes in numbing succession. The result (if
results in such a context alone count) justified
Curzon's view. I think his common sense, and his
intuitive grasp of political valuation, must always
have repelled the taste of Cato :—

> *Victrix causa deis placuit sed victa Catoni.*

It is, on the other hand, hardly possible to speak
with too much praise of Lord Curzon's work during
the war. It was unceasing, devoted, and courageous ;

no task was ever placed upon him which he was unwilling to undertake ; and he never lost his belief in the national cause at its darkest moments.

Of Lord Curzon's efforts since the Armistice I have never thought it fair to be a severe critic. The peace negotiations inevitably deprived him of a large measure of the authority which a Foreign Minister would ordinarily enjoy. And a long series of later conferences, which from time to time became necessary, raised issues which had become too grave, and too cosmopolitan, to be dealt with by any particular department. And it must also be remembered that some at least of the struggles in which he failed were determined by the swaying Russian struggle and by the Bolshevist triumph—be it fugitive or lasting—which ultimately emerged. Seldom has a Foreign Secretary been able to move with more restricted range within the ambit of that dignified building. The Coalition Government is entitled to share the praise (if there be any) for what was good (if there was any) in those difficult years which followed the Armistice. And it seems to me that that Government must also be prepared to share the blame for such failure as was avoidable. His solid and indisputable claims may well atone for a far greater number of trivial foibles than have ever been imputed to Lord Curzon. The only criticism upon this point to which, with much knowledge, I could assent is that, even allowing for all the circumstances, Mr. Lloyd George assumed too much and Lord Curzon conceded too much.

An amusing illustration of these small weaknesses was afforded at the first Lausanne Conference with the Turks, over which Lord Curzon presided.

To appreciate the full humour of the situation it must be borne in mind that the Turkish representatives at that Conference were sent to represent the wild and unsophisticated Assembly of Angora, itself elected upon no representative basis, and utterly unacquainted with the quality and finesse of European diplomatic Conferences. Soon a very remarkable circumstance became evident. No reporters were admitted to the deliberations of the Conference ; but much information was obligingly afforded by some unknown benefactor of the representatives of the British Press. And so we were indulged from day to day with vivid illustrations of the President's persuasive and masterly methods. At one moment we learned that he quelled the Turkish leaders' remonstrances with a look. At another, that an obstructive argument was swept aside with a victorious sarcasm ; at a third, that the divine gift of humour had demolished a menacing obstruction as the sun dissipates the accumulated snow. The strange thing was that these reports only appeared in the English Press. I have always wondered who gave them—obviously not Lord Curzon. It must, I apprehend, have been some loyal but slightly zealous private secretary, who could not bear that a light so superb should waste itself upon a circle so restricted. I would venture to suggest, should such a case arise again, that the publication of these dialectical triumphs might well be postponed until the result has been achieved. For the leader of the Turkish deputation might well have retorted to his august opponent :

> What are all these quellings worth
> If thou quell not me ?

But these are only specks upon the sun. When all the deductions are made, and all the pleasantries exhausted, it remains true that Lord Curzon is one of the great Englishmen of his generation. He is an illustrious Etonian, he is Chancellor of Oxford University, and his name will always live in the history of these fateful days. Of his association with the most recent political developments I need add little. He was penultimately loyal to the Coalition, and if, when it deliquesced, he found salvation a little quickly, why so, to be sure, did Balaam.

The Right Hon.
The Earl of Rosebery, K.G., K.T.

The Right Hon. the Earl of Rosebery, K.G., K.T.

WHEN, a year or two ago, the death of the ex-Empress Eugénie was recorded, the chronicler may well have been startled to remember that the illustrious lady, who was almost a centenarian, had only enjoyed her Imperial greatness for the brief period of seventeen years. When the biographer of Lord Rosebery—may his task be deferred for many a long year—sets out to occupy and exploit the rich field which such a Life will present, he may perhaps be surprised to recall that a man so deep-rooted, and so eminent in public esteem, should have been for so short a while a tenant of high office under the Crown. Such a reflection would not tend to belittle a career; it would perhaps rather magnify a personality. Lord Rosebery apparently began to attract with his first breath; he will remain attractive until he draws his last. He compelled attention in his busy noon; he cannot escape it even in his quiet evening. He always was, is, and will be, that untranslatable *quelqu'un*. And yet in some curious way he is, and always has been, an incomplete man.

At Eton, he achieved little distinction, but evoked a good deal of comment. At Oxford, where he was one of the last of the " noblemen " recognised at Christ Church, he kept little company with the intellectuals, and is said to have preferred his racing stud to his degree. But if he was impatient of

the University curriculum, it was nevertheless at
the University that he began to read eagerly and
widely, and to bring into high cultivation the resources
of what has been described as a "very elegant
mind."

He succeeded to his grandfather's Earldom
during the year of his majority, and drank freely,
but always very delicately, of the pleasures of life.
He dined and danced—especially the Scotch Reel ;
he raced and shot ; he was an ardent theatre-goer and
admitted leading actors to his friendship ; he drove
his cab—with the exception of Lord Calthorpe he
was the last to drive a cabriolet in the Park ; he was
in the innermost circle and counsels of the Marlboro-
cracy ; there were rumours of his engagement to the
most famous and beautiful débutante of her day.

He seconded the address to the Throne, and
strewed the Upper Chamber with such flowers of
oratory as " I believe that if Jupiter were to return
to earth, and recommence the courtship of Danaë,
he would woo her in a shower of diplomatic circulars."

And then, rather unexpectedly, he begins to take
himself seriously. He addresses the Edinburgh Philosophical Institution, and delivers quite a weighty
speech ; he presides over the Social Science Congress
at Glasgow ; he learns his lessons in Liberalism
through close acquaintance with such men as the
artisans in the Clyde shipping works; and vows
unswerving devotion to his emotional political father,
Mr. Gladstone ; he goes to Canada—it was whispered
(by those who did not know) on a secret mission
—and the Canadian politicians said, " If this young
man lives, he will be the Prime Minister of England."

And then in 1878 there comes the event which

determines and consolidates his future life : he marries the only child of Baron Meyer Rothschild, whose immense fortune and large estates she had already inherited.

The marriage, though not unexpected, provoked eager discussion (especially among people whom it did not in the least concern), and it was, perhaps, not viewed on either side with entire satisfaction. It was the fourth case of a Rothschild marrying out of her community ; and the *Jewish Chronicle* was moved to an article which opened with " Alas ! what degeneracy do we behold ! " Nor were the riches and the noble qualities of the bride altogether sufficient to overcome the earlier prejudices of the bridegroom's family. The old Duke of Cleveland was congratulated on the brilliant match his stepson was making. " Thank you," was the cautious reply of the venerable aristocrat ; " I do not know the young lady personally ; but I am told that the family is well-to-do in the City." And a certain sense of incongruity was perhaps not absent from the couple themselves. Lady Rosebery may have resented the fact that scarcely any of her family attended the Church of England service, and Lord Rosebery's family did not, I believe, overcrowd the synagogue. But however the alliance was regarded from outside, it resulted in a union of unalloyed and unceasing happiness ; and when, twelve years later, Lady Rosebery succumbed to typhoid fever, her death dealt a blow from which her husband never wholly recovered ; and left a blank which it never occurred to him to fill.

In 1880 came the Midlothian Campaign, and in what was perhaps the hour of Mr. Gladstone's greatest triumph, Lord Rosebery was alike his constant companion and his genial host. With the formation of the Government he was asked to accept the Under-Secretaryship for India, of which Department Lord Hartington had been given the portfolio. Lord Rosebery would have liked to say " Yes," if only to establish himself early as a speaker in the Lords. " An official pitted against Salisbury, Cranbrook and Lytton," he wrote, " could not have been disgraced, and might have earned distinction."

He said " No " because he did not wish it to be thought that he had received remuneration for services rendered. This was an idle view. In politics every sensible man looks to advancement for services rendered. But a year later the Under-Secretaryship for Home Affairs was vacant, and Lord Rosebery was persuaded to take it, just when the Home Secretary, Sir William Harcourt (surely a paradoxical double harness), was about to receive the Freedom of Glasgow. His subordinate was present on the occasion, and carefully alluded to himself as " part of the furniture of the Home Office, and very dingy furniture it is." A year later Lord Rosebery resigned his modest place—the temper of the House of Commons being that it should be occupied by a Commoner. He thereupon toured Australia. He returned to reaffirm his allegiance to Mr. Gladstone, and to be constant at his side, even when the tragedy of General Gordon made hostesses declare it difficult to make anyone dine to meet the Gladstones.

The fall of Khartoum brought with it a personal grief to Lord Rosebery. Through his influence, his brother, Colonel Primrose, then Military Attaché at Vienna, had been allowed to accompany the Nile Expedition, and, when Commandant in Lord Wolseley's camp, died a victim to a specially virulent attack of enteric fever. To a young Guards officer who was able to arrange his decent burial in a remote part of the desert, Lord Rosebery telegraphed : " Call upon me if ever I can do anything to show my gratitude "—a promise which in flux of time was to be amply fulfilled.

Lord Rosebery has only once contested an election, when he scored the instantaneous and complete success which has usually dogged his steps. By a majority of five-sixths of the Council, he was elected the first Chairman of the London County Council, which he had nursed through all its anxious beginnings, and in so doing wholly belied the gloomy predictions of the minority—of whom Mr. John Burns was one—that a brilliant orator was sure to make a bad chairman. He would not, in my judgment, ever have been Prime Minister had he not graduated in this Municipal School.

In Mr. Gladstone's brief Administration of '85-6, Lord Rosebery held—but for so short a while as to make little mark—the post of First Commissioner of Works and the Seals of the Foreign Office ; in 1892, Mr. Gladstone offered the latter to him again. For awhile Lord Rosebery hesitated—he often seemed to hesitate when the blossoms were waving their sweetness to him from the bough—" he was out of health, oppressed with insomnia, not disposed for exertion," all recurrent phases with him ; but he crossed to Paris, received medical assurances that the work would be beneficial rather than otherwise, and closed with the Prime Minister's offer—to become, according to a weighty contemporary opinion, "the best since Canning."

His merits had been suggested four years earlier, when his efforts were far happier and more fruitful than those of Lord Salisbury in enabling Major Kitchener and Monsieur Raffray to hold their own against their aggressive and impudent German colleague on the Commission for the limitation of the Sultan of Zanzibar's territory.

The underlying principle of his Foreign Office administration was to be a sane and sound Imperialism; and this often in the teeth of much opposition within the Cabinet. He would have nothing to do with those who, in season and out of season, urged Mr. Gladstone to retire from Egypt; and to his imperishable honour he remains personally responsible for the retention, even now with some measure of control, of what is still strategically one of the most important dependencies of the Crown.

In 1892, the question of the evacuation of Uganda was acute; the Government did not see its way to help the British East Africa Company, which had reached its pecuniary limitations—a fertile and fragrant province was to be left to its fate. Happily, the final appeal fell on Lord Rosebery's willing ear. He ordered the brilliant young Consul-General at Zanzibar, Sir Gerald Portal, to proceed to Uganda and send in an independent report of the value, and the promise, of the land. Portal had no hesitation. The country, he urged, bore every mark of prosperity and revival. Uganda must remain a British possession, and a railway to the Lake should be begun forthwith. The Foreign Secretary recognised all that the report advocated and insisted on its adoption.

Posterity may be disposed to think that no better contribution has been made to Empire than Lord Rosebery's addition of East African territory.

Another of his successes was in the conduct of the Siamese negotiations with France, carried on under the old-fashioned diplomatic conditions,—so old-fashioned that it was not until all danger was over that the public learnt how, but for the courtesy and firmness of the Foreign Secretary, grave trouble with an ally, at that moment a little incalculable, might have seriously threatened.

Embedded in his tenure of office was an incident which testified to a shrewd knowledge of humanity. In November, '93, the great Coal Strike was causing widespread misery and unrest. The representatives of masters and men were called to meet the Foreign Office; two hours' animated, if disjointed, talk occurred, without the slightest sign of any prospective settlement. " Gentlemen," said the Convener genially, " there is some cold meat in the next room; shall we adjourn for a quarter of an hour ? " The delegates obligingly agreed and found a luncheon of Lucullus awaiting them; on their return to the Conference, questions which, before the interlude, bristled with difficulty, seemed quite simple to solve.

Lord Rosebery's Liberalism has appeared at times to oscillate between his original aristocracy and his fiftul adventures into Radicalism. Certainly London Radicals were his keenest supporters, when in March, 1894, he succeeded Mr. Gladstone as Prime Minister. Mr. Gladstone is said to have taken the opinion of the Cabinet on the successorship, and to have found that the only supporter of the claims of Sir William

Harcourt was Lord Rosebery himself. I do not believe this story. But whatever rancour Sir William Harcourt felt, he directed against anyone rather than against the man who was elected as much by the acclamation of the people as by the will of the Sovereign, and whose only opponents were the small group who objected to a peer-Premiership, reinforced apparently by the Archbishop of Canterbury, who wrote in his diary " R. would be ill-advised to take the Premiership."

" Let him win the Derby and dissolve upon it ; the General Election will be a gift for the Liberal Party." Such was the opinion of enthusiastic sportsmen ; and if, when Ladas was victorious in 1894, Lord Rosebery had accepted the advice, he might perhaps—even if against his will—have remained in office for longer than the fifteen months allotted to him. But Lord Rosebery had made a bitter and implacable enemy in the son of William Harcourt. Lulu Harcourt was neither a great statesman, nor a great minister, nor a great parliamentarian : but he was a great son ; a great wirepuller ; and a great enemy : and his fangs, however subterraneously, were always at work on some portion of the Rosebery anatomy. He was : " *Impiger, iracundus, inexorabilis, acer.*"

In June of the following year a stumbling Government was brought to its knees by an adverse vote on the supplies of war munitions, and its Prime Minister retired into welcome ease and well-loved literature. In letters he has, perhaps, found the chief solace of his leisure. His Georgian and early Victorian Political Memoirs are better known, but not better written, than his " Preface to the List of Persons concerned in the Rebellion of 1745 "; his Pitt is not more admirable than the exquisite fragment which supplemented Mr. Winston Churchill's admirable life of his father. His Essay on Peel is on the same high level of prose as his very occasional excursions into journalism. He " can cause dead and vanished things to live in the spoken word." He has read, perhaps, as much as any man of his day; and, I believe, still points to Shakespeare and Surtees as his favourite authors. Social contrasts were often his refreshment; and he would with equal pleasure, and on the same day, discuss racing with his staunch friend Matthew Dawson; international politics with his equally good friend Count Herbert Bismarck; and art and letters with Lady Holland in the great house where he was always the most cherished guest.

It is strange that a man of such brilliancy should have achieved, in a high perspective, so little. He was indeed Prime Minister; but so have others been. The truth is that he could never make up his mind completely upon any subject. He wrote, indeed, admirable prose; but he could only begin Chatham, and end Napoleon. He is like Mr. Britling in this sense, that he did *not* see it through. His famous speech at Glasgow made it certain that a hesitating Conservative Party must throw out Mr. Lloyd George's Budget in the Lords. But when the battle developed Lord Rosebery was not in the thick of it.

And yet he allied to an unerring instinct in Imperial affairs vivid oratory, robust patriotism, and a subtle imagination. His misfortune was that he was seduced by youthful credulity, by his own emotional and sometimes splendid rhetoric, by the magnetism of Gladstone, into membership of a party with which he never really agreed; and with which he was therefore one day bound to quarrel.

For many of the errors which have disfigured the Liberal tradition, and in their reaction destroyed Liberalism, he must bear a deep responsibility. For he surrounded the folly of an emotional, a hysterical, and a dying creed with the prestige of an aristocrat and the pen of a Man of Letters. That he had grave shortcomings is plain; which of us has not? But the remark may be recalled which a great French lady made to a friend in the Tribune at Chantilly: "*Ah, ce Rosebery; voilà le vrai type de gentleman anglais.*"

The Right Hon.
The Earl of Reading

The Right Hon. the Earl of Reading

RUFUS DANIEL ISAACS, First Earl of Reading, Viscount Erleigh, First Viscount Reading, was born in London on October 10, 1860. He is therefore to-day in his sixty-fourth year. His father, Joseph M. Isaacs, was a merchant in the City of London.

There have in the history of English law been greater lawyers and greater advocates, but it is, on the whole, doubtful whether any English judge has lived a life so various, adventurous, and romantic.

Forty-seven years ago he sailed up the Húglí River, voyaging to Calcutta, a boy before the mast in a great sailing-vessel. If it had been predicted of him then that his next visit to India would be acclaimed by the artillery salute which is reserved for Viceroys alone, he who predicted it might well have been assigned to Bedlam.

And yet this strange thing has actually happened. Compared with its romance, the story of Richard Whittington fades into pale ineffectiveness. He was born a Jew; and has always had the manliness to accept the disadvantages, without rejecting the advantages, which membership of this ancient and tenacious branch of the human family carries with it. Everyone knows the advantages who has studied the clannishness and esprit de corps of this homogeneous race. The disadvantages are not so clearly appreciated, except by those who are themselves

Jews. Somebody once said that every country has the Jews it deserves. Great Britain deserves good Jews, and on the whole gets them. I have often been struck by the strange contrast between the social position of those who belong to this fellowship in Great Britain and in the United States of America. In the United States no Jew can belong to a decent club. He may be a good sportsman, a good fellow, a gentleman, and a millionaire; but the portals of exclusive American clubs none the less frown irrevocably upon him. This has always seemed to me a harsh decree, though in its own social laws every country has the right of exclusive judgment.

In this country—much less exposed to a wholesale immigration of cosmopolitan Hebrews—it has been possible with great advantage to ourselves, if with some slight compensating disadvantage, to assimilate Jews in the social and political life of the country. And many of the most meritorious citizens, highly contributory to the national wealth and prosperity of the Empire, have belonged and belong to the Chosen People.

Indeed, it would be strange if in England, and particularly in the ranks of the Conservative Party, a different view prevailed. For that party, though not specially loyal to Disraeli in his lifetime, has increasingly since his death tended to look to him for inspiration. And nobody has forgotten the unwilling tribute which his personality extorted from the great Bismarck at the Berlin Congress: " The old Jew : that is the man."

Rufus Isaacs had to contend not only with his nationality, but also with an unfortunate start in the City. Through no fault of his own, he failed, and was " hammered " upon the Stock Exchange for a large amount while still a very young man. Inexperienced, penniless, almost friendless, it might have seemed that his career was ended almost before it was begun. But it was at this point that the resource and the resiliency of the young man first made themselves felt.

With incredible difficulty he procured the means necessary to qualify him for the Bar. He read in the chambers of that great veteran, Sir Harry Poland —destined, I hope, to reach his century—and in these learned chambers acquired a considerable mastery of the principles of criminal law.

In due course he was called to the Bar by the Benchers of the Middle Temple ; and thereafter commenced a career of brilliant forensic achievement. In five years he had paid every penny of his Stock Exchange indebtedness. It was an effort made in the true spirit of Sir Walter Scott.

Allowing for the difference between pre-war and post-war remuneration, I should, on the whole, imagine that Rufus Isaacs made more money than any common-law practitioner at the Bar has ever made. For it must be remembered that, in the case of the indispensable few at the head of the Bar, fees have increased by at least 50 per cent. since the days of 1914. It is extremely difficult to analyse, or quite fully to explain, the causes of this extraordinary success.

Rufus Isaacs, though a very adroit, acceptable, and persuasive counsel, was not a great advocate in the sense that Erskine, Russell, and Carson were. But he never made a mistake. He never bullied witnesses. He was always incredibly tactful. He never asked a question which, viewed from any conceivable angle, could produce an answer injurious to the interests of his client. And he always preserved relations of the utmost courtesy and friendliness with those before whom he practised. He contrived, indeed, as much by reticence as by anything that he actually said, to convey the impression to the jury that his client's case was a very reputable case, presented by a reputable advocate to a very reputable jury. He never rose to great heights of eloquence. He had, indeed, an agreeable natural fluency and a very attractive and self-possessed manner ; but his vocabulary was poor and limited. Few men, indeed, have risen so high whose spoken words possessed so little literary distinction.

He owed much to a very distinguished appearance and to an undefinable charm of style. This charm was innate, not acquired. It was genuinely expressive of a delightful temper and disposition. No great leader at the Bar has ever been more popular with his juniors. For he threw around their errors the protection of his own great reputation ; and he was always the first to recognise and dwell upon their merits in the presence of the common client.

He acquired an immense practice, disputed only by Lord Carson—but very effectively disputed—in *causes célèbres*. But on the whole it may be claimed that his success was even greater in the argument of elaborate points of law. In such matters he developed a subtlety, an ingenuity, and a capacity for intellectual legerdemain, which has not often been surpassed at the Bar. He was, indeed, infinitely dexterous in any matter which required the nice discussion of a point of construction; or the subtle discrimination between a long *catena* of authorities.

But of any case which required the examination of ledgers or accounts, he was the supreme master of the English Bar. He seemed, indeed, almost to think in terms of double entry. His extraordinary gifts in this kind of case were vividly illustrated in the Whitaker Wright prosecution; though a hundred other instances could be given by anyone who studied, however superficially, his forensic career.

He was at the head of the English Bar—for Finlay and Carson were Law Officers—when he entered the House of Commons. He sat for the Borough of Reading from 1904 to 1913. It was expected that he would repeat in the House of Commons the brilliant rhetorical successes of his forensic career. But his was to be the fate of Erskine and of Charles Russell. The master of so many juries was denied the gift of acceptable speech in the Mother of Parliaments. No one can confidently say of a great lawyer before he enters Parliament whether he will succeed there or not. Some fail because they are too flamboyant; others because they are too arid; a few, like Erskine, and perhaps Isaacs, because too much was expected of them.

But although he was thereby denied the laurels of a great Parliamentary success, his performance was sufficient, when considered side by side with his immense forensic position, to make him, in the year 1910, Solicitor-General. In the same year he was promoted to the position of Attorney, which he held until 1913.

To this period belongs the poignant Marconi story. I say nothing of it here, except that everyone who knew Rufus Isaacs—personally or politically— knew that he was one of those men who are absolutely incapable of doing any act which they believe to be wrong. He never sought to deny or to palliate an admitted indiscretion. His was, in fact, the case of a lawyer who brings the sagacity of Solon to everyone's business but his own ; and thinks that the odd moments of a scanty leisure are sufficient for the stewardship of his own affairs. To a man of scrupulous integrity and of an almost feminine sensitiveness, the months that passed must have been somewhat like a long and terrible nightmare. But he was supported by the legal world, by a large majority in the House of Commons, and by the general sense of the fairest public opinion in the world. He paid none the less a penalty, cruel in its intensity, for what was only an error of judgment.

And, accordingly, when he was made Lord Chief Justice of England, in the year 1913, the objections, though shrilly and spitefully expressed, particularly, of course, by the *Morning Post*, were neither serious nor widely spread. In that high office he displayed many admirable qualities. He was always courteous, patient, assiduous, and industrious. But he did not, perhaps, realise upon the Bench the high expectation of his juridical qualities which his skill in arguing legal points had seemed to justify. Indeed, to argue points of law with high distinction does not always make it certain that he who so argues will deliver judgments with equal distinction. It may be that, if events had allowed him to end his career in the placid atmosphere of the Law Courts, he would have become a great Lord Chief Justice. But the constant interruptions and preoccupations of his judicial career, produced partly by the war, but partly, I think, by his own impatience of a sedentary judicial career, denied the opportunity of creating a lasting judicial reputation.

With the outbreak of war his financial gifts found employment at the Treasury, where he co-operated closely with Mr. Lloyd George in the masterly financial measures which first relieved, and then ended, the formidable crisis in the City. In 1915 he was made President of the Anglo-French Loan Mission to the United States. In 1917 he was sent again to that country as Special Envoy. And in 1918 he became High Commissioner and Special Ambassador to that country.

Lord Reading may not have been a very great lawyer; but he was undoubtedly a very great diplomatist. His charm, his tact, his patience, his lucid intelligence, and his incredible grasp of detail combined to give him an equipment which few diplomatists, even among the greatest, have enjoyed. I have spoken of the prejudice which exists in the United States against Jews. He completely conquered it. I had occasion myself to visit the United States while he was there as Ambassador, and, having had some opportunity of making comparisons, I doubt whether any representative of this country at Washington has won more affection, or attained to a greater general popularity. And at a most critical time in the relations between the two States his practical mastery of the questions, which from day to day required discussion and decision, was of the utmost service to both countries in the most critical stages of the war.

There came a time when it seemed that his special usefulness in America was exhausted, and that his own judicial duties in this country required his return. And so once again we behold him in the Lord Chief Justice's Court in the Strand. But I doubt whether he was ever really happy there, nor perhaps were all his *Puisnes* completely happy with him. They thought—and in ordinary times there is everything to be said for their view—that the duties of the Lord Chief Justice of England are to be discharged in the Law Courts, on circuit, and in the House of Lords. In normal times there is, of course, everything to be said for this view. Perhaps they made too little allowance for the abnormality of the times; and he too little for the exigent obligations of the high office which he held. There were many, for instance, who thought—in my judgment unreasonably at such a time—that absences so protracted in the United States should have involved the resignation of so high a judicial position.

But these criticisms—often prompted, though never among his colleagues, by malice—became out of date when he was offered, and accepted, the high position of Viceroy of India.

In accepting this office he gave up one of the greatest judicial positions in the world; and also a pension which he had done much to earn.

He undertook great risks at a moment when he was no longer in his most vigorous youth. The troubles which have beset British rule in India in the last few years are well known to most people. They are particularly well known to those who have held high office in successive Governments during the relevant period. Lord Reading was compelled to undertake the task of giving effect to the Montagu-Chelmsford reforms, upon which he had not been consulted, and in relation to which his views were and are unknown. And side by side with this work of dangerous transition he has been forced to combat disaffection and even to resist treason.

This is not the moment to attempt a final estimate of his career as Viceroy. But this much can be said, and ought to be said now : Few Viceroys, even in the long and anxious history of Anglo-Indian relations, have been confronted with a period of greater difficulty and menace. The tact and diplomacy which played so great a part in his legal career, which were the sure foundation of his brilliant American success, have not failed him in India. So far as the Viceroy is concerned, indeed, the voice of detraction has hardly been heard. No greater tribute could be paid to one who in dark and perilous days has walked amid pitfalls discreetly, delicately, resolutely. When he returns to England his career will be by no means closed. Both in the House of Lords upon its judicial side, and in the Committee of the Privy Council, it will be in his power to continue to render great public service. Indeed, he might establish one new record. For should he ever sit upon the Judicial Committee of the Privy Council when it is constituted to hear Indian appeals, he will be the first ex-Viceroy who has ever assisted in this task.

I have spoken of the personal charm of Lord Reading. If you strip Tito Melema of his moral infirmities, you have something of Rufus Isaacs left. He adhered to, and adorned, the highest traditions of the English Bar, by whom he was beloved, and few great English figures have maintained so many friendships—some of them humble—with more warmth, affection, or fidelity.

The Right Hon.
Winston Spencer Churchill

The Right Hon. Winston Spencer Churchill

IT will, I think, be generally agreed that Mr.
Winston Churchill is one of the most remarkable men now living. Many will dispute about
many of his qualities. Some will praise one; others
will disparage another. But no one will dispute
that that strange and brilliant complex which is
Mr. Churchill is as arresting and as bewildering as
any in the world.

His great intellectual qualities were not discovered at an early age. Harrow, great as it was
and is, neither observed nor elicited his intellectual
quality; so that he very narrowly escaped a humiliat-
ing experience which is known in different slang at
every public school to those unhappy boys who
depart prematurely through poverty of scholarly
achievement.

And it would even appear that Lord Randolph
Churchill died in complete ignorance of the fact that
he had produced a son intellectually greater than
himself. He placed Winston in a Cavalry Regiment;
and there can be little doubt that if he had lived
he would have kept him there. He discerned nothing
remarkable, nothing of singular promise in a very
remarkable and original boy. There is still extant
a letter which he wrote shortly after his last tragic
visit to South Africa (when the hand of Fate was
already heavy upon him) in which he asked a great
magnate of that Dominion whether he could find
an opening for Winston, inasmuch as he did not

believe that he would make any career for himself in England.

But Lord Randolph died. The boy became captain of his own destiny. Thereafter (until, quite lately, he succeeded to a considerable family patrimony) he was dependent upon his own exertions. Nor did his talents prove inadequate to the task of providing him with surroundings which might satisfy a disposition easily contented with the best of everything. The boy thought stupid at Harrow ripened into precocious cleverness at Sandhurst, when confronted by congenial tasks wherein he detected the promise of advancement in what then seemed to be his career. And thereafter, with every year that passed, his mental stature and his taste for literature, adventure, and politics grew and prospered. Cavalry subaltern, soldier of fortune, journalist, author, politician, and artist, he has achieved distinction in all these versatile branches of human intellectual endeavour. He has touched many departments of combative literary and artistic effort, and has not failed to adorn each in the process.

To those who know him well it is very remarkable how complete is the public misconception of the man. He is looked upon as reserved, insolent, and even domineering. For these illusions his own demeanour is (unintentionally) much to blame. He has no small talk ; and says everything which comes into his mind. Sometimes caustic and disagreeable things come into it, though in private life this very seldom happens. He walks through the Lobbies of the House of Commons with an air appropriate to Napoleon Bonaparte on the morning of the crisis of the 18th Brumaire. He does not mean to be either reserved or rude; but he contrives to give the impression to those who know him little that he does not desire to know them more. Only his friends understand him well. And they know that there is no man in public life in England with a heart so warm, with a simplicity so complete, with a loyalty so unswerving and so dependable. He has, indeed, in the intimacy of personal friendship a quality which is almost feminine in its caressing charm And he has never in all his life failed a friend, however embarrassing the obligations, which he felt it necessary to honour, proved at the moment when he honoured them.

There is about him a simplicity which no other public man of the highest distinction possesses. Lord Morley said of Lord Randolph Churchill that if you educated him you would ruin him. Winston's education has been extremely partial, but he has attained by the force of sheer genius to a mental equipment more complete than most Senior Wranglers and most Heads of Colleges. It is reported of him, and I believe truly, that a friend once lent him Welldon's translation of Aristotle's " Ethics," with a particular request that he should carefully study what that friend (rightly or wrongly) believed to be the greatest book in the world. Winston read it (or read part of it) and is reported to have said that he thought it very good. " But," he added, " it is extraordinary how much of it I had already thought out for myself."

His political career is well known in its general features to all. When he entered the House of Commons he had already long before entered the homes of the people. He had served as a soldier of fortune with the Spanish forces at Cuba; he had taken part, a reckless subaltern, in the glorious charge of Omdurman; he had effected a romantic and wonderful escape from the jail at Pretoria; and he was Randolph Churchill's son. A more promising introduction for any Tory recruit in the House of Commons would have been difficult to imagine. And at the General Election at which he became Member of the House of Commons for Oldham, he was already so great a popular figure that both Arthur Balfour and Joseph Chamberlain invited this brilliant young man to speak for them in their respective election campaigns. But when the House of Commons met, the besotted folly which has always induced the Tory Party to discourage young men of genius unless they happened to be heirs to a Dukedom once again reproduced itself. " He can wait," has always been the Tory formula which has chilled the hopes of young and able men. Liberals have never been guilty of this colossal error. And so chance after chance of modest promotion went by. And all the time the Tory Party was committing one folly after another, until even Lord Hugh Cecil was driven into nominal if not actual opposition.

Winston characteristically jumped the whole fence. That he should have done so is one of the tragedies of modern politics, simply because fundamentally he has always been, of our generation, the most sincere and vivid believer in the stately continuity of English life. Like Disraeli, indeed, he believed that this continuity required a restless humanitarian solicitude in the interests of the humbler classes. But he was like a restive young thoroughbred. He had an extraordinarily thick-witted and clumsy rider, and he jibbed tragically. I suspect without knowing, that he has always regretted it. If he has true perspective he ought to regret it, because he took a sudden, and it may be an irretrievable, step which placed him out of alignment with his natural allies. And his combative qualities being what they are, it was quite certain that he would be betrayed more and more into extremes of denunciation and invective which would make the breach between himself and the Tory Party more and more difficult to reconcile.

Paradoxically enough, he always based himself, as a moral justification for his change of party, upon the Tariff Reform controversy. He has clung to this as a moral *tabula in naufragio*. For the new economic proposals enabled him to leave the Conservative Party with the claim that a wholly novel issue justified his defection. Mr. Lloyd George is not in the least a Free Trader; he is in economics an opportunist, as every sane man ought to be; for economics are not a static but a dynamic science, and the whole truth of the dismal business is that any man is a fool who dogmatically proclaims himself to be either a Free Trader or a Protectionist. But Winston Churchill is and has to be a dogmatic Free Trader, because, being in the very essence of himself an honest man, he must cling to an honest justification for a change of Party which I cannot doubt that he has always bitterly regretted. And consider how poignant in its consequences that unfortunate change was. Who can doubt that he would have succeeded to Arthur Balfour's sceptre? In the Parliament of 1906 he would have entered into his kingdom. His audacity, his Parliamentary *flair*, his amazing industry, would have carried him far beyond any of his rivals; and when the Great War began he would, in my judgment, unquestionably have been the Leader of the Unionist Party.

It may not unplausibly be retorted that the war found him First Lord of the Admiralty, with a reasonable prospect of being the greatest War Minister in history before it ended. Everything smiled upon him in August, 1914. He became a popular figure; and many of the shrewdest judges of political forces predicted that he must emerge from the war recalling and repeating the triumphs of Chatham. But surely some malignant godmother, quarrelling with the shining gifts given to this astonishing child, must have added a discordant note of malevolence at his birth. His work at the Admiralty and his general conception of the strategy of the war were alike admirable.

But his able, restless, ambitious temperament was hardly content with its own legitimate ambit. He saw too much, and he tried to do too much. No one department, hardly one war, was enough for him in that sublime and meteoric moment. His fundamental conceptions were sound and even brilliant; but they marched too far in front of the material resources which even he could command. He was right about Antwerp; he took great personal risks to make the Antwerp policy successful; but it was doomed to failure before the attempt was made. His conception of the Dardanelles adventure was daring, brilliant and masterly. If successful, the attack, as he conceived it, would have shortened the war by two years; there would probably have been

no Revolution in Russia and no Bolshevism, with
all which this would have meant to the civilisation
of Europe and to the security of the world.

And had he only been supreme with the uncon-
trolled power of appropriating from the Western
front what was necessary—and it was so little—to
make the Dardanelles campaign a certain success,
he would have been acclaimed to-day by the whole
world as the statesman whose brilliant and intuitive
genius won the war. *Dis aliter visum,* and from
First Lord of the Admiralty, with the formation of
the first Coalition Government, he declined to the
position of Chancellor of the Duchy of Lancaster.

His tenure of this minor office was not to be of
long duration. He was given command of a Battalion
in France, which he held for many months, and,
indeed, until the unit was disbanded. When this
happened, the Government and the Allied cause
were alike sagging; and Churchill was advised by
critics as acute as Lord Carson that his place was in
the House of Commons. One story survives of his
active service which is worth recording. When
holding the Ploegsteert line the Battalion H.Q. occupied a very disagreeable farmhouse (I once had
occasion to visit it) which from time to time was
heavily shelled. A General on a round of inspection
remonstrated with Winston, pointing out the danger
of the position. Winston replied by making it plain
that there was absolutely no other place available
which would enable him to retain the necessary
contact with his officers and men. The General
did not attempt to make any suggestion, but repeated insistently and a little petulantly, " I tell
you it is a very dangerous place." To whom Win-

ston, most respectfully—" Yes, sir ; but, after all, this is a very dangerous war."

Mr. Churchill, who at this time was being pursued by Mr. Gwynne of the *Morning Post* with the fussy, feeble rancour which that gentleman employs from time to time according to feminine orders, in the man-hunt of the moment, was not included in Mr. Lloyd George's Government at its formation. But an opportunity of adding to the Cabinet a mind so constructive and so suggestive was found when Dr. Addison left the Ministry of Munitions.

Here Winston was in his element, and the immense value of the public services he rendered, though well known to Sir Douglas Haig and his Staff, has never been sufficiently appreciated at home. The War Office still preserves a comparative chart illustrating the output of destructive agencies when he went to the Munitions Office and when he left it. Had he done no other work in the war he would have deserved well of the nation. His new office afforded unlimited scope alike for his ingenuity and his driving power. It may incidentally be observed that as First Lord of the Admiralty he had done more than any other individual to procure the adoption of the tank conception. I remember him describing to me its possibilities when I was on leave from France early in 1915. With his usual rhetorical brilliancy he depicted these great caterpillars marching over No Man's Land, eating up trenches, climbing hillocks, and jeering at every material obstacle. I thought he was mad ; but, as I was his guest, I thought it polite to listen. I was, however, completely ignorant of the possibilities of mechanical locomotion of this kind. It was more serious that others who ought to have known better derided and disparaged the idea.

I still have a copy of a Cabinet paper in which Winston urged upon his colleagues the immense contribution to the war which machines of this kind might render. It was always his strong desire, when they were at last produced, that they should not be used until they were assembled in such numbers on the Western Front as to win a great, if not a decisive, victory. But the soldiers who had previously derided the invention—one sapient General describing it as " Winston's folly "—when once they were in possession of the tanks, could not wait. And accordingly the greatest mechanical invention which Great Britain or any other combatant Power contributed to land warfare was almost squandered by its employment in insufficient force. Safeguarded and multiplied, the tanks might yet have reproduced the victorious destructiveness of Hannibal's elephants.

It is of interest to note that in this matter at least contemporary justice was done to Churchill. The Committee which was appointed by Mr. Lloyd George's Government to report upon the credit and value of many different inventions made during the war measured in weighty language, which must have delighted him, the value and the force of his contribution to the discovery of tanks.

I do not propose to examine here Mr. Churchill's work since the Armistice. I was never able to share the sanguineness with which he surveyed each new attempt to dislodge the Soviet murderers. But, at least, his impulses were sound and his miscalculations —if they were miscalculations—will not, perhaps, be too severely censured at a moment when the whole world has so recently been shocked by the judicial murder of high ecclesiastical persons.

Of the man as he is known to his friends this is hardly the place to speak. He is generally supposed to be aggressive and truculent. He has many of the conversational powers of Dr. Johnson, and could be both if he wished. But no man living is more tolerant, more easy, more companionable, in social intercourse. And his charm and friendship are as well known as his genius. He is indeed *anima candidissima*. He is almost the only man whom I have ever known who simply could not speak or acquiesce in, an untruth on a matter great or small, however convenient it might be.

Churchill fell with those of his colleagues who did not in a flash find salvation with Mr. Bonar Law. With his defeat at Dundee there passed for the moment from the Parliamentary scene a memorable, formidable, and vivid personality. He was, in my judgment, before he left it, the most powerful controversialist in the House of Commons. His form was literary and even classic; his arguments were lucidly conceived, logically arranged, and massively produced. In the Cabinet he was always an arresting, original, and eloquent adviser. It was not always necessary or perhaps wise to adopt his view, but no Cabinet could afford, and ours never did, to decide against him without giving the deepest consideration to the brilliant argument which rendered it so plausible.

An extreme section of the Conservative Party, to whom, paradoxically enough, he bears no small affinity, has definitely repelled him, with others, from the army which must hold the economic fort, upon which the commercial greatness of this country depends, from those who would subvert it. This is the fight—and this is the only fight—of the future.

With characteristic courage and independence he has chosen his side indifferent to the taunt that no man in English politics can change his party twice. Every fibre of his being is individualist; and in office or out of it—in Parliament or out of it —his sword will be flashing in the struggle which awaits us all. And as I survey the combative qualities of those who, equally with himself, are pledged to march in that crusade, I cannot think of one able to bring more decisive qualities to the issues which will so soon determine the genius of our people and the future of our civilisation.

The Right Hon.
The Earl of Derby

The Right Hon. the Earl of Derby, K.G.

THE subject of these observations belongs to one of the most ancient and distinguished families in England. The very names of his ancestors recall the romance of the English people; and their careers from the date of the Norman Conquest have kept pace with the developments of that people. So long ago as the year 1066 Adam de Aldithley marched with Duke William to England from Aldithley in Normandy. Partners in his adventure came two stout sons; the elder was Lyulph; the second was Adam de Aldithley the Second. The lineage of the Derby family is concerned with the second of these two sons. He became the father of William de Aldithley, to whom Thomas Stanley of Stafford gave his only daughter and heiress, Joan, in marriage.

There followed a long succession of knights and baronets each in his day and generation making proper and often notable contribution to the fortunes of contemporary England. Perhaps the most distinguished of these was Sir John Stanley, Knight of the Garter, Lord Deputy of Ireland in the early fifteenth century, who obtained a commission to seize on the City of York and its liberties, of which he duly availed himself. Not content with this, he obtained leave to possess himself of the Isle of Man on the forfeiture of Henry Percy, Earl of Northumberland. The fortunes of this particular Stanley waxed in the reign of King Henry IV. He became Treasurer of the Household to the King, and obtained license to fortify a house in Liverpool with embattled walls. In the same year his hold upon the Isle of Man was made regular and legal, for he was granted in fee that isle and castle, with the isles adjacent, and all the proper regalities and franchises.

Passing rapidly through the centuries, we may recall the memory of that Sir Thomas Stanley, the first Lord Stanley, who was Lord-Lieutenant of Ireland for six years from 1432, Controller of the Household and Chamberlain to Henry VI., and a Knight of the Garter. It is not possible within the limits of this article to mention, even with brief reference, all the members of this illustrious family who have played their part in English life. But some mention must be made of the Fourteenth Earl of Derby, scholar, orator, statesman, and Minister. At Christ Church, Oxford, he gained by his poem " Syracuse " the Chancellor's Prize for Latin Verse. He sat in the House of Commons successively as member for Stockbridge, Preston, Windsor, and North Lancashire. In 1844 he was summoned to the House of Lords in his father's barony, and in 1859 was made a Knight of the Garter. He was Under-Secretary of State for the Colonies under Lord Godrich ; Chief Secretary for Ireland from 1830 to 1833 ; Secretary of State for the Colonies from 1833-1834, again from 1841 to 1845, and First Lord of the Treasury in 1852, 1858, and 1866.

Enough has been said to make it plain that any man who is called Earl of Derby, if he is to emerge with distinction from the long line of those who have preceded him, must make a very decisive individual contribution. It is hard enough even to live up to the battle-cry, " On, Stanley, on ! " For myself, I regard it as frankly debatable whether it is a greater benefit or injury in life to be born of a stock, however illustrious, from which so much is expected.

The present Lord Derby has responded with every capacity which he possesses, or has been able by application to acquire, to the obligations imposed upon him by the traditions of his family. He is Chancellor of Liverpool University. He has been Lord Mayor of Liverpool. He represented for many years in the House of Commons a Lancashire constituency. He is an honorary colonel of I know not how many Lancashire regiments.

His connection with racing began in 1893, when, on the accession of his father to the title, both he and his father commenced a small racing stud.

Lord Derby (then Lord Stanley) began with a small but very lucky purchase. He bought from Count Kinsky a grey horse called Greywall, and with that horse he won the first race for which he ever ran a horse, and at the place where he would most wish to win a race—Liverpool. It is curious that his son, the present Lord Stanley, also won the first race for which he ran a horse, Young Pegasus.

The year 1911 marked the high-water mark of the successes of the Stanley stable, a total of £42,000 being the value of the stake money won.

In 1913 Stedfast, Dan Russell, Light Brigade, and others won the respectable total of £17,500.

Lord Derby has yet to achieve his great ambition to win the classic race founded by his ancestor.

He breeds practically all his own horses, and has a large stud both at Newmarket and at Knowsley. The only Derby ever won by his family [1] was won by the

_____

[1] This was written in 1923.

Lord Derby who started the race, and who won it with Sir Peter Teazle in 1787. And, although there seems a fatality against a member of the family winning the race named after them, Lord Derby does not despair even now of a prize which has eluded him so long.

We pass now to graver topics : *paulum majora canamus.*

Lord Derby was private secretary to Lord Roberts in South Africa. He was Junior Lord of the Treasury from 1895 to 1900, Financial Secretary to the War Office from 1900-1903, and Postmaster-General from 1903-1906. His tenancy of this office furnished almost the only infelicity of his career. He was entirely right in strenuously opposing the claims of the Post Office employees in the year 1905 ; but he was extremely unwise in branding those whom he had successfully resisted as bloodsuckers and black-mailers. This mistake perhaps cost him his own seat, and certainly threw the whole Post Office vote all over England against the Government in the election of 1906. But it was a solitary error of tact and judgment, and it does not happen to many politicians who have lived their lives in the searchlight of publicity to make so few.

In 1916 Lord Derby became Under-Secretary of State for War and Vice-President of the Army Council. In 1916 he became Secretary of State for War and President of the Army Council, an office which he held with complete adequacy until, in 1918, he became Ambassador Extraordinary and Plenipotentiary to the French Republic. The importance of his functions in this last office was somewhat obscured by the fact that so many conferences took

place in Paris which were attended by Cabinet
Ministers of the highest consequence. But he nevertheless played a great part in Paris, and his name will
certainly be recalled at the Quai d'Orsai with those
of the long succession of English Ambassadors who
by bonhomie, tact, hospitality, and charm have
endeared themselves to a nation which they perfectly
understood.

This preface has been long. But it is by no means
easy to dismiss in a few words a pedigree the roots of
which are thrown so deep in English life, and which
has contributed at every stage so many illustrious
citizens to that life. The competition is severe, but
I cannot doubt that the present Lord Derby will rank
very high even in the records of the Stanley family.
I have known him for thirty years. I can only
recall one very unimportant difference of opinion with
him during the whole of that period. I am bold
enough, therefore, to think that I have some knowledge of him, his aims, and his character.

Attempting the kind of superficial analysis which
is all that is possible within the compass of these
articles, I say without hesitation that his most striking
and admirable characteristic is his sense of civic
and public duty. Everything in life was given to
him which in a weak and self-indulgent man might
have paralysed initiative and labour, and might in
the end, in a less conscientious man, have corrupted
the spirit of public service. He inherited a noble
name, wealth beyond avarice, and several palaces.
He has never ceased to labour as constantly, and,
I believe, as disinterestedly, for what he believed to
be the good of his country, as if his daily bread had
depended upon his daily exertions.

He has been a Conservative all his life. To his labour is largely due the position of the Conservative Party in Lancashire, and particularly in Liverpool. He has not obtained a position so dazzling by the facile gift of eloquence, to which he himself, though quite a genial and painstaking speaker, would lay no claim. He has attained it in the first place by self-denial and by dogged tenacity, by sacrificing his social life to irksome political engagements, by making long train journeys to attend meetings which must often in perspective have seemed trivial and unimportant, counting his own leisure and enjoyment as absolutely unimportant, if and when these came into collision with his sense of public duty. And he has been aided always by a natural kindliness and charm which are kindly and charming simply because they are so spontaneous. He is extraordinarily human; and the explanation of his success with the democracy of Lancashire is that he has never been the victim of the delusion of caste. He quite genuinely sees in every man an equal and a possible friend. From the first word to the last Thackeray's " Book of Snobs " had nothing to teach Lord Derby.

It would be surprising if qualities so charming had not their antidote. Lord Derby finds it more difficult to refuse than to give. The same temperamental weakness has brought many delightful ladies, from Moll Flanders onwards, to disaster. And it has occasionally in Lord Derby's case produced the distressing consequence that he has promised two quite different people, who want quite different things, his warm support. And the resultant crisis has always caused him genuine pain.

He has, indeed, a loyalty to colleagues which a

little exceeds his loyalty to causes. For instance, he knew three months ago that Lancashire would not in existing circumstances give the slightest support to a general tariff. And he knew also that to attempt to impose it upon the Conservative Party in Lancashire by a swift election was sheer madness. He could probably have prevented the campaign; he could certainly by the threat of resignation, have forbidden the election. But while Lord Derby is working with and for a colleague whom he likes, the warmth, simplicity, and likeableness of his temperament are apt to impair a critical faculty which, when not so affected, is of high quality. He saw, or thought he saw, that the Conservative Party was committed to the campaign. He would not face the risk of disrupting the party by standing aloof even with a solid Lancashire rallying more and more behind him. If he committed an error of judgment at all, it sprang from a generous weakness. And three or four times a day, as long as the battle lasted, he was found on Lancashire platforms compromising that which could not be compromised, and explaining that which could hardly (in his view) be explained. No candidate at the election made greater personal exertions than Lord Derby who was not a candidate. And if the Lancashire campaign was disappointing, it ought to be remembered that if Lord Derby had actively opposed, or even stood aloof, there would not have returned to Westminster ten Conservative members from Lancashire.

He has, of course, all his life had the very great advantage that he is not by temperament a self-seeking man. He likes influence, but is largely indifferent (as he can afford to be) to ambition. He has been known to say that he had two ambitions in life : the first, to win the Derby ; the second, to become Prime Minister of Great Britain. I rather doubt whether he has very seriously entertained the second. For he is essentially a modest man, and I suspect that his own estimate of his qualities and powers would be lower than many others who know him well would form. But he has qualities which, if a suitable crisis arose, make it quite conceivable that he might climb (or be placed) to the highest position of all in the State. These rewards come sometimes as the result of the ambitions of a lifetime. We know, for instance, that they were the dream and inspiration of Disraeli's incredible efforts and unforgettable career. But different men have different gifts, and different destinies. All that can be said of Lord Derby in this connection is, that he brings to the booths, if ever an election takes place in which he is a possible competitor, an almost unequalled record of public service, immense personal popularity, and a character for simple and sincere friendliness which has not often been surpassed in the records of British statesmen.

The Right Hon.
Sir Robert Horne, M.P.

The Right Hon. Sir Robert Horne, M.P.

SIR ROBERT STEVENSON HORNE was born
in February, 1871. He is to-day, therefore, in
his fifty-fourth year. He has had a very interesting and a very varied career. His education was completely Scotch; he was brought up
upon porridge and upon Scotch stories. He was,
indeed, so much a Scotsman that he never forgot
the road to England. At Glasgow University he
was President of the University Conservative Club
in 1891, and President of the Students' Representative Council in 1892. Nor did politics exhaust his
energies. In 1892 he was elected John Clark Scholar
in Philosophy. He obtained first-class honours in the
Department of Mental Philosophy in 1893. He won
the Ewing Fellowship in 1894. He graduated for
his future close association with Mr. Lloyd George
by becoming Lecturer in Philosophy in the University
College of North Wales in 1895. From 1896 to 1900
he was Examiner in Philosophy in the University of
Aberdeen.

In the midst of these somewhat high-browed
activities, he found time to be called to the Scottish
Bar in the year 1896. He subsequently attained to
a very considerable rank at that bar, obtaining his
patent as King's Counsel in the year 1910; and thereafter reaching a position among the first five or six
of the very competent men who lead the Scottish
Bar.

In order that this quite remarkable record of

achievement may be made not less complete than the somewhat tedious catalogue of the Allies who invaded Troy, it may be added that in the year 1917 Sir Robert became the Inspector-General of Transportation, embellishing this appointment with the rank of Lieutenant-Colonel : that in 1917 he was made Director of the Department of Materials and Priority at the Admiralty : that in 1918 he rose to the position of Director of the Admiralty Labour Department : and that he became in the same year Third Civil Lord of the Admiralty. Nor was the swift and agreeable course of promotion closed by his tenure of these important but secondary offices. In 1920 he was appointed by Mr. Lloyd George (who was the first to discern his great gifts) President of the Board of Trade, holding this office until the year 1921. In 1921 he was promoted, again by Mr. Lloyd George, to the high office of Chancellor of the Exchequer, a position which he occupied until the fall of the Coalition Government.

This recital, inevitable, if rather tiresome, has made it plain that we are dealing with a very unusual, if with a singularly fortunate, man. For his activities and his successes have by no means ended with the temporary interruption of his political career. Our philosopher, lawyer, and politician immediately cast his eyes about for new worlds to conquer. The City of London, after all, since the days of Richard Whittington, has afforded an attractive lure. And many of our Scottish friends travelling the broad road, which Dr. Johnson loved to describe as the only good road in Scotland, have responded alike to the attraction and to the lure. Sir Robert Horne has attempted many occupations in a career of comparatively brief duration ; and he has not failed to adorn each in the process.

And, accordingly, when the break up of the Coalition left him a free man, he devoted himself, as Mr. McKenna had done before him, to the activities of business life. It is a tribute to remarkable versatility that his success in these novel fields has not lagged behind the many various performances of his earlier life. He is to-day a director of the Suez Canal Company, and of the Great Western Railway Company. He is also a director and vice-chairman of Baldwins, Ltd. ; and in many undefinable ways he has stamped himself upon the City as a political importation who must be both respected and recognised.

No man could have lived a life at once so various and so successful who did not possess many very enviable qualities. Indeed, upon the whole Sir Robert Horne must share with Sir Eric Geddes the distinction of being one of Mr. Lloyd George's two greatest war discoveries. Unlike Sir Eric, Sir Robert was a politician from youth. He was born and bred a Scotch Tory. His University record makes that plain. Unlike Sir Eric, all whose interest lies in business, Sir Robert is deeply concerned in politics. For his political advancement he was very much indebted to the War, but not less indebted to his own extraordinary qualities.

But for the War, indeed, he might never have emerged at all into that larger British atmosphere which the ablest Scotsmen alone think worth breathing. For in both the elections of 1910 he stood as a Conservative candidate and was defeated. He would, indeed, be the first to own that his chance of playing a conspicuous hand in the greatest game of all was given to him by Mr. Lloyd George. The ex-Premier, indeed, delighted in him, and believed in him, from the first moment when they made acquaintance. Efficiency, anecdotage and humanity brought them together ever more closely. Horne, indeed, became the man whom the King delighted to honour. And the younger, and less experienced, man responded and developed with the encouragement and promotion which were so bountifully and swiftly afforded him. The intellectual qualities were always there. They often are, and yet he who owns them not unfrequently goes to his grave undiscovered and undistinguished. And so it might easily have happened that the very remarkable services which Horne rendered in various capacities in the War would have received only subordinate rewards, had it not been for the estimate formed of his ability by Mr. Lloyd George, then at the zenith of his power and of his prestige.

So high, indeed, was that estimate that Mr. Lloyd George made Sir Robert Horne Chancellor of the Exchequer at a moment when most people thought that that office would have fallen to Mr. Winston Churchill. This promotion, remarkable as it was, excited little jealousy and no opposition. The duties of the office were, at the moment when Sir Robert assumed them, extraordinarily arduous. He was never overwhelmed by them ; and he always contrived to give to his colleagues the very comfortable impression that he was master of the difficulties which beset him. He struck out no new line ; he adhered to the sound policy of debt reduction which Mr. Austen Chamberlain had initiated ; and he was always the vigilant critic of excessive expenditure. And yet in that criticism, applied as it always was to a wholly exceptional period, he never allowed himself to decline into pedantry. As Chancellor of the Exchequer, he was competent, intelligent, firm, and yet open to conviction. The finances of this country would not have suffered had he been afforded a longer reign. Nor do I think that the American settlement would have been less favourable to the finances of this country had he remained at the Exchequer.

The warmth of Mr. Lloyd George's recognition —with all that it involved—was never forgotten by Sir Robert Horne ; and it is on the whole true to say that, strong as were the political ties which bound Mr. Chamberlain and myself to Mr. Lloyd George at the moment when the Coalition fell, equal political ties and at least as strong associations of personal friendship connected Sir Robert Horne with the ex-Premier. It was therefore inevitable that he should throw in his lot with those who, when their advice was rejected by the Conservative Party, found themselves unable to serve in the Government of Mr. Bonar Law, and had consequently no share in the misfortunes which followed (as we had foretold) upon the formation of that Government.

But it is the special quality of Sir Robert Horne's temperament—a very valuable one—that he never makes enemies, and it is therefore always certain that, without the slightest disloyalty on his part to any associates, he will always have friends in both camps. Indeed, why should he have any enemies ? He never says a bitter word about anyone. I doubt, indeed, whether he ever thinks bitterly about anyone. He never, so far as I have learnt, has ever cherished a single animosity. We have seen indeed that he is a philosopher; but surely he must belong to the school of the Laughing Philosophers. If the achievements of his life had not proved him to be a serious man, in the sense in which the French use the word serious, it would sometimes have seemed difficult to make this acknowledgment in his favour. For his temperament is compounded of gaiety. If you did not know how much serious work he had accomplished, and how efficiently, you might be tempted almost to dismiss him as a *flâneur*. And yet he is conscientious even in his levities. For no man could make so many jokes, and tell so many stories, who had not made a serious, if subordinate, business of collecting jokes and stories.

And I myself find Sir Robert Horne's zest in social life very attractive. If that life absorbs too much of the time of a Minister his devotion to it becomes a weakness. But Sir Robert never made this mistake. His work, punctually and conscientiously discharged, was always put first. Only when that was done, and well done, has he given play to the lighter side of his temperament. Mankind will always be divided into different types. Some draw refreshment from the delights of social gaiety; others from a morose and unbroken absorption in the severity of official duty. Sir Robert has never even affected to belong to the second of these classes. But he has none the less done work worthy of the most solemn Puritan who ever frowned upon the Embassy Club.

Whether he is ever depressed or not, I do not know. I have myself enjoyed association and friendship with him for some years, and I have never known him in anything but uproarious spirits. And of this I am sure; that when the last dread passage in Charon's boat (I hope it will be long postponed) confronts him, as it must confront us all, he will with characteristic Scottish prudence have disposed of his last obol before leaving the world; but will pay his fare by a Scotch story which has already by much repetition gained the meed of mundane applause.

It is very easy to overrate a dull plodding and learned man; just as, in my opinion, the contemporaries of Sir Charles Dilke exaggerated the merits of that tiresome and encyclopædic statesman. It is just as easy to under-estimate the merits in statecraft of one who laughs and jests and unbends in every social situation which affords him the excuse. Personally, I greatly prefer lively men to dull men; and informal men to pompous men. Sir Robert is both lively and informal. And it is to me his chief attraction that he combines what his great countryman Stevenson called " a little judeecious levity " with qualities as solid as are possessed by any man in public life to-day.

His earlier career exhibited no small capacity for abstract thought. His progress at the Bar marked his possession of many valuable practical qualities. In the great political world hardly anyone of our generation has made progress so swift and so deserved. That world to-day is in flux. It is difficult in our Party to write of one that his career is finished; or of another that his career is beginning; but of Sir Robert Horne it may be moderately claimed that, if and so long as his interests are centred in politics, there are hardly any limits to the ambitions which he may legitimately entertain.

And he possesses this very great advantage over many men whose success has been swift and unexpected. His head has never been turned ; his un-affected good humour has never been deflected ; his dazzling and swift promotion has left him the same simple and merry companion that he was when he first entered the House of Commons. It is quite true that he is *bon homme ;* but this quality does not spring from calculation, but from the very nature of the man. For he genuinely radiates an honest merri-ment and good humour which are the true fruit of a gay and sunny temperament. Sir Robert Horne, in a word, has contributed much to the liveliness, to the charm, and to the good humour of English political life in dark and lowering days when those who could offer these gifts have been rare and shining figures.

Field-Marshal
The Earl Haig of Bemersyde, K.G.

Field-Marshal the Earl Haig of Bemersyde, K.G.

IT is on the whole true that for one person who can say off-hand that Lord Liverpool was Prime Minister in June, 1815, a million could name the man who crossed swords with Napoleon that year and won the fight of Waterloo. Soldiers to-day, therefore, entertain themselves by the surmise that a century hence, when the man who held the political wheel will be recalled only with an effort of memory, the name of the man whose hand was weighty to thrust a tyrant from his throne will leap to the lip of an intelligent schoolboy. They are, perhaps, too sanguine. The reputation of Lord Chatham has overtopped that of his generals. The plain truth is that in time of peace the most eminent generals comport themselves with great civility to politicians. In time of war they never mention the noun " politician " without the adjective " d——d." But the paradox of the matter is exhibited by this indisputable circumstance, that wherever an intellect of incomparable valuation has been devoted to the science of war, he who has possessed it has been alike a statesman and a politician. If Hannibal, Julius Cæsar, Oliver Cromwell, Marlborough, Clive, Napoleon—all those men who have left behind them a very memorable political record—had none of them ever placed his hand upon his sword, they would still have bequeathed to history the names of accomplished politicians.

It is, however, worthy of comment at a moment when every notable individual has his biography announced before his burial is complete, that fifty years elapsed before any Life of the Duke of Wellington appeared ; nor, indeed, was it until after the issue of Mr. Fortescue's later volumes that the full scope of the Duke's earlier energies was ever disclosed. If it be true that Lord Haig has confided important documents into custody, with imperative instructions that a long period is to elapse before they are publicly dealt with, it is evident that an interim study of his career cannot be profound. It is, however, to be hoped that the matters so bequeathed are not very controversial, for that would be a little unfair to others possibly affected, who might wish to make a reply, and who, if the period be long enough, will undoubtedly be dead.

If the biography of Lord Haig is to be reserved for the future, it may be noted that he has lent himself very sparingly to the ear of the chronicler. Few men, indeed, have attained so considerable a position in public esteem while appealing so little to the public eye. If he has not actually shrunk from publicity, he has never made the slightest attempt to secure it. His public appearances, except upon military occasions, have been few ; his utterances brief, and usually marked by little resonance. In private conference he has indeed occasionally given the impression of being almost tongue-tied. His excursions into fields outside his own province have been closely restricted. In his life, of which he has scarcely passed the prime, ambition may—or may not—have been a motive power ; he has at least never allowed ambition to carry him outside the range of professional duties, although he has himself carried these duties to the highest level a soldier can occupy.

Lord Haig's birth, of highly considered Scotch parents, the easy circumstances of his boyhood, helpful though these and other conditions may have been, furnished him with no passport to special favour; if he was to achieve military fame, he must carve his own way to it. Nor was there any particular promise of future distinction in his career either at Clifton or at Brasenose. The first note of real promise was sounded at Sandhurst just forty years ago. Soon after his entrance there a visitor inquired of one of the officers whether there were any cadets who seemed to stand out from their fellows.

"Well," was the reply, "there is a cadet here called Douglas Haig, a Scotch lad, who is top at everything—books, drill, riding, sports and games; he is to go into the Cavalry; and what is more, he will be top of the Army before he has finished."

Ten years later Sir Lonsdale Hale, the military critic, wrote from the Staff College: "There is a young Cavalry officer here, Haig, of the 7th Hussars, who, if I mistake not, will go very far indeed."

But, before that prediction had been made, the story had run in India that the Adjutant of the 7th Hussars had set a new standard of Cavalry efficiency; that he was proving it possible to combine keenness for sport with serious study of the science of war: and that Captain Haig was a marked man for the higher branches of Staff work. For thirteen years he was to see no active service; and it was not until the advance to Omdurman in the summer of 1898 that he was able to exhibit military quality, and, incidentally, to bring himself under the notice—never afterwards relaxed—of Lord Kitchener. For some reason no official narrative of this highly organised campaign was ever produced, and Mr. Churchill's " River War " stands as the only real record. A year or two later, however, there was published " An Account of the Work of the Egyptian Cavalry in the Atbara and Omdurman Campaign." The pamphlet appeared over no signature, but it was notorious among soldiers that Douglas Haig had made his first effort as an author.

A well-known man of letters was responsible the other day for the dictum that " a soldier almost always writes well." I believe this generalisation to be completely untrue ; whatever truth it possesses is due to the obligation imposed upon soldiers of drafting concise and lucid reports and orders. It may, of course, be less indulgently said that soldiers never attempt to write unless they are an exception to their order, and have some skill with the pen. Lord Haig, on the platform, is very hesitating in speech, rhetorically quite unimpressive, not too rich in vocabulary, and only carries his points by a sheer honesty of purpose plainly ingrained in every word he utters. On paper—I am told that in this field he never asks or accepts advice—he is clear, easy, enamoured of his subject, and quite readable. He was wise in taking the unusual (if not unprecedented) step of securing the copyright of his despatches, which will take their place—apart from their professional and historical value—among the widely-read books of the day.

After the Calipha had been crushed and the

Sudan redeemed, Haig passed at once from North to South Africa, and there, in that long and dreary warfare, from the Colesburg operations down to the Peace of Vereeniging, he established himself as a fighter of the first order. After two years' command of the 17th Lancers he proceeded to India as Inspector-General of Cavalry. From which office, despite some opposition in high places, he pronounced himself as an incorrigible upholder of shock tactics and arch-apostle of the *arme blanche*.

In the Great War, rightly or wrongly, he resisted all inducements made to him to send home this branch; and at a dinner given shortly after the Armistice he vehemently protested against cavalry being lightly dismissed as an obsolete instrument. He insisted that they were indispensable services in the retreat from Mons, and that their part in the final advance from Amiens was of itself sufficient to justify their retention in the theatre of war. Most instructed critics have reached the conclusion that the cavalry in France played and could play no part adequate to their numbers; that there were throughout those continuing crises theatres of war in which they could have been more usefully employed; and that the fact that the greatest infantry war in history was almost entirely conducted by cavalry generals led to immense wastage of man-power.

The South African War had shown that military training on the scientific side left much to be desired, and at the end of it for three years Lord Haig dedicated himself as Director of Military Training and Director of Staff Duties at Headquarters to this subject. The military schoolroom which he then occupied was to furnish many apt scholars, and the hand of the instructor could be traced in much of the work which proved of sterling merit in the years to come.

Meanwhile there occurred an event lighter and more romantic. On his return from India Sir Douglas Haig was the guest of the King and Queen at Windsor Castle for Ascot races; before the week was over it was known that a marriage had been arranged between the already famous soldier and the Queen's highly attractive Maid of Honour.

A further brief period in India as Chief of the Staff was marked by continuous efficiency, but was cut short to enable him to assume the blue ribbon of War Office appointment—the Command at Aldershot. Two years only were allowed to prepare that command to take its place in the miniature Army which in 1914 was to bear the brunt of the German attack; but these two years were sufficient to polish a slender weapon to the highest pitch of perfection, and to set up a standard which the Kitchener Armies observed and maintained.

In the summer of 1915 it was generally realised that a change was imminent in the Command on the Western Front. The succession was a theme of anxious discussion. The choice was thought to lie between Sir Douglas Haig and Sir William Robertson. As a matter of fact the choice, if any existed, lay between the selection of Haig and a request to the Secretary of State to assume the post himself. The actual dilemma, however, never arose. Lord Kitchener's own vigilant survey of Haig's work allowed no room for doubt that Haig would on the whole prove adequate even to the immense situation by which he was confronted.

It is not within the scope of this paper even to touch on the operations which for nearly three years Haig was to direct ; beginning with the relief that enabled the French to hold Verdun, and ending with the final plan of attack which the French Commander-in-Chief frankly preferred to his own. Haig's massive endeavour, absolutely direct in purpose and complete in result, marks a military period which for interest has never been approached, and will perhaps never be rivalled in our military annals.

And in this connection the statement of Marshal Foch will be recalled, that his admiration for the courage and endurance of the British soldier was not greater than his appreciation of the skill of their leader.

It is not, of course, pretended that his leadership was not disfigured by many terrible errors Indeed, few of the Higher Commands in any of the armies of the world can be protected from this charge. The whole Paschendaale offensive, vehemently, but vainly, protested against by the Cabinet, futile in its results and bloody in its consequence, was a tragic illustration of obstinate error. And equally, the pointless prolongation of the Battle of the Somme —entirely defensible in its inception—was one of the greatest follies of the war. Two Englishmen were destroyed for every German who perished in that struggle.

Haig would certainly endorse Macaulay's axiom that " to carry the spirit of peace into war is a weak and cruel policy." War is a desperate remedy, of which the very essence is violence, and it is no doubt true that languid warfare tends not to save blood but to squander it. Any fruitless sacrifice of men was abhorrent to the British Commander, but he never shrank from putting down what he believed to be the price of substantial success. The trouble was that quite often he and his Staff officers were entirely mistaken. But he cared for his men—for their health and welfare—no less than for their steadiness and stability. Indeed, ungracious though it may sound, he cared for them more than they cared, or could perhaps reasonably be expected to care, for him. He was never actually inaccessible, but he was always quite remote. There have often been men in high places—and he was one of them—who from sheer selflessness cannot understand the value which attaches to a genial air; to a familiar nod of the head; to the motion of an outstretched hand.

The coming of Haig would never—like the coming of Roberts—light up faces in the camp. But if he did not win affection, he enjoyed the confidence of every individual on the Western Front, from the Army Commander to the last-joined recruit. And as the Commander-in-Chief gave, so he expected to receive, the best that lay within the powers of subordinates. Slackness in work, sloppiness in appearance, were insupportable to him; plain incompetence he pitilessly rejected as prejudicial to the public service. But if never fluent in praise, he was slow in reprimand, especially for what seemed an error of judgment. Rebuke was infrequent, and reserved for flagrant neglect. But when it came, it was scathing in text and tone. Yet often then, so strict was the judgment he passed on himself, that if he felt he had exceeded what the occasion called for, he would let the culprit know his regret for an expression which even by a hair's breadth seemed on reflection excessive.

And above all and accounting for all that he did and dared must be remembered Haig's serene outlook. Unruffled by rumour, he never permitted himself to be fussed or flurried. However tempestuous the conditions, he never deprived himself of the leisure of mind necessary to form a decision ; the decision once formed was irrevocable. As he was patient to wait, so he was prompt to act. His habitual calmness was that of a strongly controlled, not of a passionless or apathetic nature. In his darkest hour there was no despondency ; in the hour when his final success had become certain there was no undue elation.

History, moving with passionless ease among facts and figures, now scarcely attainable, will assign their just due to the men to whom was entrusted the conduct of the Great War. Military history will draw perhaps with greater particularity a distinction in merit between the commanders on whose skill hung the fate of bloody battles. Some of these will perhaps be found among that pathetic company who spent themselves in their country's service, but to whom no justice was done until long after they passed away. The calm courage of the Grand Duke Nicholas will one day stand out in high relief ; the exploits of Cadorna will some time be fully realised ; Joffre, whatever his shortcomings may have been, will be, and deserves to be, immortal as the Commander-in-Chief who won the Battle of the Marne. Nivelle's defence of Verdun will be remembered long after his failure in Champagne has been forgotten. Foch will stand on a pinnacle all his own.

And under the clear light which posterity will enjoy, it will, I think, be written that the strength and endurance of the British leader, fortified by his confidence in the strength and endurance of his troops, were finally strong to drag down the strongholds of German resistance and to thrust an implacable enemy from the fair fields he had despoiled.

It has often been suggested that if the assassin's bullet in Paris had cut short Wellington's career at its zenith, he would have died in public esteem a greater man. It would seem that Lord Haig has decided that the fame he has achieved matches his ambition, and that the autumn of his life shall be spent in retirement. But such retirement sets no abrupt term to the loyal activities of a soldier. As a field-marshal he remains an officer on full pay, liable and eligible at any time to be called upon for any and every military duty.

But for the past five years, and probably for all the years to come, a self-imposed duty has filled —and will fill—all his time and thoughts. He took up his high command as a simple and sacred duty. He did the right; he conquered and he had reason to rejoice. But the victory which he won was won in dust, blood, maiming, and agony; Lord Haig has stood solid and four-square, the stern and unbending champion of the rights of the men who in those fateful years trod the *Via Dolorosa*. His place among military conquerors may be undetermined; but there is assuredly reserved for him an even nobler title. Justly proud of his soldierly honours, he may yet be prouder of having proved himself the Soldier's Friend.

And to conclude this sketch of one who was in obstinacy, in courage, and perhaps even in unimaginativeness, the very type of those whom he commanded, I may perhaps record a letter—I believe at present unpublished—which he wrote to the Secretary of State for War on the Christmas Day of 1918, enclosing a map which made plain the final operations :—

Dear Mr. Churchill,—

The enclosed map shows the eight great battles which we fought between Amiens and Auvergne, and the results.

You will also see from the same table, that the British Army took more prisoners in the period under consideration than all the other Allies together.

Wishing you the best of good luck in the coming year,

I am,

Yours very truly,

Douglas Haig.

In this, the very culminating crisis of the war, the British Armies took 188,700 prisoners and 2,840 guns ; the French Armies 139,000 prisoners, 1,880 guns ; the American Armies, 43,300 prisoners and 1,421 guns.

The Field-Marshal underwent dark and doubtful days in the long period of his stewardship ; he had many critics ; but seldom, in spite of them, deviated from his plans. The culmination of the Great War placed him, with whatever limitations he had, among the Immortals. And his name will go down to history as one of the conquering generals of the British Empire.

The Right Hon.
Lord Buckmaster

The Right Hon. Lord Buckmaster

LORD BUCKMASTER of Cheddington was born on January 9, 1861, so that he is to-day in his sixty-third year. He was educated at Christ Church, where his career was distinguished. He was junior student, and is to-day an honorary student, of that ancient foundation. He was called to the Bar in the year 1884. He was elected, like Mr. Ramsay MacDonald, Mr. Snowden, and other distinguished people, a member of the House of Commons in 1906. The unstable constituency of Cambridge abandoned him in 1910 ; but the Keighley Division of Yorkshire provided him in 1911 with a seat which he held until 1914.

In 1911 he was appointed Counsel for the University of Oxford. In 1913 he became Solicitor-General. In the critical years of 1914-1915 he discharged, with incomplete success (as others had done before him), the unthankful duties of Director of the Press Bureau. The formation of Mr. Asquith's first Coalition Government made it plain that there existed an unconquerable Tory proscription of Lord Haldane. So far as it is known, or has ever been suggested by anyone except the Editor of the *Morning Post*, no single point of conduct or opinion distinguished Lord Haldane from either Mr. Asquith, Mr. McKenna, Lord Buckmaster, or Sir Edward Grey. But it had been spread about—and was commonly believed—that Lord Haldane, who had done more to win the war than any identifiable Die-hard, even including Mr. Gwynne of the *Morning Post*, was the friend of Germany. And accordingly he was thrown to the wolves. Lord Buckmaster thus, when Sir John Simon decided upon a political career, somewhat unexpectedly, and in a singular and complicated moment, took his seat upon the Woolsack.

Unlike most of those who have been the subject of the sketches which I have heretofore attempted, Lord Buckmaster's name, though, of course, well known, is not of national notoriety. And yet it is a name which deserves to be, and ought to be, very well known by his countrymen. He was far the most successful practitioner of his day upon the Chancery side. He was, indeed, an advocate of unmatched learning, ingenuity, and lucidity; and of a mental and verbal readiness which recalled the fact that he had been trained in the rough and tumble of the Common Law.

Had Lord Buckmaster refused the Woolsack, it is as certain as anything can be that he would to-day be earning an income of £30,000 or £40,000 a year. And yet the particularly mean taunt is still made against him, as against others, on Labour lips, that he is a pensioner upon the charity of the State. It is time that Lord Haldane and Sir Patrick Hastings enlightened the more ignorant of their colleagues upon a somewhat elementary matter. For eight years Lord Buckmaster has never refused to sit in the Final Court of Appeal, either in the House of Lords or on the Judicial Committee, when requested to do so by the Lord Chancellor of the day. Indeed no ex-Lord Chancellor in my experience —which extends over a period of five years—has ever refused to do so, unless disabled by health. The pension of an ex-Lord Chancellor who sits, when engaged upon these duties, to revise the decisions of the Lord Chief Justice and the Master of the Rolls, is considerably less than the emoluments of either of those distinguished men. Indeed, his pension is exactly equal in amount to that of the *puisne* judges who comprise the original court in which litigation of consequence commences.

And yet it is spoken of, by men who ought to know better, as if it was an abuse that a man who could, by general admission, earn £30,000 a year at the Bar, and whose services are indispensable, if the final Court of Appeal is to be efficiently manned, receives an emolument of £5,000 a year. The Bench and the Bar of England are fully aware of the unfairness of this particular recrimination. It may perhaps be moderately hoped that the existence of a Labour Government, and the experience which it has gained, may in compensation for its obvious mischiefs, make away with a taunt as ignorant as it is foolish.

Lord Buckmaster has many qualities which entitle him to be even better known and more widely respected than he is. He is in the first place unquestionably one of the most gifted living English orators. He possesses not only the eloquence of the spoken word, but also that of the underlying literary quality which re-creates without disillusion that which was heard, when it is read in print.

He was in the House of Commons an unfrequent speaker. But he never interposed in debate without decisive effect. In the 1906 Parliament a violent party debate took place upon the alleged partisanship of Mr. Justice Grantham in trying election petitions. Mr. Justice Grantham was a rugged, attractive Tory gentleman, unconventionally, but according to type, appointed to the Bench by Lord Halsbury. He was utterly incapable of giving any consciously dishonest decision upon any matter, whether it were political or non-political. But it unfortunately happened that his mind was so rigidly constituted that it was entirely impossible, in its view, for the Tory Party, or any member of that party, ever to be wrong; or for the Liberal Party, or for any member of that party, ever to be right. And his selection, therefore, for the task of trying election petitions was perhaps a little unfortunate. Certainly his conduct of a particular election petition, and the remarks made by him in the course of its hearing, were open to critical comment. And so a very heated debate arose in the House of Commons.

Far the most striking speech in the debate, and one which perhaps averted a decision involving an address from the two Houses for the removal of the learned judge, was made by a comparatively young King's Counsel, who had not hitherto intervened in debate. He spoke with so much eloquence; and placed upon so lofty a ground the importance of assuming, however difficult it might be in an individual case, the impartiality of the judicial atmosphere, that he dissuaded his fellow-Liberals from a course which must have made the Bench, with disastrous results, the centre of fierce political controversy.

I wish to make it plain that my recollections of this crisis, and of the debate to which it gave birth, are not in their essence derogatory to the great common sense and the many admirable qualities which the late Mr. Justice Grantham possessed. He was, on the contrary, the very type of an English country gentleman. In dealing with issues of fact he possessed considerable acuteness. But he was not sufficiently a craftsman in the science of the law to make the idea ludicrous, as it is with those who are the true children of that science, that when they sit upon the Bench they should allow their legal minds to be deflected even a hair's breadth by any non-legal, still less by any political, consideration.

I did not hear Mr. Buckmaster speak for many months after that first debate. But when Mr. Lloyd George introduced his notorious Budget, that strange Bill was found to contain a clause which substituted for the ordinary law courts a kind of civil Star Chamber, which was to determine the rights of citizens upon many vital points, thereby depriving them of their access to the courts of law. Here again, Mr. Buckmaster made a decisive intervention in debate. He spoke against his own leaders and against the official proposal. And he produced so deep an effect not only upon the opponents of the Budget, but upon its official supporters, that the objectionable clause was almost completely withdrawn.

But it must be freely admitted that his speeches in the House of Commons, admirable as they were, had given little indication of the great rhetorical qualities which his personality in the House of Lords, and his contributions to its debates, have made it plain that he possesses. His tenure of the Chancellorship was too short to afford him any great opportunity for distinction except upon the judicial side of his duties, of which I will say something hereafter.

When the Asquith Government fell, it fell so

rapidly and so unexpectedly that no provision was made for giving Lord Buckmaster a step in the peerage : perhaps in any event the short period of his office would have made such promotion difficult ; but the consequences have been unfortunate. A word of explanation may be given here to those who are not familiar with the technical rules of precedence among judges in the Final Court of Appeal.

It may in the first place be made plain that the conduct and the promptitude of business in that assembly depend a great deal upon the qualities of the presiding judge. In the House of Lords, and in the Judicial Committee, ex-Lord Chancellors preside over all other judges in virtue merely of the fact that they have once occupied the Woolsack. But precedence amongst ex-Lord Chancellors is determined, not by their seniority as Lord Chancellors, but by the rank which they hold in the House. And therefore Lord Buckmaster, though senior in the date of his appointment to Lord Finlay, to myself, and to Lord Cave, is junior to each of us for the purpose of presiding ; though, of course, he is senior to any other member of the court. I shall not be thought to reflect upon the acknowledged competence and learning of those distinguished judges whom I have mentioned when I make plain my opinion that neither the House of Lords nor the Judicial Committee would have lost anything had Lord Buckmaster more frequently presided.

He is indeed, in my opinion, a consummately-equipped judge. He has a profound grasp of the fundamental principles of the law, and he is able to elucidate and apply them with equal swiftness and cogency. I have already made it plain that no contemporary Chancery practitioner was his rival, or anything like his rival. But I choose to think that he owes much of his efficiency to the fact that in his forensic youth he was almost equally bred upon the Common Law. His mind moves so swiftly, and yet so directly and accurately, that he is sometimes apt to be impatient of those who are accustomed to a more leisurely progress. Indeed, if upon his judicial side he has a fault, it lies in a slight tendency to impetuosity. Now an impetuous judge, who is incorrigible when once his mind is made up, is a public danger. But Lord Buckmaster's impetuosity is not of this order. His legal intellect is far too manly and self-confident to be embarrassed by any petty vanity. And so it has happened, over and over again, that even where he has seemed to commit himself (perhaps a little prematurely) to a conclusion, he has himself been the first to reconsider, and even abandon, his attitude when confronted with an argument which convinced his fine and impartial intellect.

He has been a judge now for nearly ten years. He has lavished the resources of a mind richly endowed by nature, and much reinforced in the field of technical law by industry, upon his judicial duties. The law reports are read only by an instructed and critical few. But they are read, and used, and applied by others who have no choice because, after all, they are binding upon all inferior courts throughout the Empire. And I greatly doubt whether of all the distinguished men who sit in the final tribunal, which in the last resort administers justice to populations so diverse and pronounces upon systems of law so dissonant, there is one who in calm perspective, of our generation, will command more weight with posterity than Lord Buckmaster.

His chief quality as a judge is to be found in his immense passion for the very spirit of justice, operating upon a technical mastery both of the details and the principles of the law, which has taught him with precision how far hardship in an individual case may be corrected, without the greater mischief of violating an indispensable general rule.

The same sense of justice made him a passionate and eloquent champion in the House of Lords of the reform of our Divorce Laws. Here he ranged himself constantly and fearlessly against inveterate prejudice; and against the organised battalions of the Church. Not for the first time the House of Lords proved itself to be more enlightened than the House of Commons. I have little doubt that on a secret vote the majority of the House of Commons would range themselves in support of Lord Buckmaster's Bill. But the organisation of the Church is very strong in many constituencies; it seems certain to a calculating member that a vote in favour of the Bill will excite many animosities; it is quite uncertain how many friendships it will create. And so countless tragedies, easily curable, are made perpetual, in adjustment to the cruellest niceties of the party game.

Lord Buckmaster's general political views are of considerable, though it would seem of declining interest. He is a resolute supporter of Mr. Asquith. Presumably he approved of that fatal and incredible error of judgment which placed the Socialist Government in power. He will be rewarded, it seems to me, by seeing in the near future the Liberal Party split into fragments. An extreme section—not inconsiderable in numbers—will join the Labour Party. Many others will recognise the truth, vainly preached by some of us years ago, that the future only holds room for two political parties; and that of these two, the Liberal Party is not one. If these anticipations are well founded, it is unlikely that Lord Buckmaster has any considerable political future before him. But his lofty and resonant eloquence will always make him a formidable critic of those from whom he differs. And it is quite certain that he will always differ from many people. His learning as a lawyer will maintain his reputation throughout the British Empire.

Of his personal qualities a short word, consistently with my practice in these articles, may be added. On a superficial acquaintance he has sometimes given the impression that he would adorn a stained glass window. No suspicion could be more unjust. He is a keen sportsman, and he carries into his general outlook upon the problems and difficulties of life that atmosphere in which alone a genuine sportsman can live. He is loyal and warm-hearted; tenacious in friendship; politically enduring in resentment. But a kindly word, or a warm-hearted appeal, will disarm him at once. Brilliant, impetuous, learned, a little wayward; a little too sure of himself; in some of his impulses almost like a child, Stanley Buckmaster will live in the judicial history of our day. On such an issue the Bench and the Bar of England are alone entitled to vote. And from their expert decision there will be few dissentients.

The Right Hon.
The Viscount Grey of Fallodon, K.G.

The Right Hon. the Viscount Grey of Fallodon, K.G.

VISCOUNT GREY OF FALLODON was born in the year 1862. To-day, therefore, he is 62 years of age. He was educated at Winchester and at Balliol, and in many respects is a typical product of both these admired institutions.

He has, as all the world knows, played a conspicuous part in English public life for more than thirty years. In 1892 he became Under-Secretary for Foreign Affairs; in which capacity it became the fashion in the Liberal Press to compare him, much to his own advantage, with Mr. George Curzon. He imported into the discharge of his duties a portentous gravity which many people who admired his undoubted qualities thought excessive in the case of an Under-Secretary.

Indeed, in his whole public career he has owed singularly little to the quality of levity. Whenever he advanced to the box he contrived to disseminate an atmosphere of pontifical correctitude which not only silenced criticism, but rendered it almost indecent. Indeed, if any human being in the whole world of either sex had actually been as impeccable as Lord Grey contrived to appear, he or she might very reasonably have acquired a separate heaven for ultimate habitation. I remember a passage in Robert Louis Stevenson's "St. Ives," in which the hero was unhappily detained, in circumstances of

163

some convenient clandestinity, in a hen-house. He found the experience depressing. He was a Frenchman. He observed that there was something incorrigibly respectable about a hen, although he had never observed that in her own little affairs she was more particular than another. " But conceive, my friends," he said, " a British hen."

And yet it gradually became apparent that the political world was not merely contemplating an impressive external façade ; but that a man of great, if measured, power of speech and debate ; of original political outlook upon Imperial and Foreign affairs had emerged a little paradoxically and even more unsuitably from the womb of the Liberal Party. The South African War, as everyone remembers, divided the Liberal Party into two bitterly opposed sections. Mr. Lloyd George has recently pointed out, whether in eulogy or in censure of that rapidly disappearing but historically interesting segment of political thought I do not know, that every great war always disunites the Liberal Party.

The criticism implicit in this generalisation is perhaps a little serious. But I am at the moment concerned not so much to pursue it as to recall that Sir Edward Grey committed himself definitely and irrevocably to that patriotic section of the Liberal Party which realised that some time or other the South African situation had to be cleared up. It is still a fashion in certain sections of Liberal writers to give the impression that the South African War was a guilty adventure. History, however, is gradually making it plainer and plainer that the claims of President Kruger were wholly irreconcilable with the retention of any part of South Africa within the

British Empire. Year by year that crafty and Puritan-like old dissembler increased his secret armaments; year by year he stiffened his treatment of the citizens of Johannesburg. It became evident that, disagreeable, tiresome, inglorious, costly, and even perilous as the adventure must prove, the matter had to be fought out.

Many distinguished Liberals accepted this view. All the world knows that Mr. Lloyd George was not among their number. He honestly dislikes wars, immense as is his gift for conducting them. But the idea of a war against a small agricultural community plunged him into an intense and bitter antagonism. Even Sir Henry Campbell-Bannerman, who went as far as most Liberals thought desirable along the pro-Boer road, was not spared the lash of this caustic tongue.

On the other side were Lord Rosebery, Lord Haldane, Mr. Asquith, and Sir Edward Grey. From the point of view of those who were convinced that the war was just and necessary, it is proper to pay a high tribute to the attitude of these four men. The Liberal Party, taken as a whole, has always, throughout its history, tended to conclude that the views of this country must be wrong in any international controversy in which it has become involved. Obviously, therefore, all four were running considerable risks when they had the temerity to allege that England was, for once after all, right. To their colleagues, however, the matter, strangely enough, presented itself in a slightly different light. They knew that at the moment the " jingo " fever of the nation made the war popular; and the view which the Liberal Party as a whole took of the matter was that these four men found it more agreeable to swim with the tide than against it. The gravity of the offence was increased by the circumstance that they monopolised all the bouquets which were available from their old opponents for political ornamentation.

And so there began a feud, bitter and durable, culminating, and reaching a temporary decision in 1906, but only to be finally adjusted when Mr. Asquith a year or two later became Prime Minister. The differences in the Liberal Party were unhealed when Mr. Arthur Balfour resigned and Sir Henry Campbell - Bannerman was called upon to form a Government. It then became evident that if the Conservative Party had grossly under-estimated this pawky Scotsman, the Imperial Four had, with less excuse, committed the same error. It is paradoxical, looking back, to recall that the first Labour Lord Chancellor was to be the eupeptic trophy around which the contest revolved. The Imperialists were determined to make Lord Chancellor, upon Imperialist grounds, him whom the Socialist Party now delights to honour. Sir Henry Campbell-Bannerman and his friends were equally determined that Sir Robert Reid, afterwards Lord Loreburn, should be placed upon the Woolsack.

It is a profound political truth that, when parties prosper, those who in the earlier moments of adversity have contended for the extreme party position will always be triumphant. Every party is cursed with, and ultimately destroyed by, its own Diehards. But at certain moments in the history of all parties the influence of the extreme section becomes irresistible. And so it happened here. Sir

Henry Campbell-Bannerman, who had been as completely underrated by Mr. Arthur Balfour as Mr. Bonar Law was later to be by Mr. Asquith, proved to be master of the situation. Sir Edward Grey and his friends estimated the situation so wrongly that they conceived themselves strong enough to insist upon Sir Henry Campbell-Bannerman accepting a peerage, leaving the leadership in the House of Commons to Mr. Asquith. As a collateral perquisite they insisted upon the Woolsack. Sir Henry Campbell-Bannerman, strongly assisted in this decision by the resolute indignation of his wife, firmly and successfully rejected both proposals. For a day or two it was uncertain whether the Ministry would include these four important personages or not. And it rapidly became evident that as far as the political exigencies of the moment were concerned, it mattered very little whether they were included or not; for nobody particularly cared. The Liberal Party was so strong in the constituencies that an enormous majority was returned, completely in sympathy with Mr. Lloyd George and his friends, and openly contemptuous of certain Liberal leaders, whom they could never forgive for having formed the view that their own country had been right in an international quarrel.

Fortunately for England, the matter was accommodated. Lord Rosebery was indeed left philosophising out of the Cabinet; but it was not deprived of the services of Mr. Asquith, Mr. Haldane, or Sir Edward Grey. To do them justice, each of them thereafter rendered very great service to the State; each of them repeated on a larger and more vital stage the loyalties which had ranged against them the malignant hatreds of an insane and pacifist party. Mr. Asquith, indeed, though not the author of it, must bear the responsibility of having supported that campaign of class hatred which men still rightly associate with the People's Budget; he must still support the charge that he destroyed the House of Lords, without putting anything in its place. He must still concede that he provoked the whole Irish crisis by including Ulster in his Home Rule proposals, although he and every one of his successors have since admitted that the attempt forcibly to include it was a mad and wicked error. But it must none the less be remembered that his own services to the nation in a dark and terrible hour were supreme and indispensable. He brought a united nation into a necessary war at a moment when disunion must have meant disaster and ultimately the destruction of the British Empire.

Lord Haldane on his part rendered services at the War Office which I have more particularly recorded in the brief sketch which I have already attempted of his career.

Lord Grey's association with, and responsibility for, the events which preceded the war were individual to himself and far greater than that of any individual colleague, or of the Cabinet as a whole. From 1906 onwards I think that Lord Grey was a man wholly free from illusion upon the realities of the European situation. I think that he plainly realised very early in the history of that Government that his country was confronted with one of these recurrent crises in which everything must be resolutely put to the hazard, or everything alternately must be lost. He clearly perceived the reality and the terribleness of the German menace. He must, I think, have formed the view that France and Russia alone would not be strong enough to resist their defined enemies. And the construction of the German Fleet convinced him that the ultimate victim of a German triumph in the earlier Continental warfare which he foresaw, but conceived of as a stage only, must be the British Empire. When once he had formed this clear view, with characteristic courage he began to take the same risks, which he had faced in the South African War. But in the later case the risks were, of course, immeasurably greater.

I have often amused myself by speculating what his reception would have been in the mad House of Commons of 1906 if he had informed the collection of hysterical sentimentalists who kept him in office of his conversations, at the time when they took place, diplomatic and military, with the French nation; and of the commitments deeply rooted in honour, if not in formal documents, in which he was gradually, formidably but rightly involving this people. The necessity, however, for such confidences did not, happily for the interests of the world, appeal to him, and therefore for eight years everybody was satisfied. He and Lord Haldane, with the knowledge of Mr. Asquith, made preparations for the war that followed; their followers made perorations on behalf of the peace which preceded.

When the crisis came, as it did, swiftly and suddenly, in August, 1914, it found the Liberal Party as usual disunited. Every great national crisis always has found the Liberal Party disunited.

For the members of that party can never agree, upon any issue, that their own country has been right in an international quarrel. Several Cabinet Ministers resigned. Several more very nearly did. In fact, on one day there was very nearly an ugly rush from the Cabinet room for the door of No. 10. But once again the tact, prudence, patience, and negotiating quality of Mr. Asquith saved the situation. It is right, however, to make it plain that had England failed to respond to an obligation which Sir Edward Grey conceived to be equally founded upon honour and upon every consideration of public safety, he at least would no longer have continued to be responsible for the conduct of public affairs. He never wavered in that dark and fateful moment. He realised that Great Britain must once again fight for its life, or perish. He furnished, indeed, a shining example of a great man who took a clear, if grave, decision without perplexity because he saw no other course which could be reconciled with the traditions, the history, or the security of his country.

I put this on the whole as the greatest moment of Lord Grey's life. His courage, and his clearness of insight, were both put to the test at a supreme moment. Neither failed.

I do not, however, think that the historian, patiently sifting hereafter his vast materials, will assign to him an equally high place as a war diplomatist. In fact, the developments which accrued in Greece, Turkey, and Bulgaria would have seemed absolutely incredible if anyone had predicted in 1914 that they might possibly occur. We estranged Greece, and lost the help which she offered us ; we even succeeded in throwing Bulgaria and Turkey,

divided it might have seemed by ineffaceable antagonisms, into the same camp. It is indeed hardly
too much to say that if Lord Grey had devoted
himself to producing every conceivable diplomatic
disadvantage for the purpose of menacing our fortunes, the result would not have been very different.
The difficulties were of course immense; but it
cannot, I think, be reasonably claimed that the conduct of the Foreign Office at this critical time produced even the attainable minimum of success. Our
arms indeed triumphed, but the victory came late;
and it was deeply compromised by the diplomacy of
the first year of the war.

Then there came in domestic politics that collapse
of the First Coalition to which I have so often referred. Mr. Asquith fell, and with him Lord Grey
fell too. Lord Haldane, it will be remembered,
had fallen a little earlier, although with ponderous
agility he has picked himself up a little earlier too.
But with the collapse in 1915 the ministerial life of
Lord Grey probably reached its close.

He was indeed appointed Ambassador Plenipotentiary at Washington. Although struggling with
characteristic courage against the threatened loss—
since happily averted—of his eyesight, he undertook
at the request of Mr. Lloyd George this great diplomatic burden. It was reasonably hoped that his
great prestige, high character, and universally admitted ability would have enabled him to render
much service to this country; but unfortunately
President Wilson was so busy at the time that for
some months he found himself unable to receive Lord
Grey. The health of the President was indeed at
that moment failing; but it did not prevent him

from giving interviews which upon this side of the water at least did not on the whole seem more important.

I have sometimes thought that a certain letter which Lord Grey wrote to *The Times*, which had incidentally the effect of torpedoing the League of Nations in its largest conceptions, and which I have the best reason for supposing was specially unwelcome to President Wilson, may perhaps have reflected in some degree the memory of an unfruitful intercourse. And I like to believe this; for it is pleasant to reflect that some human element of resentment may flicker for a moment even in the most blameless breast.

Since his return to England Lord Grey has not indeed taken a specially conspicuous part in public affairs; but he has devoted himself in a very leisurely way to shepherding the scanty flock which bleats a discordant allegiance to the Liberal Party in the House of Lords. He was, indeed, in the time of the late Conservative Government, the official leader of the Liberal Party in that calm assembly. He simplified his problems, however, in the first speech which he made when Mr. Bonar Law became Prime Minister, by observing that he did not intend to oppose him; and that he anticipated that the Conservative Party would enjoy many years of power. I did not agree with him; and took leave to say so. His attitude in relation to the present Socialist administration has not, perhaps, been very fully disclosed; nor, indeed, does he indulge his followers with elaborate or frequent declarations of policy. Personally I regret this. For I should like to hear his candid opinion of Lord Haldane as much as I should like

to hear Lord Haldane's opinion about him. But
Lord Grey would never begin; and Lord Haldane
would never end. And so this contest of giants
must be indefinitely postponed.

In fact, Lord Grey's leadership of the Liberal
Party in the House of Lords has very closely resembled the general leadership which in so short a
time has brought a great party to the brink of destruction. There is no reason to suppose that he was not
a party to the fatal decision which placed the Socialists
in power, with the resultant paralysis and swift
dissipation of Liberal strength. Lord Grey, with
the other Liberal leaders, must support his share
of the responsibility for these disasters.

His career has been vital and arresting. At
one of the greatest moments in history he was called
upon to fill (and he did not fail) a shining part. But
those who had been opposed to him for many years
in domestic politics had always believed that there
lurked behind the grave and imperturbable composure of his public manner the germs of no inconsiderable weakness. Had he, for instance, been the
man he seemed, he of all men could never have run
the risks involved in the attempt to place Ulster, if
necessary by force, under a Parliament sitting at
Dublin.

Lord Grey has, in fact, been resolute in patches;
it is the good fortune of this country that at the
greatest moment of all neither his courage nor his
insight failed. And for this reason alike in achievement and in general quality he will always be counted
a great Englishman.

The Right Hon.
The Marquess of Salisbury, K.G.

The Right Hon. the Marquess of Salisbury, K.G.

JAMES EDWARD HUBERT GASCOIGNE CECIL, fourth Marquess of Salisbury, was the eldest son of that great and dignified figure who was so long leader of the Conservative Party and Prime Minister of England. He is the head of one of our old English families. The founder of that family, Lord Burghley, was the greatest man whom it produced until the late Lord Salisbury Indeed, those who are curious in studying the reproduction of family qualities over a long period of time may trace considerable points of resemblance, making allowance for the day and environment, between the great Lord Burghley and the father of the present Lord Salisbury. But it must be added that there were many notable points of difference. Sir Robert Naunton, in his "Fragmenta Regalia," gives an entertaining if a homely account of Lord Burghley's emergence :—

> On the death of the old Marquess of Winchester [he writes] he came up in his roome, a person of a most subtile and active spirit.
> He stood not by the way of constellation. He was wholly intentive to the service of his Mrs., and his dexterity and experience and merit therein challenged a roome in the Queene's favour which eclipsed others overseeming greatnesse, and made it appeare that there were others steered and stood at the helme besides himself, and more stars in the firmament of grace than Ursa Major.

He was borne as they say in Lincolnshire, but as some aver, upon knowledge, of a younger brother of the Cecills of Hartfordshire, a family to my owne knowledge, though now private, yet of no mean antiquitie, who being exposed and sent to the citie, as poore gentlemen used to do their sons, he became to be a rich man of London Bridge, and purchased in Lincolnshire, where this man was borne.

The younger son of Lord Burghley, and the founder of our branch of the family, was Robert Cecil, who was knighted in 1591, was Principal Secretary of State from 1596-1612, Chancellor of the Duchy of Lancaster from 1597-1599, Lord Privy Seal 1597-1612, Lord Treasurer 1608-1612. He was created on May 13, 1603, Baron Cecil of Essendon, Rutland ; advanced to the Viscounty of Cranborne, Dorset, in 1604 ; and created Earl of Salisbury on May 4, 1605.

The seventh Earl of Salisbury, who was Lord Chamberlain to George III. from 1783-1804, became the first Marquess.

The family produced many useful citizens with a very respectable record of public service, in the period between the death of the first Earl and the birth of the late Lord Salisbury. But, on the whole, no injustice is done to the generations which intervened by the statement that the family, after a long period of tranquil usefulness, underwent a new, and still continuing, efflorescence some sixty-five years ago. It is not my purpose in this article to attempt an estimate of that weighty and massive statesman, of whom I have written elsewhere, who confronted Gladstone for so long, who fought Disraeli unsuccessfully, Randolph Churchill with better fortune, and who succeeded in the end to an almost supreme political dominion, equipped with a mordant tongue, a brilliant pen, and immeasurable sagacity. He left behind him many very remarkable children. Three Privy Councillors, a General, a Bishop, a gifted daughter-biographer afford some comfort to those who in a sceptical generation still believe that there is something, in human beings as in horses, to be said for the hereditary principle.

Three of the late Lord Salisbury's sons have attained to the highest eminence in the State. Viscount Cecil, better known to us all by the name of Lord Robert, was in Opposition one of the most accomplished Parliamentary dialecticians of our day. No one who sat in the House of Commons from 1906-1910 will ever forget the services which he rendered to that scanty and demoralised Opposition. He went out, as the saying goes, in all weathers. But, somehow or other, he never completely realised his high Parliamentary promise. Mr. Joseph Devlin once, with a characteristic gibe, dismissed him as a man who had one foot in the Middle Ages and the other in the League of Nations. Though, in fact, a very direct and straightforward man, he had a method of presenting an argument which somehow or other suggested a touch of Jesuitry ; and while his devotion to, and work for, the League of Nations contribute a shining page to the history of human idealism, it is probably true that his complete absorption in this subject, weakened by an estimate far too sanguine of that which at the moment was attainable, has somewhat affected his reputation as a practical statesman.

Far the most brilliant of the brothers was, and is, Lord Hugh. And, indeed, at his best, the youngest of the Cecil brothers has, in my judgment, been the greatest master of rhetoric at once spoken and literary in our generation. While still a very young man, speaking upon the subject of religious education in the schools, to a House almost one-half of which was repelled by his views, he held it hushed, almost awed, for nearly an hour by the sublimity of his conception and by the nobility of the language in which he clothed it. It is, indeed, an almost insoluble question why Lord Hugh Cecil has never attained to that position in English public life for which his shining gifts, by universal admission, equipped him. One says that he is impracticable ; another, angular ; and a third, that he cannot work easily in association with colleagues. Perhaps all three criticisms really amount to one. I express no conclusion upon this point, but record my clear conviction that the public life of England has been made less vivid and less interesting by the fact that Hugh Cecil has never been a Minister.

The present Lord Salisbury has not been either impracticable or a visionary. He is to-day in his sixty-third year. In the South African War he commanded, with the rank of lieutenant-colonel, the Bedfordshire Regiment, and was mentioned in despatches. He represented the Darwen Division in the House of Commons from 1885 to 1892 and Rochester from 1893 to 1903. He was President of the Board of Trade in 1905, and in the Conservative Government which recently disappeared from the scene he was Lord President of the Council and Deputy Leader of the House of Lords. He owns some 20,000 acres, and the prudent stewardship of his estates has occupied no small part of a very conscientious life.

Right Hon. the Marquess of Salisbury, K.G.

Activities so varied, and discharged with so much merit, indicate a man at once practical, able, industrious, and many-sided. I had myself, at no period which was relevant, any opportunity of influencing such matters ; but I always regretted that Lord Salisbury was a member neither of the first nor of the second Coalition. We should have gained by his inclusion. And I think that he would have gained something too. For he would have realised (he never quite did) at once the immense difficulties in which the country was placed, and to which it was so long to remain exposed ; and he would, I think, or, at least, he might, have realised that, in the attempt to solve those difficulties by the painful reconstruction of our national life, there was much to be said for a postponement of our old party strife. It may at least be moderately claimed that up to the present the other view has not been conspicuously successful.

Lord Salisbury is a very effective and forcible debater in the House of Lords. And if the material is sometimes a little thin, and its presentation a little acrid, he none the less enjoys in that assembly an influence largely due to his vigorous speeches, but perhaps not less to the fact that everyone likes, respects, and trusts him. It is, for instance, never possible to doubt, when you listen to him, that here is a man, whether he be right or whether he be wrong, who is attempting to offer the best counsel in his power in the spirit of one who has no desire except to help his country. The only criticism which can reasonably be made of his Parliamentary judgment and his presentation of a Parliamentary case is that he is apt to be too impetuous. Sometimes the vocal emphasis—always a marked feature of his rhetoric —ceases to be forcible, and almost threatens to splutter. And yet few men in either House of Parliament excel him in the art of putting his side of a controversial case cogently, concisely, and acceptably.

If, however, he has ever been able to realise that whatever disadvantages were incident to a Coalition, that form of Government had nevertheless some element which made for good, he would not have made what I deem the fatal error of rejecting the Coalition proposals for the reform of the House of Lords. Lord Curzon, Mr. Austen Chamberlain, Mr. Churchill, Mr. Fisher, and myself had spent many months in discussing these problems. We had arrived, however meagre the result, at the largest attainable measure of agreement between men of different parties. We proposed a reduction of the number of legislative peers to three hundred, affording thereby a mode of selection which would have protected the Lords in future from the most obvious and bitter attack to which they are at present exposed. We should, at least, have ceased to be an unpurged House. We offered them, instead of the certificate of Mr. Speaker, to determine the character of a money Bill, the decision of a Committee equally chosen from both Houses of Parliament. And we offered them, further, this great consideration— that the Parliament Act should never be amended under its own terms, but only after an election upon a specific issue. And at the same time we caused it to be known that if the proposal were welcome, we saw on principle no objection to conceding to Ministers a right of audience in both Houses.

I know the difficulties too well seriously to blame
our successors for their failure to produce a reform
scheme while they still had the power to give effect
to it ; but I cannot help reflecting how much stronger
in defence would have been the position of the House
of Lords at this moment ; and how much more
secure the country, had Lord Salisbury and his
friends found it possible to co-operate with us in
order that this modest instalment of reform might
immediately have been placed upon the Statute
Book.

But he had other views ; he preferred to move a
series of resolutions of his own, which were no doubt
much more meritorious than ours, but which, unlike
ours, had the small disadvantage that no one but
an extreme section of the Conservative Party would
ever agree with them. I have had occasion since
to re-read the debates which took place upon the
subject. More and more I have been driven to the
conclusion that Lord Curzon and I had obtained
the most favourable scheme—for the country, to
the House of Lords itself, and for the Conservative
Party—that will ever be produced as the result of
agreement. And, failing agreement, this ancient
assembly may one day disappear completely in the
crash of destruction. Indeed, the soundness of this
view was made plain when Mr. Bonar Law formed
his Government and Lord Salisbury became a member
of the Cabinet. We had been told by him and by
Lord Selborne, in season and out of season, that
the settlement of this Constitutional problem admitted of no delay. Yet almost the first announcement of the Government was that it did not intend
to deal with this subject for two years. I ventured

to point out that, to put the matter mildly, there was no certainty that the Government would be in existence in two years. But this caution was contemptuously waved aside.

It is my wish, however, to make it plain that I do not, on cool reflection, think that Mr. Bonar Law was wrong in postponing the matter. For I do not believe that a Conservative Government acting alone could ever be strong enough to introduce a reform sufficiently acceptable to general public opinion to afford any prospect of continuity when that Government gave way to another. The mistake was in not welcoming at once the moderate measure of reform which we tendered, and which we were in a position to carry through both Houses by large majorities.

Lord Salisbury was indeed the principal enemy of the Coalition. I am not concerned to deny that on more than one important subject he made good his criticisms. Neither the Coalition nor, I may add, any of its three successors has been immune from grave error. The plain fact, however, remains that the tactics and the policy of those who destroyed the Coalition, with all its faults, have placed a Socialist Government in power in so short a period. The easy optimism against which I protested when the older parties connived at this surprising result is rapidly passing away. More and more it is being realised that the time, in Mr. Asquith's ill-starred phrase, is not so particularly " safe " for the experiment of a Socialist Government. With the exercise of reasonable common sense, whether the Coalition had survived or not, the formation of such a Government could have been postponed for ten years. I have no doubt that the present hideous outbreak of industrial unrest is mainly attributable to the fact that we have in office a Socialist administration. The spirit abroad is : " We have our own friends in office ; now is the time to enforce our demands ; this Government, at least, can neither quarrel with the strike policy nor take effectively the steps which are necessary for the protection of the public."

I am very willing to recognise that we are probably too close to the events of the last two and a half years, and still too much under the influence of prepossession, perhaps of prejudice, to give any of us the right of forming too dogmatic a conclusion. Lord Salisbury formed a different view from ours ; he became the leader of the Die-hards ; and, having formed that most reactionary opinion, he adhered to it with his usual force and tenacity.

I cannot believe that one so experienced, and with the reputation of a Free Trader, could have agreed with the policy of the premature election upon the issue of a general tariff. And I have often wondered in his case, as in that of Lord Derby and Lord Curzon, why these members of the Cabinet, whose experience and responsibility were so great, made no effective effort to defeat the unhappy rush tactics of our Younger Statesmen. In fact, Lord Salisbury wrote one colourless letter, went to the Riviera, and returned when the election was over.

It remains only to attempt the kind of general estimate which I have presumed to make in closing many of these sketches. Enough has been said to show that Lord Salisbury has already played a very considerable part in the public life of this country. Nor is there any reason to suppose that he will not do so in the future. I have spoken already of his argumentative gifts, and of his devotion to the public service. To these qualities he adds a remarkable infusion of common sense. I do not suppose that he has a personal enemy in the world ; and I should doubt whether he has a political one. Although warm-tempered, he is extremely generous and courteous in debate, responding in a flash to any civility or kindliness from an opponent. Whether you agree with him, or whether you disagree with him—and to me it has often happened to do both—you are bound to admit that here is an Englishman, strenuous, single-hearted, and efficient, without whose point of view the public life of this country would be definitely the poorer.

The Right Hon.
J. H. Thomas, M.P.

The Right Hon. J. H. Thomas, M.P.

WHEN Mr. Ramsay MacDonald undertook to form the first Labour-Socialist Government he was evidently confronted by a task of unusual difficulty. His supporters were drawn from diversified political origins, ranging from the moderate trade unionist to the street-corner revolutionary subsidised in many cases from Moscow. The mere task of creating even the appearance of unity among elements so discordant was very great; the graver task of producing unity, in fact, will probably exceed the ingenuity of Mr. MacDonald and his principal advisers.

There is, however, one among those advisers whose help must have been extraordinarily valuable to Mr. MacDonald in the last six weeks.[1] The Right Hon. J. H. Thomas is unquestionably the cleverest politician hitherto produced by the Socialist Party. His career has been an astonishing one. He was born forty-five years ago in the town of Newport (Monmouth), on the banks of the River Usk. He has recently recalled with manly pride that as he drove quite recently from the station in his native town he passed the drapery establishment where, thirty-two years ago, he was employed as an errand-boy; that he saw the brass plate which that boy had cleaned; and that he vividly remembered carrying the rivets for the construction of the Alexandra Docks. Nor did Mr. Thomas shrink from the political moral which his surprising elevation

[1] Written seven months ago.

in a period comparatively so short makes it proper to draw. " One must feel proud," he has said, " to live under a Constitution which enables a humble boy with a meagre education, surrounded by poverty, to become in so short a time one of His Majesty's principal Secretaries of State."

Nor has the avenue over which Mr. Thomas has forced his road to fame been the primrose path of the Independent Labour Party along which many have dallied, not uncomfortably, with the aid of journalism and lectures until the day of official opportunity dawned. Young Thomas had to fight every yard of his way. He passed from a chemist's shop to a draper's stores, and thence to a firm of decorators, where he became skilled in the art of mixing paints.

From the decorators he proceeded to hard manual labour at the Alexandra Docks shops. And it was when so employed that he first felt the fascination of the steam engine. We next find him employed by the Great Western Railway as an engine-cleaner. He held this office for some years, and it was while still so employed, at the age of fifteen, that he organised his first strike among his fellow-cleaners. The merits of this long-past dispute—it was, I think, concerned with the appropriate allowance of tallow for each boy—are long forgotten, but, if I remember the story right, the justice of the revolting cleaners was recognised by the concession of the company.

The limits of this article do not make it possible for us to trace the career of this active, industrious, and ambitious young man from cleaner to fireman, from fireman to engine-driver ; from engine-driver through all the anxious stages which intervened before he reached the immensely responsible position of Chairman of the National Union of Railwaymen. But one interesting incident may be preserved. On June 10, 1901, a high official on the Great Western wrote to a lower, " Please write across this by return post saying who and what the Mr. J. H. Thomas is whose name is reported as having taken part in the recent meeting." The meeting related to some trade dispute; and it is amusing to notice that Mr. Thomas at that date was not even worth a separate sheet of notepaper. The answer is to be sent, and was in fact sent, written across the short inquiry. In it he is described as a young engineman in the locomotive department of Swindon ; and it is pointed out that the young man's activities were even more formidable than had been supposed, for he had actually visited Plymouth for oratorical purposes on the previous Sunday.

The rise from the position of junior engine-driver to chairman of the mightiest trades union of all undoubtedly required, and must in the future require, an amazing combination of qualities. If the head which wears a crown lies uneasily, we may believe that that of Mr. Thomas has not always enjoyed undisturbed nights. All trades unionist leaders who sit in these exacting days in the House of Commons are exposed to the difficulty that their prolonged absence leaves the path clear for younger rivals who, to put the matter moderately, could easily be persuaded to fill their places. A man who has kept himself in the saddle of an extremely restive horse as long and as surely as Mr. Thomas is evidently a jockey of the highest quality. He has all his life been a vehement champion of the trades

union movement. He has believed, and probably
still believes, that in the last resort the weapon of
the strike must be kept unimpaired in the hands
of Labour. I should doubt whether he believes
that any device—arbitration, mediation, or legislation—will, where grave issues have developed,
take the place of the strike.

But while he holds these views, he has on many
occasions shown great courage, and run extreme
risks, in fighting the men where he thought they were
in the wrong. It will, for instance, be recalled how
in September, 1918, an unauthorised railway strike
of alarming dimensions broke out in South Wales.
Mr. Thomas did not stay in his London office wringing
his hands. He rushed off to the scene of disturbance,
harangued the strikers in firm and uncompromising
language ; and demanded the immediate resumption
of work. Four days' fierce struggle followed between himself and the unofficial leaders. His energy
and courage were rewarded by victory, and the
malcontents returned to work.

And then Mr. Thomas did rather a remarkable
thing. He announced that if he had so little control
over the union that a great strike could be organised
and take place without his approval, and almost
without his knowledge, he was not prepared to hold
the responsibility of chairman. This decision was
made public. Within a few days 950 branches of
the union, representing 350,000 railwaymen, for-
warded resolutions of confidence in the late chairman,
who, fortified by so singular a demonstration of
loyalty, withdrew his resignation.

The official railway strike of 1919 is within the
memory of us all. It is not my object here to ex-

amine the wisdom or the merits of this strike. It is sufficient to notice that it was official, and was, therefore, led by Mr. Thomas. Here, as always, he insisted upon the maintenance of law and order ; there were no injuries to persons or damage to property ; neither soldiers nor extra police were employed. He has, indeed, even where the situation has seemed most menacing, always ranged himself boldly on the side of obedience to law. His moderation in this respect has naturally excited hot resentment in the minds of extremists, and in 1921 the *Communist* attacked him for his part in what was known at the time as " Black Friday." Mr. Thomas was awarded £2,000 by a jury, which he proceeded at once, though by no means a rich man, to distribute among railway charities.

I can only trace in his career one episode which sharply conflicts with the estimate of his character which I believe to be true. In an unfortunate moment for his own reputation ; and in one alike dark and dangerous for his country, he harnessed his influence and prestige to the menacing movement, subversive of all our institutions, which became known as direct action. The movement was, in fact, revolutionary. I know not what influences seduced an intelligence ordinarily so collected, sane, and acute, but I am in my own mind persuaded that the Mr. Thomas of 1924 would not repeat an error so grave and so inexcusable.

But a candid narration must record the fact that it was Mr. Thomas himself who moved the resolution on August 13, 1920 : " That this conference approves of the action of the three national bodies in forming a Council of Action to deal with the present situation arising from the policy of the Government towards the Russian-Policy war." Even the memory of this half-baked and hysterical folly has almost perished. An England, sane, whole, and non-sectional, which is learning to understand and admire Mr. Thomas, asks nothing but to forget the whole miserable incident.

And on the other side must be set the great and courageous stand he took in April, 1921. This was the gravest moment in all the post-war industrial crises. The miners' strike was continuing its menacing progress. The Triple Alliance had given formal notice of a sympathetic movement. At this moment Mr. Thomas did not hesitate to fight every extremist in the Labour Party upon the issue that it was the duty of the miners' leaders to undertake further negotiations with the employers. It was a typical and courageous action, abundantly justified at a later date by the remarkable article written by Mr. Frank Hodges condemning a section of his executive for prolonging the strike.

The man of whom the things set out above can be truly said was unlikely to feel any doubt as to the road of duty when this country was forced into the Great War. He threw himself with characteristic energy into the work of recruiting. He did as much as any man in England to bring home to the trades unions the reality of the war and its causes. He was sent to America on an important mission; was publicly thanked by the Government on his return; and was created a Privy Councillor. He was a member of the Port and Transport Committee; of the Treasury Retrenchment Committee; of the Board of Trade Railway Committee; and Chairman of a most important Reconstruction Committee set up by the Government during the war. And it should be added that twice while the war lasted he was offered Cabinet rank, and twice refused because he believed that he could do his country better service by maintaining at a far lower salary his position and influence in the railway world.

The foregoing account makes it plain that we are dealing with a very unusual man. He is sane, sagacious, balanced, patriotic. It will be supposed that it is not my present purpose to injure Mr. Thomas, but I will nevertheless take the risk of stating that in my opinion he is no more Socialist than, say, Lord Parmoor or Mr. Winston Churchill. I am persuaded that whatever he once believed he knows now that for this country to socialise the means of production, distribution, and exchange, whilst other countries adhere to individualist systems, would at once involve us in devastating ruin. And like the Roman augurs, I suspect that Mr. Thomas must sometimes smile at the programmes and the promises with which some of his colleagues (particularly at election times) are so profuse.

But, after all, the smile must be kept to himself. For Mr. Thomas is as astute an electioneer as this country possesses. He knows well—none better—whence comes the driving power which produced so many Labour victories in the last two elections. And yet in his case I do not believe that the moderation and public spirit of his Ministerial utterances are the result of tactical subtlety ; they are, on the contrary, on the whole, consistent with the history and the tenor of his whole career. It would indeed be interesting to hear from Mr. Thomas, speaking frankly and in the temple of truth, the future of politics as he foresees it. Does he, for instance, believe that the extreme and moderate elements in the Socialist Party can continue to co-operate? Perhaps—though I think it unlikely—he holds this view. If not, does he, I wonder, contemplate, as many Liberals undoubtedly do, a new political alignment by which the right of Labour may coalesce with elements of the Liberal Party? I do not know Mr. Thomas's views upon these matters; but that he has views is certain, for his mind is restless, speculative in the non-philosophical sense, and fore-seeing. I make, however, the prediction confidently that whatever party changes may take place Mr. Thomas will never become responsible for proposals which repel on the economic side a very robust common sense; and which his conscience teaches him are fraught with injury to the larger interests of his country.

This sketch has been mostly concerned with public activity; but it would be incomplete without a few words in relation to Mr. Thomas's individual characteristics. He is affable and not bashful. He is a warm friend and a clean opponent. He is an adventurer precisely in the sense in which I am myself willing to be called an adventurer. And the great Disraeli did not disdain the name. Life is, in fact, an adventure, and he who (starting from nothing) fights hard, while conceiving ambitiously, must be an adventurer. Mr. Thomas knows several Dukes by their Christian names. He has established an affinity (literary or what-not) with Mr. Edward Marsh. He has a mastery of the more robust vernacular beloved by our forefathers beside which

Sir Robert Walpole would have paled his ineffectual fires. He enjoys all that is enjoyable in life with an unconcealed and rather attractive zest. He is an extremely agreeable, if not over-silent companion; and in the merry company which the genius of Rabelais imagined he would, I think, have found himself in almost all respects well-equipped and at his ease. He could, for instance, have talked without much risk of mutual misunderstanding with Friar John. Nor do I believe that in the moon-bathed gardens of Boccaccio's romances he would have been embarrassed by the company, the narratives, or even by the nightingales. Whether his fellow-revellers would have been embarrassed when it fell to him, in his turn, to propose his own *conte* I cannot tell. But the standard of that delightful company was admittedly relaxed.

Enough has perhaps been said to make it plain that a draper's boy does not rise to be Secretary of State for the Colonies by accident; and that Mr. Thomas's dazzling success is the reward of extraordinary talent, energy, and variety of character.

The Right Hon.
Lord Carson

The Right Hon. Lord Carson

THE career of Lord Carson is one of the most interesting, as it is certainly one of the most romantic, of the last thirty years in either Irish or English politics. He is sprung from a very old family of South of Ireland Protestants; he is steeped in the atmosphere of the Southern minority; he has imbibed its traditions and its loyalties, and has responded to them, right or wrong, throughout his career, with all the resources of a chivalrous heart and of a strong intelligence.

He was educated at Trinity College, Dublin, where he was a fellow-student with the late Irish Lord Chancellor, Lord Glenavy and Mr. Oscar Wilde. Trinity College, Dublin, then, as always, was one of the most distinguished Universities in the world, and Carson held his own, and perhaps a little more than his own, in the society of very remarkable and brilliant young men. He was destined for the law, and in due course became a member of the Irish Bar. Forensic gifts like his are phenomenal; and his success was extraordinarily rapid. His career in Ireland coincided with the long Unionist tenure of power, and in due course he became Solicitor-General for Ireland. The Attorney-General was the present Lord Atkinson, one of the most learned lawyers on the Bench of the Empire; and it is an astonishing circumstance that a Bar so limited in numbers should have produced, in a single period, two figures so outstanding. When Carson was

Solicitor-General the office was no sinecure. His duties were discharged under the régime of " Bloody Balfour."

It is quite certain that this resolute and subtle Minister could have found nowhere in the Empire an instrument more suitable for his purposes than the young Solicitor-General. He did not know what fear was ; he was in constant danger of his life ; armed policemen displayed their revolvers in Court in order to make it quite certain that the forensic eloquence of the prosecutor would not be interrupted with impunity ; he was daily and even hourly threatened with assassination. But he did his duty, and did it extremely well. And by doing so, oddly enough, he greatly endeared himself to the incomprehensible Irish race. It is, in fact, a paradoxical truth that Edward Carson was never really unpopular with the Nationalists, and was almost popular with the Sinn Feiners. They all liked an Irishman, and they all liked a man. And he was a typical Irishman, and no one who knew him ever disputed that he was a man.

Qualities such as he possessed could not be confined within the relatively narrow limits open to Irish ambition. And so in the year 1892 he was elected as the representative of Trinity College, Dublin, to be a Member of the British House of Commons. Here, as always, his strong and arresting personality made itself felt at once. The picturesque appearance, the soft, captivating brogue, the romantic personality, the force behind the man, made him almost at once a commanding Parliamentary figure. Most of his early speeches were made against the Government, of which he was a nominal supporter. He has often told me of his friendship at this period of his life with Randolph Churchill. The latter took him home to dinner one night after a stormy debate. The child Winston had been among the audience. " What did you think of it all ? " asked the Irishman. " Sir," replied the boy, " I think that the ship of state is moving in troubled waters."

Carson had then (he has always had since) an obsession. Who knows whether from his point of view he was right or wrong ? I have never been quite sure all through his career. But he has always had the enormous advantage of knowing his own mind, which gave precise, if passionate, expression to convictions which were, at least, as much the result of breeding and of tradition as of reason and logic. But I am not myself prepared to` affirm dogmatically that he has ever been in the wrong ; for the issues with which he and I have had to deal have been far too obscure and speculative to recommend dogma. However this may be, his early guerrilla warfare did not stand in the way of Parliamentary advancement, and when a vacancy occurred in the office of the Solicitor-General, his claims were preferred to those of no mean opponent, the blameless Lord Parmoor. He had in the meantime already established a great reputation as an advocate at the English Bar. No other Irish barrister has ever supported the translation to an entirely different atmosphere so successfully ; none has ever come so immediately into an alien forensic kingdom.

This reflection leads me naturally to an estimate of Carson's qualities as an advocate. He frequently led me, and I was often opposed to him in very important cases. I have no doubt whatever that he was the most formidable opponent upon issues of fact that I have ever encountered at the Bar. His speeches lacked the literary quality of those with which Sir Edward Clarke delighted his hearers. They were not, indeed, as formless, and, it must be added, as cheap (from the point of view of the reader) as those with which the late Lord Russell of Killowen garnished his advocacy, without losing verdicts. But he was a great master of the emotions. He was a consummate judge of human nature. He knew exactly the point of view which would appeal to a juryman. He was never a bully. A junior who appeared against him was treated with the same respect as a distinguished Leader at the Bar. And always he possessed, like the great Erskine, the incommunicable and almost divine gift of flinging his own personality around his client's case, so that it was independently fortified and enriched without any necessary relation to its own deserts.

I cannot speak of Russell's advocacy from personal experience. I never, in fact, heard him or even saw him. But I have read most of his chief forensic speeches, and whilst I acknowledge that no man can judge of his quality as an advocate who had not heard him, I still adhere to the opinion that Carson was the greatest advocate the English Bar has produced since Erskine. And if all-round merit is to be examined in this disputable comparison, it must be admitted that the claims of Lord Carson become stronger and stronger. Lord Russell was a complete Parliamentary failure ; and, indeed, in order to obtain audiences who would listen to his views upon political subjects he had to make fatiguing journeys to provincial towns. Carson from the first, on the contrary, was a vivid and arresting Parliamentary figure. He never lost his mastery in the House of Commons, and he has gained for himself a very considerable, if a very unconventional and sometimes disturbing, position in the House of Lords.

This is not the place to trace in detail the story of his political life, but some of its more salient features must be hurriedly examined. The great fight of his life was, of course, against the Home Rule Bill, which followed upon the election of 1910. The tactics which he set himself to destroy were simple. There was no majority either in the House of Commons or in the country for a Home Rule Bill. Mr. Asquith and his friends accordingly, by a campaign almost obscene in its class hatred, set themselves to destroy the House of Lords, in order to give the Home Rule Bill the only chance it could ever have of becoming law. They avoided the unpopular; they embraced the popular campaign.

The reckless wickedness of the attempt to force Home Rule upon an unwilling Ulster cannot be better illustrated than by the fact that the two ablest Ministers in Mr. Asquith's Government, Mr. Lloyd George and Mr. Winston Churchill, were against it from the start. They were overborne by a majority; and thereafter by a majority vote the Cabinet proceeded on its guilty and perilous course. Every Minister involved, whose opinion matters to anyone, has since admitted that Home Rule cannot be forced upon Ulster against the will of Ulster. But the Government of the day, taking their orders from the Nationalists, upon whom their majority depended, chose to involve themselves in this crazy and criminal gamble. But they had completely underrated the resources and the personality of Carson. He transferred his allegiance from the South to the North ; he was elected the leader of the party of resistance in Ulster ; he sacrificed his practice ; he underwent the risk of prosecution on behalf of a cause which he knew to be just, and which, courageously directed, he believed must be triumphant.

It is as certain as anything in politics can be that if the war had not intervened he would have been successful in his campaign. For all the moral strength of the position was with him. The Government, which was gambling with the currency of tragedy, knew that their proposals were not only morally indefensible, but were incapable of fulfilment. They only adhered to them because this adherence was the necessary price of a vilely dishonest party bargain.

Then came the war. It did not, indeed, solve the Irish question, or perhaps very much affect it. If you ask an Ulsterman to-day which was the greater battle — the Battle of the Boyne or the Battle of the Somme—he would laugh at you. And yet in the Battle of the Somme the Ulster Division covered itself with unforgettable glory, suffering so much only because in this desperate offensive it charged so far. But Carson now devoted his great gifts to the purposes of the war. In doing so he became a much greater man. He left parochialism far behind him, and devoted a competent mind to Imperial issues upon an Imperial scale. He became a formidable critic of Mr. Asquith's Government. He had, indeed, joined it as Attorney-General in May, 1915 ; but he convinced himself, rightly or wrongly, that that Government could not win the war, and after three months' tenure of office he resigned his position.

Thereafter, a minor Clemenceau, he became Chairman of that Committee of Unionist members which attempted to add driving power and imagination to the official conduct of the war. The fall of the first Coalition was in no small measure due to the organisation hostile to that Government which Carson had created. The relations between himself and Mr. Lloyd George, before the war most antagonistic, had become, under the stimulus of national peril, warm and even sympathetic. It was therefore no surprise to anyone when it was announced that Carson had become First Lord of the Admiralty in Mr. Lloyd George's first administration. He was, indeed, with Mr. Bonar Law and Mr. Lloyd George, one of the band of three which was responsible for determining the personnel of the new Ministry; so that aspirants to office were summoned by Mr. Lloyd George to his room at the War Office, where they were interviewed and, so to speak, reviewed by the body which became known to Under-Secretaries as the " Big Three."

Of his work as First Lord of the Admiralty this is not the place to speak. He held that office at a very dangerous and critical period. He came to it with no special qualification or training, bringing to it little, as it would seem, except a high spirit of patriotism and a strong native intelligence. So far as I can judge, he decided that, on the whole, his duty could be best discharged by supporting in their difficult task the experts over whose deliberations he presided. It would be very rash to say that he was wrong. Expert advisers may quite

easily be right in their opinions ; it is even more
certain that they may be, and often are, unani-
mously wrong. But, on the whole, and certainly
in war-time, it is more probable that they will be
right than amateur strategists. Such, at any rate,
it is believed was the reasoning which recommended
itself to Carson. In time Mr. Lloyd George became
anxious to avail himself of Lord Carson's general
services in the War Cabinet, a commitment which
could hardly be reconciled with the exacting daily
duties of the Admiralty. And so Sir Eric Geddes
became First Lord of the Admiralty. Carson retained his position as a member of the War Cabinet,
rendering valuable services, until Ireland made
herself once again inopportunely felt. There was
talk—and more than talk—of an Irish settlement,
and he felt that his position had become impossible,
and so he resigned—I am sure unwillingly—because,
and only because, he thought that the retention of
office would involve him in the clash of combative
loyalties.

Then the war ended. The Irish Government Act,
which I conducted through its various stages in the
House of Lords, seemed for the moment at least
to have made an end of this immortal question.
Ulster was safeguarded in her own boundaries by a
measure which Carson did not seriously affect to disapprove. His controversial career he may and indeed
must have believed was closed. His active fighting
life had come to an end, and he was well entitled,
after so many and such constant exertions, to look
for repose. A vacancy occurred in the Law Lords,
which he was admirably qualified by his high previous achievements to fill. He decided to hang

up his spear and his shield, so that he might devote what was left of his life to the majesty of British justice in its Imperial Court of Appeal.

And then again perverse Fate intervened, with malignant consequences. The Irish Act failed completely in the South. Weekly and daily the crisis grew, and finally a conference was convened to discuss the terms of a final settlement. This is neither the time nor the place to argue either the merits or the justification of that which was done. That task awaits the patient and impartial historian, if and when such an one is found. I am only concerned here to make it plain that I myself neither misunderstood nor resented the attitude which Lord Carson felt himself called upon to take in the House of Lords. Being what he was, he could take no other. He only accepted high judicial office in the belief that the struggle of his life was ended. Decisions for which I was largely responsible, but which I knew and know to be disputable, had produced a revival of the old mediæval antagonism. I thought then, and I think now, that Lord Carson, in the perspective of the whole tangled situation, was wrong. But I have read Irish history too closely to be quite certain that he was entirely wrong. Whether the whole—the ultimate—truth in this controversy be ever found or no, this at least is certain, that no man has ever in the history of Irish politics flung all his powers, all his eloquence, and all his health more recklessly into the Cause in which he passionately believed than Lord Carson.

His Excellency
Timothy M. Healy

His Excellency Timothy M. Healy

HIS EXCELLENCY TIMOTHY MICHAEL HEALY, K.C., M.P., first Governor of the Irish Free State, a Bencher of Gray's Inn, was born in the year 1855. He is therefore now in his 70th year. He had great experience of Irish constituencies in his stormy political career. He represented Wexford from 1880 to 1883 ; County Monaghan from 1883 to 1885 ; South Londonderry from 1885 to 1886 ; North Longford 1887 to 1892 ; North Louth from 1892 to 1910 ; and North-East Cork from 1910 to 1917.

Dr. Johnson once said of someone, " I like the fellow; he flatters me." When, therefore, I write of Mr. Healy, I recall a little crumpled note passed to me when I sat down after my first speech in the House of Commons, prophesying extravagant things for the future—and ending with the sentence : " I am old, and you are young ; but you have beaten me at my own game."

And again I recall an occasion when Mr. Amery's admirable book on the South African War was made the subject of a libel action by a non-commissioned officer whom Amery charged, perhaps a little crudely, with cowardice. In my closing speech for the defence I made a contrast between the gallantry of the British Army generally, and that of the soldier who was Mr. Healy's client, closing with the lines :—

> " On Fame's eternal camping ground
> Their silent tents are spread ;
> And Glory guards with solemn round
> The bivouac of the Dead."

Again I received from my opponent a pencilled note : " I did not think that any barrister in England knew the lines except myself. Who wrote them ? " to which question I whispered across the Court the words, " Theodore O'Hara, New York." With such friendly acquaintance, forensic and Parliamentary, I must confess myself disabled from touching with very dark pigments the canvas of his career. What has that career been ?

A lad of humble rank, he left school at thirteen, and became immersed in business and journalism in his early years. That boy, with so little help, has crowned his career with the position of Governor-General of his native land. I am not certain whether, had the Coalition Government which made the Irish Treaty with Arthur Griffiths and Michael Collins not been displaced, by the fateful vote against Mr. Chamberlain at the Carlton Club—I am not, I say, certain whether we should have had the courage to nominate Tim Healy to that great office. Mr. Bonar Law boldly did so after the General Election of November, 1922 ; but peers like the late Lord Shaughnessy of Canada or Lord Granard were earliest in our minds.

I asked Mr. Bonar Law afterwards what had decided him to risk the disapproval of his Party by appointing Healy. He replied that the latter had come to him a week before on a matter affecting British Government stock and their inscription at the Bank of Ireland. Some Treasury official, now in India, proposed to withdraw from Dublin the facilities which stockholders there have enjoyed for a century—although I believe they have not been extended to Scotland—of a special register for

British Funds, whereby Irish holders can immediately turn them into cash without being compelled to resort to meticulous formalities in London. Mr. Bonar Law found in Mr. Healy's mind so complete an acquaintance with the procedure as to registration and sale of Government stock that he was satisfied from his argument that it would injure British interest on the Irish market if the Treasury proposals were carried through. This, added to his previous appreciation of Healy's mind, turned the scale in favour of an appointment for which Mr. Cosgrave was earnestly pressing. Healy has always made it plain that he thought Bonar Law both generous and courageous. The late Prime Minister might easily have reproached him with a mistake in judgment of Irish affairs, because he urged upon him the release of de Valera and his accomplices in the 1916 rebellion. The older generation of Irish politicians, in fact, knew as little of the rising generation as did British statesmen themselves.

Healy tells that when he went to seek mercy for these prisoners, he found Bonar embedded in clouds of smoke in his room behind the Speaker's Chair. He assured him that prisoners enduring penal servitude suffered so terribly that for their own sakes, and the sake of their families, they would not again be likely to enter upon violent courses. There is no doubt that this advice was honestly tendered; but it was based upon the experience of an earlier generation, and went back to arrests and trials in 1865 and 1867, without any acquaintance with the minds of the Irish youth of our own day. It is certainly arguable that if de Valera and his abettors had endured a while longer the sentences which justice awarded, the course of Irish affairs would have flowed in different channels. Mr. Healy had no acquaintance with any of the prisoners who benefited by his advocacy. The Prime Minister of the day, however, consented to their discharge.

I myself found nothing to regret in the part I played in the great drama which led to the treaty of 1921; nor, I suspect, has the subject of this sketch. It is not, however, as Governor-General of the Irish Free State that I propose to analyse his career.

The public, I think, will be most interested in a criticism or an appreciation of his Parliamentary method; and, above all, of the part played by him in the downfall of Charles Stewart Parnell in 1890–1891.

A scrap-book of mine dealing with Irish affairs contains a sketch taken from the *Daily Telegraph* of Monday, March 10, 1924, by my friend T. P. O'Connor, on Sir Henry Campbell, late Town Clerk of Dublin, and formerly member of Parliament for Fermanagh. It is there asserted by T. P. O'Connor, who should be a well-equipped authority on Parnellite history, that Healy broke with his chief as secretary during Parnell's visit to America in the spring of 1880. Mr. O'Connor's words are : " Something happened in America that produced some disagreeable impression in Parnell's mind, and he did not employ Mr. Healy again. It was a decision which in time was to bring tragic consequences, especially to Parnell."

Knowing little of the events of forty-four years

ago, but having heard Mr. Healy give another and more tragic explanation, I thought it not improper to submit to him Mr. O'Connor's narrative.

The Irish Governor-General informs me that it has no foundation, although, of course, he does not question Mr. O'Connor's good faith. He says that he was never " employed " by Mr. Parnell; that he threw up his position in London on receiving a cable from him in February, 1880; and acted in a volunteer and unremunerated capacity as his secretary during the remaining months of 1880. In January, 1881, on the arrest of Michael Davitt, a meeting of the Land League Executive was called in Paris to fill Davitt's post. Parnell's intrigue with Mrs. O'Shea had commenced, but was then unknown to his colleagues. Healy however was in possession of a still more anxious, sinister, and analogous, secret connected with his chief; and brought to Paris a number of letters to Parnell, unopened, which made that secret plain.

In Paris the Land League Executive, including men like Mr. Dillon and Mr. Biggar, to the number of a dozen, were kept dangling about the boulevards for a week by Parnell, who preferred the attractions of Eltham to politics in the Rue de Rivoli. Alarmed and mystified by Parnell's failure to arrive, the Executive questioned Healy straitly; and then formally passed a resolution requiring him to deliver to them a letter which might afford a clue to Parnell's whereabouts.

Nationalists looked upon this Executive as their only valid authority. Parnell's absence at a moment so grave might easily involve a tragedy holding incalculable political consequences. The secretary was at that moment comparatively uninfluential. Healy therefore gave up a letter, stating, however, that although he acted under the orders of the Executive, he could not after a violation of correspondence continue to act as Parnell's secretary. The letter, surrendered in these circumstances, was charged with vital consequence; and betrayed a secret at once destructive and discreditable.

Parnell arrived in Paris the next day; and one of the group informed him of what had taken place. Later on Parnell unjustly blamed Dillon for tampering with his private letters. His relations continued to be friendly with Healy, who asked Parnell to allow him to substitute as his secretary a friend to whom Healy had taught shorthand in Newcastle-on-Tyne. This was Henry Campbell, who as the late Sir Henry Campbell became the subject of T. P.'s sketch. Parnell, who appreciated what underlay the change, consented, and matters went on as smoothly as before.

The tragic consequences which separated the two men politically arose over the Galway election of February, 1886, when Mr. T. P. O'Connor requested Biggar and Healy to oppose Captain O'Shea, Parnell's nominee for that seat. O'Shea was not merely the husband of his mistress; but was to some extent, it would appear, a confidant of the late Mr. Joseph Chamberlain, who at one time contemplated his appointment as Under-Secretary for Ireland. Mr. O'Connor was desirous that a friend of his own should fill the vacancy caused by his double return for Galway and the Scotland Division of Liverpool. Biggar and Healy were brought in between the hammer and the anvil.

In 1888 the famous *Times* Commission, consisting of Justices Hannon, Smith, and Day, was appointed to examine into the genuineness of the letter, forged by Richard Pigott, which a great organ was betrayed by its own credulity into publishing in the hope of destroying Parnell. The presumed object was that the Crimes Act of 1887 might pass into perpetual effect in Ireland ; and the letter, congruously with this purpose, appeared on the day fixed for the Second Reading. Parnell's solicitor in the case was Sir George Lewis, of Ely Place, London, a most acute and experienced lawyer. Lewis retained for the defence the late Lord Russell, the late Lord Loreburn, the late Sir Francis Lockwood, Mr. Asquith, Arthur O'Connor, Mr. Healy and T. Harrington. Not all these counsel were to appear for the same defendants ; but all were substantially briefed in the same interest.

Suddenly after the names of the counsel had been published in the Press, and without a word of explanation, Sir George Lewis was ordered to inform Healy that his retainer was discharged. Lord Russell was dismayed and indignant ; but Healy did not demand an explanation, knowing that it was the vengeance of Mrs. O'Shea for the Galway incident. Parnell's allies put it about that Michael Davitt had objected to him, and that this objection led to his extrusion from the case. Such an allegation actually appears in Barry O'Brian's life of Parnell published ten years later. Davitt, on seeing it, wrote a pungent denial, declaring that he had advised Parnell the other way.

O'Shea's divorce proceedings were begun a year after Parnell's vindication against *The Times*, and caused his downfall. Healy was absent from Westminster through illness, when Mr. Gladstone wrote the famous letter which caused the Irish Party to change its decision of loyalty to Parnell as chairman ; and he had nothing to do with the initiation of the proceedings to evict that statesman from the chair of the Irish party. When a majority asserted itself against Parnell, Healy came from Dublin to Westminster and thereafter became his most formidable opponent.

Barry O'Brien records (on page 334) that " an old Fenian " (who can be identified as Mr. John O'Leary) said to Parnell, " Healy seems to have the best political head of all these people "—to which Parnell rejoined, " He has the only political head among them."

Such was the history of the relations between Healy and Parnell.

I have not space here to attempt any adequate examination of Healy's chequered and tempestuous career.

His Parliamentary gifts were individual and extraordinary. He possessed the power of mordant and corrosive sarcasm, the like of which I have never met elsewhere. I can still see him standing up to address the House, his chin aggressively protruded, his expression one of melancholy gravity, pouring out a long succession of bitter, cruel and wounding insults. His wit was as extraordinary as his invective. He possessed, too, another quality not less effective in his oratorical stock-in-trade. He was amazingly *arresting* as a speaker. When Healy was speaking, you had to listen to him all the time, whether you wanted to or not. Had

Edmund Burke added this quality to his superb intellectual equipment, we should, perhaps, not have lost the American Colonies.

Those who formed their judgment of Healy's nature from his public utterances alone, or, I may add, from his public actions alone, would, indeed, have been mistaken in their judgment of the man. For concealed within this strange personality by his public ferocity are the heart and the temperament of a warm-hearted child. His is, indeed, the disposition of a man who unites a steely resolution to his other qualities; and has found himself compelled to act fiercely and speak fiercely in antagonisms which themselves were very fierce.

Those who have known him best have always realised how faulty an impression his public activities created. No friend ever went to him in vain for help which he was able to give; none ever went for sympathy or affection without receiving both in generous profusion; and he has mellowed with success and with advancement. His reminiscences are a joy; and he ought, while he still retains so much vigour and a memory unimpaired, to collect them in the interests of those who love good stories; a vivid pen; a stirring and brilliant narrator.

The Right Hon.
Reginald McKenna

The Right Hon. Reginald McKenna

MR. REGINALD McKENNA was born in the year 1863, so that he is to-day in his 61st year. He was a Scholar, and is an Honorary Fellow, of Trinity Hall, Cambridge. He rowed bow in the Cambridge University Eight of 1887; and in the same year he rowed in the Grand and Stewards' Cups at Henley; thus early in his career exhibiting in the field of athletics that stocky stubbornness of fibre which he has since exhibited on many larger theatres.

He was Financial Secretary to the Treasury in 1905; President of the Board of Education, 1907-1908; First Lord of the Admiralty, 1908-1911; Home Secretary, 1911-1915; Chancellor of the Exchequer, 1915-1916; and to conclude a record both varied and very distinguished, he has since 1919 been Chairman of the London Joint City and Midland Bank.

So large a measure of achievement could only be explained by the possession of remarkable qualities. I should suppose that Mr. McKenna's strongest points are a very orderly, clear and well-arranged mind; immense industry, and an intuitive logical faculty. He occupied the highest offices of the State, without reaching to the first rank of Parliamentary debaters; although within a certain range of subjects he was unsurpassed in the House of Commons. And while a very competent platform speaker, he never belonged—perhaps it is to his

credit—to the band of "spell-binders" who storm
the doors of promotion by tempestuous public
rhetoric. And yet, as we have seen, he has filled
with distinction many, almost most, of the great
offices of State.

His career has exhibited many strange and
incalculable vicissitudes. When I first entered Parliament in 1906 he was, on the whole, one of the most
unpopular Ministers in the eyes of the rank and file
of the Conservative Party. His manner was precise,
attorney-like and irritating. And in the eyes of men
who did not know how much charm and geniality he
possessed in private life, he seemed jejune in his conceptions ; and rather petty in their presentation.
An occasion is still recalled on which he announced,
at a moment when political feeling was much em-
bittered over the Welsh Church controversy, what
he evidently believed to be a brilliant—and what
was, in fact, a considerable—concession. " I am
in a position," he said, " to reassure those who believe that it is not our intention to act generously :
I am prepared to meet them in the matter by offering them 6s. 8d." The ambiguity of this announcement, and the paltry county court atmosphere which
has long surrounded this particular sum, produced a
degree of laughter and ridicule which I do not think
that even up to the present day Mr. McKenna has
completely understood.

The first change in the view which the Tory
Party as a whole took of Mr. McKenna was observable when he became First Lord of the Admiralty.
I remember the late Lord Fisher, who liked his political
" chiefs "—if in such a connection the noun may
be allowed—to be combative in the warfare of

Parliament, told me in reference to the appointments of Mr. McKenna and Dr. Macnamara, that he had now obtained the services of the two " Fighting Macs." Both of these Ministers justified the confidence of the First Sea Lord. Dr. Macnamara was to hold his responsible office with great public advantage for many years ; perhaps longer than any Minister has ever held it. Mr. McKenna was to fight a great fight, not yet forgotten at the Admiralty, in order to maintain the British Navy at the minimum strength imperatively required, at a moment charged with crisis, by the safety of the Empire.

The atmosphere of those days seems now so remote that men have forgotten how difficult was McKenna's task ; and how steadfastly he discharged it. The swollen Liberal majority of 1906 contained, as I suppose, a larger number of wordy men wholly ignorant of international politics, and of the affairs of the world, than any House of Commons within living memory. Its members, or most of them, were drugged by the poisonous influence of pacifism. They refused to believe that it was conceivable that Germany would ever take a desperate aggressive. They ignored the strength of the German Army ; and smiled in a superior way when reminded that the greatest military nation in the world was deliberately challenging our supremacy on the ocean. It was a House of Commons at whose hands even the bland unintelligibility of the present Lord Chancellor hardly availed to extract sanction for the creation of the Territorial Army. Lord Haldane was, in fact, looked upon as a dangerous Jingo.

McKenna applied his cold and passionless mind

n the first place to a conclusion upon the merits of the Admiralty claim. Having reached a conclusion in its favour quite clearly, he thereafter turned neither to the right hand nor to the left ; but with the same doggedness which he had shown in youthful days on the Cam, he set himself to the fight which lay in front of him. He fought it well, courageously and successfully ; not only against doctrinaires in the Commons, but also against doctrinaires in the Cabinet. And when men throw their minds back to those who, labouring greatly and taking great political risks, combatted the contemporary miasma of folly, the name of Mr. McKenna may worthily be recalled with that of Lord Haldane.

I had at that time no official channels of information. And, like the rest of the world, I can only conjecture as to the circumstances in which Mr. McKenna left the Admiralty. It was, however, freely stated that his strategic preparations for a war probably imminent and ever menacing, were less complete than those which were concerned with material and personnel. And this might well be the true explanation ; for I should very much doubt whether Mr. McKenna, who unites to high logical quality, both clear-sightedness and modesty, ever regarded himself as a gifted strategist.

In 1914 came the War, justifying for ever and ennobling the great fight which he had fought and won. Soon it became evident that Mr. Lloyd George had even more striking services to render to the nation than those which were bound up in finance. He weathered indeed, with equal imaginativeness and resource, the storm of the first few weeks ; but when this was weathered became convinced that, great as the financial anxieties of the War must continue to be, other problems even more vital awaited both his daring resources and his driving-power.

Mr. McKenna held the office of Chancellor of the Exchequer until the first Coalition Government, over which Mr. Asquith presided, fell in inextinguishable ruin. To that ruin he made perhaps no inconsiderable contribution. The relations between himself and Mr. Lloyd George, never good, had grown worse ; and he was convinced that Mr. Lloyd George could not form a Government ; and that if he succeeded in doing so it must be short-lived. His influence over Mr. Asquith at this time was very great ; and I have never been able to resist the conclusion that it was resolutely used to persuade Mr. Asquith that by declining accommodation he must after a very short interval re-assume office upon his own terms. This calculation, like so many others in the incalculable political temperature of the war, failed ; and neither Mr. Asquith nor Mr. McKenna has ever held office since.

Mr. McKenna brought to the discharge of his difficult duties all the qualities which his history would have prepared us to expect. He proved himself acute, very accurate, very thorough, and very resourceful. But I sometimes doubt whether he ever quite realised that in modern conditions, for whatever other cause wars are lost, they are seldom lost by financial stringency alone. I doubt, for instance, whether he fully realised how boundless at the moment, if a Minister of Finance shut his ears to the gravity of the post-war reaction, were the resources of this country available for the prosecution of the war. But, after all, if a Chancellor of the Exchequer does not indicate caution, and insist upon economy, his colleagues are unlikely, while war rages, or even now when peace rages, to undertake the task. Mr. McKenna brought to the discharge of his duties the most conscientious energy and all the natural resources of a fine business instinct. Even if it was unimaginative, his stewardship was, on balance, of immense service to the national cause.

And then came the collapse of which I have already spoken. It might have seemed that an ex-Minister in his 54th year was trying destiny rather high when he attempted a career in the City, which lay almost wholly outside anything in his previous experience. He began life as a practising barrister, and continued to practise until he entered Parliament. So far as I know, the only business or financial experience which he had ever enjoyed was derived from the high field of important politics, which has not always proved a fruitful avenue to success in the City. No higher tribute could have been paid to his reputation than that he should have been offered the chairmanship of the London Joint City and Midland Bank ; no higher tribute can now be paid to his abilities than to record the fact that by universal admission he has discharged the duties of that high position with incomparable distinction. Indeed, from the moment that he entered the City, his prestige, which had by no means been universally admitted, continuously grew. He became recognised as one of the men who counted in the City of London, not merely in virtue of his titular position, but of his natural or acquired qualities.

Right Hon. Reginald McKenna

A very surprising and paradoxical recognition of his growing reputation was not to be long delayed. The collapse of some Coalition or other seems naturally to presage a strange change in Mr. McKenna's fortunes. The ruin of the first took him into the City; the ruin of the second nearly brought him out of it. A homogeneous Conservative Government obtained a serviceable majority; and Mr. Bonar Law soon disclosed his purpose of inviting Mr. McKenna to take high office in his Cabinet. The discussions were for various reasons protracted; but with the death of Mr. Bonar Law, Mr. Baldwin, his successor, definitely announced that he intended to invite Mr. McKenna, and that Mr. McKenna had agreed, to accept the office of Chancellor of the Exchequer in a Conservative Government.

The larger ironies of politics have seldom received a more vivid illustration. The Minister who had been howled down with contemptuous derision by the Tory benches as the " Six-and-eightpenny man " was now fêted and welcomed by a Diehard Government, who had come into office upon the basis that they could no longer co-operate without contamination with Liberals. Nor am I aware that Mr. McKenna has ever made a public recantation of his own political views. I doubt very much whether in post-war conditions he was ever a supporter of the McKenna Duties. It was, indeed, even stated, without contradiction, in the recent debate upon these duties in the House of Commons, that Mr. McKenna had made his acceptance of office in a Conservative Government conditional upon the withdrawal of these duties.

The situation, however, in circumstances within

the memory of all, never developed. It is believed that Mr. McKenna's ambition was to be elected by acclamation Independent Member for the City of London. But Lord Banbury could not tear himself away from so ancient a haunt, until he did so hurriedly some weeks later. Just in time, in a homely American phrase, to " get away " with his peerage. And it did not at the moment prove a particularly easy task to find a seat for Mr. McKenna at once easy and dependable. And so, after all these surprising negotiations, there suddenly appeared the announcement, unauthorised at first, but never, I think, seriously contradicted, that Mr. McKenna had changed his mind, and no longer proposed to become a member of Mr. Baldwin's Government.

The short summary which I have attempted of a career full of achievement shows much else, but it shows with special plainness that Mr. McKenna possesses both originality and nerve. He quarrelled tenaciously in the old days with his Tory opponents ; he was never unwilling to break a lance with Mr. Lloyd George ; and finally, as it seemed, almost without a struggle, he extricated himself from the somewhat obsolete embrace of Mr. Asquith.

It remains only to add that his responsibilities have not depressed the man ; nor his successes spoiled him. He is simple, approachable, and courteous ; in private life a most pleasant companion ; and, if such a thing may be whispered with impunity of a great financier, one of the best bridge players in London. I attempt no prediction as to his future ; for a man who has behaved so surprisingly in the past is an unsuitable subject for the industry of political prophets.

The Earl of Lonsdale

The Earl of Lonsdale

THE subject of the present study belongs to one of the most ancient and illustrious families in England. It is of great antiquity in the counties of Westmorland and Cumberland, where from almost immemorial days it has been seated at Lowther Hall.

The tenacious quality of the house in English life is comparable to that of the Stanleys, the Cecils, and the Churchills; though in antiquity it greatly exceeds the records of the last two families. I myself have a great reverence for the ordered traditions of English public life. I recognise, indeed, that you cannot keep alive upon a long and tedious record of history a family which has declined in quality; and which can no longer make a contemporary contribution in the valuation of modern life. The same is true of nations. They wax and wane just as the great families of the aristocracy wax and wane; as soon as it has become obvious that they can no longer make a special contribution there is no reason why we should concede to them a special survival.

It is, indeed, probably in the interests of the general efficiency of the nation that when the vicissitudes of time have exhausted the qualities which brought a great strain to an illustrious position in the State, it should decline in favour of your shipbuilders, your lawyers, and even your war profiteers.

For the greatness of England will undoubtedly

be maintained only upon the basis that it is as possible to found a tenacious family in the year 1924 as in the year 1324. But if I were writing the history of England in three hundred years from now I would gladly, and with adequate tribute, record the fortunes of any great House founded to-day which had played an illustrious part in the history of these Islands over so long a period.

And so in dealing, however shortly, with the history of the Lowther family, I recall with a pleasure not wholly free from irony, that the cousin and the trustee of the " Yellow Earl " was that Speaker of the House of Commons whom I now know as Viscount Ullswater, and who presided with ancient dignity over a modern House of Commons.

The age of the family with which we are concerned may be illustrated by the fact that its name occurs in connection with grants of land in the time of Henry II and Henry III. In the latter reign, for instance, Thomas de Lowther was witness to the foundation Charter of the Chantry in the Chapel of Great Strickland Hall, and to an agreement concerning the Morland Wood. Sir Gervase de Lowther, Knight, and Gervase de Lowther, Archdeacon of Carlisle, were powerful figures in the reign of King Henry III. And it is interesting to recall, in view of the celebrated French sarcasm that more than half our aristocracy was in its origin legal, that Sir Hugh de Lowther was Attorney-General in the reign of King Edward I. He became later Justice Itinerant and Escheator on the north side of the Trent ; and was promoted to be one of the Justices of the King's Bench in the fifth year of King Edward III.

His son and heir, Sir Hugh de Lowther, took

part with the Earl of Lancaster against Piers Gaveston, the favourite of Edward II, and was concerned in his death ; but was with others pardoned by the King by Act of Parliament 7 Edw. II 1313.

Hardly a generation of this illustrious north-country family passes without producing some member who would deserve to be mentioned in a longer survey ; our summary must be short.

Sir Hugh Lowther fought at Agincourt, and was Sheriff of Cumberland in the eighteenth year of the reign of King Henry VI.

In the reign of Queen Elizabeth Sir Richard Lowther was High Sheriff of Cumberland. He succeeded his cousin Lord Scrope as Lord Warden of the West Marches, and was three times Commissioner in the grave affairs that arose between England and Scotland. When Mary Queen of Scots fled into England, and arrived in Cumberland in the month of May, 1568, Elizabeth sent orders to Sir Richard that he should convey the Scottish Queen to Carlisle Castle. While Mary was still in custody, the Sheriff incurred the deep displeasure of his Sovereign by allowing the Duke of Norfolk to visit his prisoner. We are not told whether the contumacy was preceded by an interview with this beautiful and tragic Queen. But I suspect it ; and no Lowther in history, worthy of the name, and responsive to the family traditions, could or would or ought to have resisted such an appeal.

And so from knights the family grew to be barons, from barons to be viscounts, and from viscounts to be earls. To-day the head of the House of Lowther has obviously, like the head of the House of Stanley, very little to gain by any advance in the Peerage.

The present holder of the title belongs to a very individual if unhappily an obsolescent type in our English life. He is a great territorial magnate. He belongs really to the period in which illustrious noblemen drove magnificently through Europe in their coach and four; he is a very remarkable embodiment of the sporting spirit of England. The fashions of a drab age do not unhappily permit him to wear the clothes which ought to adorn a picturesque if old-fashioned body.

He was M.F.H. of the Quorn Hunt from 1901-1909, and of the Cottesmore until two years ago. There is much to be said for the view that by sustaining the Cottesmore Pack through the war he saved fox hunting in England. His stables, like everything else about him, have been conceived in a style of splendid and almost mediæval state. His coaches were always yellow; his motor-cars have inherited and even exaggerated this brilliant colour; his horses could not easily become yellow (this must always have annoyed him); but they have almost always been chestnut; they have been the best in England; and he has always had at least twice as many as he, his friends, and his staff could employ. He is included in this series because he is in many ways one of the most remarkable links between the past and the present. At Lowther Castle he lives in splendid state, and with incredible hospitality; universally beloved and respected by his farmers, his tenants, and labourers; preserving, as Matthew Arnold said of the Oxford spires, the lost enchantments of the Middle Ages; and while he has maintained so much in modern actuality of that " Young England " which filled the vain dreams of young Disraeli, while almost alone he preserves an atmosphere which to our grandchildren, alas! will be nothing but an historic dream, he has none the less, by a *bonhomie* and kindness and simplicity peculiar to the man, completely disarmed the voice of detraction and jealousy.

He is sometimes called " The Jolly Earl," " The Yellow Earl," " The Costers' Earl," but never, so far as I know, in his whole life has he been assailed by the shrill voice of class hatred. No one really would be quite strong enough to attack him. For he is, as I have plainly indicated, the idol of those in this country who pursue honest sport in the spirit of gay and adventurous gentlemen; and he who challenges that spirit, from whatever party he issues, will meet a very grave reverse.

If, indeed, I were to attempt to reconstruct the genial figure of Hugh Lord Lonsdale to a generation which will not share with me the happiness of knowing him, I should picture him immaculately dressed, radiating good humour and genial kindliness, with a large camellia in his buttonhole, and a larger cigar in his mouth. He would be either distributing prizes at Olympia, or riding gallantly over the great pastures and stiff fences of the shires, or presenting a super-donkey to a stricken coster, or observing a prize fight with the same bright and sporting eyes through which his ancestors looked over so many centuries upon bear-baiting and cock-fighting.

No one who has known him intimately has ever seen him depressed. Presumably, in spite of the fact that his life has been protected from many anxieties which surround most of us, he, like others, must have experienced troubles. If such troubles have assailed him, they must, I think, always have been repelled and dissipated by the sunny charm of an unconquerable good nature. Nor is this good nature limited to his own personal fortunes. He could not be really happy unless those around him were happy too. That section of the British public —and it is a very large one—which is devoted to sport has a sure instinct; and it has long since decided that while there are many difficulties in defining a sportsman, there is not the slightest difficulty in recognising one when you see one. And if a plebiscite of a whole nation of sportsmen were taken to-morrow to elect a president of the sportsmen of the British Empire, I have little doubt that the choice would fall upon Lord Lonsdale. His only possible rival would be Lord Desborough, who would present different but remarkable claims in an interesting competition.

He has, in fact, done many wonderful things in his life. So, it will be remembered, did Baron Munchausen. But Lord Lonsdale's achievements are more easily authenticated than those of the imaginative Baron; though perhaps the experiences of the noble Earl (and I like this trait in his character) have lost little in the telling.

He made, for instance, a memorable journey in December, 1888. He left Winnipeg in that month, travelling by dog-sleigh in the winter, up the Athabasca River to the Great Slave Lake; and afterwards the bitter journey down the Mackenzie River to its mouth. In the course of his journey an Indian deputation entreated him to divert from his direct route in order to inspect the gold at Forty Creek. There were quantities there, observable even to one without any pretension to expert gifts. Lord Lonsdale reported in this sense to Lord Lansdowne. Within a short period of time this district became the Klondyke. On the only occasion in a striking career the Yellow Earl was perhaps a little unworthy of his name. Had he chosen to decline from the rôle of adventurer into that of speculator, he could have added enormously to a great territorial fortune.

From Mackenzie River he took a whaler and went down the Channel between Banks Land and Melville Land, across to Bathurst Island ; and visited Lowther Island, a small island discovered by one of his ancestors serving generations ago in the Hudson Bay Company.

Crossing to the Yukon River he penetrated to the sea, expecting to find a whaler in Norton Sound ; travelling, now by dog-sleigh, now on snow-shoes ; but the vessel had sailed prematurely, owing to the murder by the Indians of Bishop Seager. So he proceeded down the Alaska Peninsula and then to Aleutian Island, where there are many whalers. He found one and chartered it ; but in a few days was wrecked amid terrible cold ; and escaped only after great sufferings in a small whale boat.

He crossed thereafter the side of the Alaska Peninsula, and reached a small port where he found a vessel to take him to San Francisco.

His journey of one and a-half years was ended ; for a great part of this period he and his companions had travelled and slept in a temperature of 50°-60° below zero ; and he returned in the fullest health and fitness.

These were remarkable and characteristic adventures ; and the fact that many malicious and imaginative people vigorously disputed that Lord Lonsdale had ever visited any of these countries at al shows how fierce is the light that beats about a throne : or an ancient North-country Earldom. It exhibits also the risks in which a gay inventiveness and a happy imagination may involve him who possesses them even when he is most accurate. For myself, having coolly weighed the evidence in almost a judicial capacity, I am on the whole satisfied that Lord Lonsdale did make this journey ; and that several of the incidents recorded can be verified.

I have not space here to deal with Lord Lonsdale's other memorable sporting achievements. He has shot big game in almost every part of the world. But his fame does not and will not depend upon any particular achievement. It depends rather upon the whole geniality and personality of the man. I hardly know of anyone still surviving in England who belongs quite to the same school. He was a boon companion of Squire Chaplin ; and he lived in the same wonderful world. He recreates the highest traditions of British sport ; and it is certain that he will hand on that torch to those of a younger generation, if indeed there be any such able to grasp it.

And while the spirit and the traditions for which he stood, and the genuine kindliness of heart by which he has adorned them, survive in England, this ancient country will have little to fear from the poisonous doctrines of the Bolsheviks.

In taking leave of him we salute a great aristocrat, a great sportsman, and a very kindly English gentleman.

The Right Hon.
Philip Snowden, M.P.

The Right Hon. Philip Snowden, M.P.

MR. PHILIP SNOWDEN came into the House of Commons in the same year that I did (1906), and left it for four years when I did in 1918. I went to the Upper House, and he retired owing to the view taken by his constituents in Blackburn of his war activities. But during those twelve years I had considerable opportunities of observing him as a Parliamentarian and debater. We made our maiden speeches upon the same night. He spoke indeed immediately before I did.

He always interested the House of Commons. His manner of delivering his speeches made him appear far harsher in form than he was in reality—and it was given to few to know that he possessed a milder side. He struck the outside observer as a kind of inverted Hugh Cecil—what Lord Hugh might have been had he chanced to be an extreme Socialist instead of an extreme individualist. Public opinion did not deny to either man a just tribute. It recognised that both orators were very able, manifestly sincere, and acrimonious to a point where debating scruple often disappears. Lord Hugh Cecil, mainly by his own choice, was never subjected to the test of proving the practicability of his own doctrines in office ; Mr. Snowden, on the contrary, has to answer the question how far the theories propounded by the ideologue member for Blackburn coincide with the actions of the Chancellor of the Exchequer.

One theory at least Mr. Snowden, like the Prime Minister, disproves in his own person and career. It is often said that the career of politics is confined to the families of the rich and powerful or to those endowed with exceptional opportunities for education. Mr. Snowden was born in Yorkshire, the son of a working weaver. He carried, we now know, his Chancellor's baton in his knapsack. His father was, however, well enough off to give him an education which, joined to his natural abilities, carried him into the Civil Service. And a civil servant he remained for seven years. In the ordinary course of events he would no doubt have risen to such preferment and secondary distinction as the conditions of that Service allow. He would have been a successful man known to a narrow circle.

But in the 90's there happened to him first an accident, and then a miracle. A fall from a bicycle made him for the time a cripple : a sick-bed reading of the Socialist case, undertaken in order to answer it, made him a Socialist. Bradlaugh, it may be remembered, was converted to his somewhat eccentric views on religion by a similar episode. Mr. Snowden, the convert, arose strong in the faith, if not in the body, and began to preach the crusade at first to a small body of adherents in the North Country. His very physical limitations added to the fervour of his appeal. He was seen as one in whom the desire of the soul and the mind devoured the infirmity of the flesh, and became a living flame. Instead of St. Paul at Corinth we had St. Philip at Blackburn. Nor did the new Saint forbear from a certain intolerance often found among the early Christian fathers.

Right Hon. Philip Snowden, M.P.

If you were a Socialist of some sort you might on a charitable supposition have a hope of political salvation : if you were a Liberal or Conservative you were mercilessly damned.

Mr. Snowden, whose writings in the Press and whose local speeches had attracted some attention since he had been " converted " in the sense of the older Evangelicals, came into Blackburn as a candidate in the election of 1900 as an almost unknown man. That constituency had been a Tory stronghold for nearly a quarter of a century. The tide in 1900 was setting strongly in the Conservative direction. Yet so great was the personal impression that he made that he shook the party in power ; and when the flood came with the ebb of 1906 ; and Liberalism triumphed, he was returned to Parliament. His few and original supporters had been members of the Social Democratic Federation, and many cries of treason were raised when he left the patriotic Socialists and became the shining light of the Independent Labour Party as one member of the " Holy Trinity," as it was usually termed, consisting of Keir Hardie, Ramsay MacDonald, and himself. But it must always be remembered that conversion does not eliminate altogether a longing for original sin. The Salvationist sometimes remembers the taste of strong drink, and Mr. Snowden (like Mr. Henderson) started life as a Liberal. His first Budget as Chancellor was clearly a case of an author reverting to type.

No party since the Whig-Liberal-Radical Combines of the middle nineteenth century has been so heterogeneous as the present Socialist-Labour bloc, with its outer fringe of Communists shading through the Socialists of the Chair, or the Fabians, to the individualistic Trade Union leader intent in reality simply on improving wages and conditions under the existing capitalist régime. Again, it includes members who are practically Tolstoyan in their views of war, and fiery advocates of international class war; while on the same benches sit men like Mr. Clynes and Mr. Henderson, who served with distinction in Mr. Lloyd George's war Government, and keen patriots and Imperialists like Mr. J. H. Thomas. And then apart from differences of view, there are diverging gulfs of temperament in the Socialist ranks—the men who want to go slow and the men who want to go quick; the men who wish to capture Parliament and the men who wish to destroy it; the theorists and the realists, the men of peace and the men of violence—the theoretical pacifist like Mr. Lansbury being, of course, always the most violent.

Where in all this welter does Mr. Snowden stand? Technically his position is exactly the same as the Prime Minister's. He is an I.L.P. man—neither a Trades Unionist with the associations of manual labour, nor a Fabian with the idea of a gas and water revolution painlessly and imperceptibly effected, but a Socialist of the Chair seeking to establish the new state by the rapid nationalisation of the means of production and exchange. None the less, since his temper has less flexibility than his chief's, he would be capable of playing Robespierre to Mr. Ramsay MacDonald's Danton.

No one could doubt which is by nature the more extreme in carrying a logical conception beyond the border line of safety or practicability. This difference between the two men manifested itself very clearly during the war. In theory both were out-and-out Pacifists. In actuality Mr. MacDonald " hedged," while Mr. Snowden went straight forward with a kind of implacable sincerity to damage his country in the hour of her mortal danger. He had let fall observations to the effect that since both a Prussian and a British Government were capitalist in principle, it made little difference to the British working classes whether they were governed from Potsdam or Downing Street. And he acted up to this amazing, this revolting, theory. He opposed the war ; he opposed conscription ; but he shrank back—after Kerensky's fall—from the Communism of Moscow as seen through the eyes of Mrs. Snowden. It is not considered very polite now to remind the public of the services or disservices done to the country by individuals during the war. Possibly we have not too good a conscience about our national treatment of ex-Service men. We should like to forget the whole episode—and behind this craving for a merciful oblivion both the present Prime Minister and his Chancellor have taken somewhat obsequious refuge. Everyone, however, recognised even at the time that Mr. Snowden's fanaticism and anti-patriotism were perfectly honest, even if they were insane.

It seems a curious thing to say of a man who belongs distinctly to the left, and not to the right of Socialism, that he possesses a far more " Liberal " mind than, let us say, Mr. J. H. Thomas or Mr. Clynes. He overleaps their mental position by a kind of somersault, and straddles their minds with one leg on Karl Marx and the other on Richard Cobden. Logically, of course, such a position is indefensible. But it can be understood temperamentally. Both Marx and Cobden were men ready to lay down hard and fast rules, admitting of no exceptions, for the guidance of humanity in certain political and economic matters. Free Trade or State Socialism would in their view suit any country under any conditions. No Conservative could possibly argue or think like that. And therefore it was amusing, but not so wholly unnatural as it might seem, to find Mr. Snowden sunning himself the other day in the beaming approval of the Cobden Club— the advocate of the most cast-iron economic régime for restricting the freedom of contract ever devised, surrounded by the disciples of the politician to whom Free Trade was nothing but one branch of mankind's inalienable right to complete economic liberty.

Mr. Snowden, however, had earned his dinner, for there is little doubt that it was his influence with the Government that destroyed the Imperial Preference Resolutions. In that debate we had a curious picture of the bulk of the Labour Party showing a marked tendency to take a rational view both of the problem of Empire and the question of Tariff Reform, while their "advanced" leader turned on them a mind frozen for ever in the immobility of mid-Victorian Individualism and Little Englandism.

I have written throughout of Mr. Snowden as a man by nature extreme. One curious instance to the contrary has to be noted. At a time when there seemed every prospect of the late Conservative administration remaining in office for some years, Mr. Snowden wrote a series of articles in a Conservative morning paper, predicting with considerable accuracy the actual proceedings of the Socialist minority Government to be, and breathing a general spirit of quietude and moderation. The critic deputed to answer him was so astonished that he took the line that these were not Mr. Snowden's past opinions, nor the present ones of most of his friends —and this he was able to prove.

I feel much the same about Mr. Snowden's Budget. It is perfectly true that it was in the main both sound and successful. It is also true that the remission of taxation it granted could have been made by any Liberal or Conservative Government which was not contemplating vastly increased expenditure—and should have been made by the Conservative Chancellor in the previous year. It is also true that the Liberals would have turned the Government out had they attempted a Socialist Budget. But from all these admitted facts I do not in the least draw the conclusion that the Chancellor is a moderate, except in so far as he is believed to have little enthusiasm for the Capital Levy. On the contrary, I believe the Budget to have been based on these considerations : (1) A sound instinct for finance—which Mr. Snowden possesses. (2) The necessity of preserving the Government in office. (3) The determination so to heap up the Social Reform expenditure against the Budget of 1925 that the money clearly could not be found without taxation bordering on confiscation.

Then if the Commons throw out the Budget we shall see the agitation of 1909 back again in an even more violent form. In such a battle, planned largely by his own mind, the Chancellor of the Exchequer would prove no " moderate."

Therefore I take leave of Mr. Snowden's character as I found it at the beginning of this article. Honest, visionary, implacable, a theorist in his very inconsistencies, he is a man who has fought a hard battle with life and health and won it—and in doing so has raised himself by his conspicuous courage and abilities to one of the highest places of a State in which he sees so much to disapprove.

It is not however inconceivable that he may live most grossly to abuse that position. For quick parts and madness are still close allies.

The Right Hon.
Lord Hewart

The Right Hon. Lord Hewart

LORD HEWART was born in the year 1870;
he is therefore to-day in his fifty-fourth year.
He was a Lancashire man, with a Lancashire education; he was trained in the famous Manchester
Grammar School, and proceeded thence to University College, Oxford. He was dependent for his
subsistence almost from boyhood upon his own
exertions. Nor was his academic career as brilliant as
it should have been. He missed his First Class at
Oxford by a mixture of bad luck and bad health.

He did not find himself in a position when he
left Oxford to address himself directly or immediately
to that career at the Bar in which he was later to
win so great distinction. The Bar, indeed, is a very
difficult career for those who lack a patrimony which
will support its adherents for at least ten years. And
so it happened to him—as it has happened to many
—that he resorted to an intermediate employment
enabling him to pay his way at the moment. He
became a leader writer on a daily newspaper and fre-
quented the Press Gallery of the House of Commons.
Another distinguished contemporary Judge had preceded him in this apprenticeship; for Sir Henry
Duke, the President of the Probate, Divorce, and
Admiralty Court, commenced his career from the
same exalted but unpromising situation.

And yet the position, remote as it seems from the
road of forensic success, has its advantages. The
members of the Press are notoriously warm-hearted,

and they are also clannish. And so it happens that if one of their number, whom they have liked and admired, has set out to storm even greater fortresses than those which are open to Pressmen, his old colleagues follow his career with sympathy and pleasure ; and, what is perhaps even more important, they pursue him with support. Gordon Hewart, therefore, who is a particularly affectionate and lovable man, began his legal career with this advantage, if he had no other, that there were many people who liked him and were determined that no conspicuous case in which he was engaged should be wanting in reasonable publicity.

For the career of a journalist he possessed many striking gifts. He was a good classical scholar, and had imbibed from his study of the Classics that general literary cultivation which is perhaps the overwhelming justification for maintaining in our schools the study of Latin and Greek. He not only appreciates good literature, but he writes and speaks extremely good English.

It is, indeed, an interesting study to observe the different methods by which great advocates rise to success. It happened by a coincidence that I was dining at the Mess of the Northern Circuit of Liverpool on one of the occasions on which Hewart was eating a probationary dinner. I did not know him by sight, and asked who he was. I do not think he will take offence if, with the liberty of an old friend, I state that I did not form the slightest conception of the distinction which he was one day to win.

And yet it was impossible to talk to him without realising that he was a very clever, a very polished, and a very companionable man. Indeed,

I suspect that just as the qualities which I have indicated had made for him powerful friends among the Press, they equally smoothed, in an almost incredible degree, his early struggles at the Bar. He became the pupil of the late Mr. Sutton, of Manchester.

Mr. Sutton was a man of immense learning —perhaps in his day the most learned junior at the Bar. It was his foible that he was so great a junior that he would diminish the lustre of his position by taking silk. And accordingly he lingered on at Manchester year after year, allowing junior men to take titular precedence over him ; objecting, where he could successfully do so, to the employment of a leader in the cases in which he was engaged ; and generally bringing himself into collision with the traditions and hierarchy of the Bar. But with all his foibles, Sutton was a great lawyer and a great personality. No one in the world was better suited to instruct in the Law a young man who possessed the industry, the acuteness, and the originality of Hewart.

I should, on the whole, imagine that the years which he passed in Sutton's chambers taught him almost all he knows—and it is much—of the Common Law of England. Sutton was a hard, if a kindly, task-master. He was intolerant alike of idleness and superficiality. So that any man who went through the crucible of his chambers with increased reputation, and retained the esteem of his teacher, was a man evidently marked out for promotion at the Manchester Bar. And in this way Hewart's career began. He established in Manchester, at first in the County Courts, the reputation of an adroit, subtle, industrious, and learned counsel.

And the reputation so gained spread rapidly to litigation in the High Court.

The qualities of advocates are very various. One man possesses one gift in a high degree ; another a different one, perhaps not less valuable, but still quite distinguishable. The special quality of the Lord Chief Justice must, I think, always have been his persuasiveness, his tact, and his plausibility. He never extorted verdicts by an exhibition of dæmoniac energy, like Charles Russell. He never bullied witnesses. He was never insolent to Judges. He never, in a word, set himself to storm trenches by frontal attacks. These attempts were indeed reserved for our generals in the War. But in his easy, equable, bland manner, he put himself upon the best possible terms with the Judge and with the jury. He contrived to give the impression that he was under-stating, rather than over-stating, his client's case. So that before the case was concluded the impression became general that his client, in some way or other, had been harshly used, and was entitled to the sympathy and assistance of the Court.

I should imagine that Lord Hewart had formed large ambitions, from which politics were not excluded, while he still sat in the Gallery of the House of Commons. For men at the Bar, when once success is certainly within their grasp, have a very difficult decision to make. It is, whether they shall complicate their lives, and perhaps compromise their prospects, by uniting the political with the legal career ; or whether they shall adhere rigidly to their profession. The choice is as critical as it is difficult. Many lawyers have gone to the House of Commons ; they have spent a fortune upon politics ; they have sacrificed their comforts, their leisure, and their vocations; and they have gained nothing. And yet the highest prizes at the Bar are seldom gained except by those who have not only proved themselves to be accomplished lawyers, but who have also undergone the drudgery of political service.

I cannot doubt that Hewart from the first had made up his mind to take a hand in the larger game. He contested North-West Manchester at a by-election in 1912, and was shortly afterwards given what at that time was a safe Liberal seat in Leicester. His success in the House of Commons was neither rapid nor spectacular. He seconded the Address on one occasion in a manner graceful indeed and polished, but not in the least striking. Nor had he made any very decisive impression upon the House of Commons when the removal of Lord Cave from the Solicitor-Generalship to the Home Office made him the Junior Law Officer of the Crown.

His professional advancement had fully justified his promotion. He had taken all the risks of the legal game; and played them boldly out to their extreme consequence. He took silk young; came to London; seldom went circuit; and made it plain that the only forensic career for which he cared lay in London. The outbreak of war, and its collateral results, removed many formidable rivals from his path. Lord Carson, Sir Henry Duke, Sir John Simon, and myself were, for various reasons, diverted from private practice. Sir Douglas Hogg and Sir Patrick Hastings were still juniors. And so it happened that this industrious, insinuating, adroit, and accomplished Lancashire advocate took the legal world of London by storm almost before the general public had realised his identity.

I can speak of his work as Solicitor-General with a great deal of knowledge ; for nearly three years I was, as Attorney-General, his senior colleague. It used to be said that " there are no secrets like those between a horse and his rider." It is equally true that there is little possibility as between two Law Officers of one over-valuing or under-valuing the other. Every day brings its problems, which must on that day be discussed and pronounced upon in consultation. The argument must always be insistent and closely pressed. Our period of office was particularly arduous, not only by reason of the immense burden of prize work, but also by reason of the fact that the Common Law was largely replaced by many volumes of emergency legislation, with which it was necessary that the Law Officers should be intimately acquainted. In these trying years Hewart's loyalty and friendship were as remarkable as his capacity and industry. I have, in fact (though it sounds egotistic to say so), never worked intimately with anyone whose mind marched more closely with my own upon the subjects which engaged them both.

I had not much opportunity of judging of his work in Parliament. Indeed, in the House of Commons the position of Law Officer is an unenviable one ; and that of the Solicitor-General particularly unenviable. For whenever a Minister—even an Under-Secretary—thinks that there is any credit to be gained by a Parliamentary effort, he reserves it for himself. But whenever there is a point in any Bill which he does not understand, and could never understand, he immediately clamours for a Law Officer ; and obligingly throws the duty of explaining it and recommending it upon him. If any point arises which, though technical, the Attorney-General thinks might be made the subject of an important legal allocution, he in his turn reserves it for himself. So that all that is left in the House of Commons, in normal conditions, for the Solicitor-General is the elucidation of unintelligible legal difficulties in minor and uninteresting Bills. The Attorney-General does not, as a rule, think it necessary to be present at these discussions.

I adhered loyally to the conceptions of my office which I had inherited from my predecessors, and it accordingly happened that, in the three years in which Gordon Hewart was Solicitor-General, I seldom had the pleasure of listening to his Parliamentary efforts. But I had all the time the knowledge that nothing committed to him was ever bungled ; that he developed an amazing skill in recommending the undesirable, and in explaining the inexplicable.

Larger opportunities were given to him when he became Attorney-General. The dictatorship of the War Cabinet swiftly and happily disappeared. Cabinet responsibility was restored. Emergency legislation, and the feverish unhealthy atmosphere in which it lived, became things of the past. And many occasions developed upon which, in the absence of Mr. Lloyd George at Paris, Mr. Bonar Law required help on the Front Bench. And soon it became plain that in the Attorney-General, soothing, placative, bland, and ingenious, he had discovered a very great Parliamentarian

The arts which made him successful in the House

of Commons were precisely those which had brought him to so much distinction at the Bar. Yet many distinguished lawyers have been notorious failures —as were Erskine and Charles Russell—in Parliament. Hewart was happy in that his forensic equipment did not antagonise the House of Commons ; but harmonised alike with its traditions, and with its habitual methods of expression. He was polished, suave, mildly ironic, never bitter ; he seemed, indeed (if the metaphor be permitted), to lick round a subject with the tongue of some bland serpent, all of whose poison glands had been carefully sterilised. He never offended anyone ; he always answered everyone ; and of compliments, which cost him little, he was no niggardly distributor. He certainly owed much to his deserved personal popularity—to a side of his character to which I have hitherto made no reference. He is an extraordinarily genial man. He likes company ; he likes talk ; and he does not disdain the accompaniments by which company is made more agreeable, and talk more tolerable.

And so he became, in the smoking-room of the House of Commons (where much serious business is discharged), one of the most popular and most frequent visitors. An important Minister visiting the smoking-room brings with him interest and prestige. Many Ministers have been weakened in their popularity by their failure to realise this elementary truth. Gordon Hewart not only seemed to be hail-fellow-well-met with everyone he met in the House of Commons smoking-room ; he actually was so. He missed perhaps his supreme opportunity in life by being born later than the age of those taverns in which Ben Jonson loved to talk ; of the coffee-houses in which Dr. Johnson was dictator, and of the literary club of which that great man was the most illustrious figure. You may call this very attractive quality in the Lord Chief Justice what you will. I have spoken of him already as companionable. Call him, if you choose, sociable or convivial, or clubbable. Unite what is best in all these adjectives, and you will produce—and this indeed is my purpose—a very lovable and a very human creature.

It is proper to add a word, however, carefully chosen, on the qualities of the Lord Chief Justice as a Judge. And, inasmuch as I have consistently attempted in these articles to avoid the folly of excessive praise, I shall make it plain that the time is not yet come when his judicial status can be measured. It was indeed certain when he became Lord Chief Justice that he possessed many qualities very desirable, if not indispensable, in the holder of that office. He was by nature extremely courteous. He constantly bore in mind Bacon's pregnant saying that " a much-talking Judge is like an ill-tuned cymbal." He has never thought himself competent to form an opinion until he has heard both sides. And he treats members of the Junior Bar with as much civility as the greatest leaders who appear before him. These qualities are all admirable, and not less conspicuous because some of his predecessors have been lacking in some of them. But he has confined himself so far, no doubt for good reasons, to the business of *nisi prius ;* he has gone circuit with a frequency unusual in the case of the Lord Chief Justice ; and has thereby deprived himself of the opportunities always open to him, unless the Courts of first instance are overwhelmed with arrears, of demonstrating his grasp of the intellectual problems of the Law.

I cannot doubt that, when the business of the Courts makes it possible and expedient, he will take his place on selected occasions as President of one of the divisions of the Court of Appeal. And when that day comes, and he is confronted by legal problems of delicacy and complexity, I for one cherish the confident hope that he will prove himself, even if *post intervallum*, in the true succession of Mansfield and Cockburn.

This expectation will be shared by many; this hope will be shared by all. For Lord Hewart has steered his way so smoothly and so dexterously amid the shoals and perils of forensic and political life that it is doubtful whether he possesses two ill-wishers in England. I think it possible that he possesses one; for he drove the present Prime Minister from a Leicester constituency in a speech of vitriolic and merciless polish. And the great are not always placable.

The Right Hon.
Lord Darling

The Right Hon. Lord Darling

LORD DARLING, better known to many generations of lawyers as Mr. Justice Darling, was
born in the year 1849. He is, therefore, in his
seventy-fifth year, although few who look at his
alert face and trim figure would suppose it.

Although extremely cultivated, and in many
ways very academic in his outlook upon life, he was
not, as it happens, educated at any of our Universities. He was called to the Bar in 1874, when I
myself was two years old. He was given his Patent
as Queen's Counsel in 1885. He had many years'
Parliamentary experience ; for he represented as a
Conservative the constituency of Deptford from
1888 to 1897.

In that year Lord Halsbury, then Lord Chancellor, made him a Judge in the King's Bench Division
of the High Court of Justice. His promotion was
received in 1897 with universal consternation by the
legal profession. His demission of that office twenty-
seven years later was received with a regret not
less universal. He left the Bench indeed with the
respect and affection of the whole legal fraternity.
He had in the interval silenced the voice of a very
obstinate, and not altogether unjustified, detraction.

The exercise of Lord Halsbury's patronage was
not, on the whole, the strongest side of that undaunted veteran's Chancellorships. But in this case
at least the result has vindicated his judgment. Lord
Darling would never make the claim, on his own

behalf, that he was a profound, or even a very learned, lawyer. But he proved, as time went on, that he possessed many remarkable and compensating qualities in which great lawyers are not unfrequently lacking. Indeed, I have often thought—and I was sometimes guided by this view in my own promotions—that while it is extremely important that the High Court Bench should be manned by admirably-equipped lawyers, it ought always at the same time to count among its members some who shine rather in virtue of personality than by consummate mastery of the scientific conceptions which underlie and determine the law.

The administration of law, especially upon its criminal side, requires qualities which are not to be completely learned in the commercial court; and the formidableness of the Red Judge on circuit ought not always to be exhausted by his imposing robe. The criminal classes soon become aware when a man has arisen in Israel. Mr. Justice Hawkins, with all his gross and glaring faults, was such a personality; Mr. Justice Lawrence ("Long John") was another. The last-named judge would, I think, have been extremely puzzled to comprehend, and still more to expound, any difficult principle of abstract law. But he none the less wielded the power, which many judges lack, of projecting into the Court from the Bench the force of a dignified and forcible personality. He possessed great aptitude for the rough-and-tumble work of *nisi prius*. He was admirably equipped for most of the problems which arose before a criminal judge. And on all issues of fact in civil matters he was a judge at once courteous, competent, weighty and silent.

Mr. Justice Darling soon compelled the admission from his critics that he too possessed a definite, and even an arresting, personality. Small of stature, slight of build, he none the less presented upon the Bench an appearance at once picturesque and dignified. He looked rather like a very delicately fashioned cameo. And he made it evident at once that he had his own conceptions (right or wrong) of the methods by which he might most usefully and acceptably discharge his judicial duties. He is an extremely witty man ; and his wit is reinforced both by natural culture and by wide reading. He was never at any pains to pretend that he took the view that his position upon the Bench ought to congeal his natural fountain of pleasantry ; it afforded him, on the contrary, in his view, what I may perhaps unkindly, but still intelligibly, call a more conspicuous theatre for its exhibition.

For more than twenty-five years he has been lectured for this propensity both by graver judicial persons, sitting in higher courts ; and also by the more decorous organs of our Press. Both were very likely right ; but he has never paid the slightest attention to either of them. I myself like a man who adheres inflexibly to his own standards. He has pursued his own blithe judicial path impervious alike to censure and to ridicule. *Punch* might call him " Mr. Justice Starling " ; and the House of Lords might shake grave heads over his levity. The learned Judge, quite unmoved, continued to administer justice as he understood it, but never neglected the opportunity for a *mot* or a witticism. And finally the whole legal world helplessly recognised the futility of protest and the failure of criticism.

And, the recognition once made, a balance was insensibly struck in the minds of that highly critical profession between Darling's merits and demerits; and with every passing year it became more and more clearly recognised that the merits of the Judge greatly outweighed his demerits. He possessed an arresting individuality of style, which compelled everyone to listen to him, and to him alone, the moment he raised his voice in court. This result was attained partly by an innate and rather exquisite personal distinction; partly by some very attractive quality in his voice.

And he quite soon made it plain also that he possessed more solid qualities very important in a judge. He was seldom impatient; his view in this respect being expressed by the resigned observation that if he were not trying one case, he would be trying another; and that it was very undesirable that parties to litigation should leave his court believing that their contentions had not received a full hearing. And so if occasionally the litigant who left the learned Judge's court in defeat was hardly in a mind to enjoy, as they deserved, the witticisms by which its hearing had been seasoned, he was never at least able to complain that his case had not been fully and patiently heard.

And Mr. Justice Darling possessed one other enormous advantage as a judge. He not merely was never bored with his work; he was positively enamoured of it. It became an obsession; and in the end one of the two or three hobbies of his life. He was, indeed, hardly happy off the Bench. And so it happened that on Saturday mornings, when there was sometimes a noticeable judicial exodus

from that great building in the Strand, in one court
at least, a small, assiduous, and deeply-interested
figure was to be found dealing either with the arrears
of the week, or with such odds and ends of judicial
work as could conveniently be disposed of within the
brief compass of Saturday morning. Nor did the
fountain of humour even on Saturday ever run dry;
though the Bar was perhaps a trifle less appreciative
of it than upon week-days.

Of witnesses Mr. Justice Darling, although short-
sighted, was a quick and shrewd judge. For he
has a great knowledge of human nature; and the
gift of drawing swift and accurate inferences from
facts which would afford little guidance to many
more learned lawyers. Another quality very greatly
endeared him to the Bar. He was conscious of the
difficulties in which busy counsel, often through no
fault of their own, become involved. He did not
adopt the rough-and-ready rule of saying that no
case should in any circumstances be postponed for
the convenience of counsel. Sometimes, especially in
the higher courts, such a rule must be rigidly enforced,
however moving the appeal, for reasons which need
not detain us here. But the senior judge in the special
jury list of the Law Courts, as Darling so often was,
could often without injury to anyone, and with
merciful effect upon the interests of the client,
mitigate the application of what must probably
always be the general rule. Looking back upon
the many years during which I was a busy practitioner before the learned Judge, I have many
memories of kindly indulgence and of consideration in
this respect.

I have already made it plain that Lord Darling

possesses wit in the true sense of that often misused term. And he possesses also, in a very refined degree, the quality of irony. I will even tell a story against myself in illustration of this attribute.

He once said to one of His Majesty's counsel, who repeated the story to me :—

" I would rather hear F. E. Smith open a complicated case before me than any counsel at the Bar."

Gratified, perhaps, rather than surprised, by this tribute, I asked :—

" Did the Judge say why ? "

" Yes," replied my friend. " He said that it was so interesting to discover which of two fresh minds would grasp the facts first."

It will be observed that the learned Judge did not reject even the extravagant from his ambit of humour.

I recall, too, a case in which copyright in verse was disputed. Counsel contended that poets wrote from pure inspiration, which had little contact with actual fact.

Darling J., in summing up, observed : " Gentlemen, you will no doubt consider this argument ; but remember that Gray's lines : ' Where ignorance is bliss, 'tis folly to be wise,' occur in a poem headed ' On a Distant Prospect of Eton College.' "

This observation seems to me to be extremely witty. But I wonder how many of the jury grasped it ; and I wonder a little, too, whether the judge was thinking of the jury, the Bar, or of the mere pleasure of saying something very amusing.

A Parliamentary effort is still recalled. Mr. Gladstone (growing old) led the House of Commons till dinner time; Sir William Harcourt for the rest of the evening. Questions arose as the House adjourned as to arrangements for the next day. Harcourt proved entirely lacking in information. Darling, M.P., pointed out that although there was ancient precedent for the practice, it was inconvenient to have " a greater light to rule the day, and a lesser light to rule the night." For long afterwards Harcourt was known as " The Lesser Light."

To go back still earlier, Darling—a very junior counsel—was addressing a jury at Quarter Sessions.

The Chairman : " Mr. Darling, have you noticed the position of the hands of the clock ? "

Darling : " Yes, sir ; but, with respect, I see nothing to cause anxiety. They seem to me to be where they usually are at this time of the day."

I am not an admirer of punning as a form of humour, but the following is not a bad illustration :

In a trial at *nisi prius* a witness, who was under great suspicion, said :

" I was not trying to avoid observation. I merely went into the ' Elephant ' to ask the manager if I might use his telephone."

The Judge (incredulously) : " A trunk call ? "

Another story of the Bar. Darling, a junior, was defending a thief before Cotton J. (a Chancery judge wholly inexperienced in criminal work and equally ignorant of the world). The case was uphill.

" The policeman," said Darling, " made a mistake in arresting the prisoner. The real truth, according to my instructions, is, that the thief escaped, and that the policeman seized upon the prisoner because he resembled the thief in appearance (both being bearded), and was standing near by. He appears to have applied a doctrine with which my lord is far better acquainted than I am—the *cy près* doctrine. The result is unfortunate : it is for my lord, who is an accomplished master of equity learning, and for the jury, directed by my lord, to correct the misunderstanding."

Mr. Justice Cotton, in summing up, very conscientiously explained that the Chancery doctrine of *cy près* did not apply in such a case ; and that no Court, either of law or equity, had ever attempted to extend its operation to criminal matters. He advised the jury to dismiss this suggestion from their minds, because it was founded upon a misunderstanding of Chancery Law. And the late Sir Reginald Acland, K.C., the Judge's Marshal, was never tired of telling the story that the Judge lamented at dinner that night that Common Law counsel should be so ignorant of Chancery Law as to suppose that *cy près* could be a defence to a criminal charge.

I remember one other case in which I was myself engaged before the learned Judge, as Attorney-General, in relation to proceedings for the sequestration of German assets in this country, having their origin in a German mine. The mass of documents in the case was enormous, and their character extremely technical. In spite of the slighting observations of the learned Judge, to which I have already referred, I had spent about ten days in mastering the facts ; and had set aside a week to conduct the case. It was to begin on Monday morning. On

Friday afternoon counsel for the defendants applied for three months' adjournment, on the ground that the documents in the case were extremely bulky, were all in highly technical German, and required a very expert translator.

The Judge asked my view. I curtly objected, pointing out that all parties concerned had had warning for six weeks that the case would be reached about the date proposed; and that the law officers had reserved the week for the hearing.

Darling J. turned to counsel making the application, and said:

" I can understand that you should apply for some delay; but why three months ? "

To which counsel : " Because, my lord, the documents which require translation are so technical."

Darling J. : " Rather a good idea has occurred to me. *Why not go to someone who knows German already ?* "

I have already called attention to the fact that the learned Judge possesses great literary gifts. He has written many charming verses. His volume, " On the Oxford Circuit," was published many years ago; and has recently been republished with some delightful additions. I have here little space for quotation. But when I recall that day on which the Judge left for the last time the Law Courts, in which he had sat, a conspicuous and unconventional figure, for twenty-seven years; where he had witnessed so many dramas; where he had contributed (as a judge must) to so many tragedies; I recall, and conclude this article, by his lines recently published and entitled :—

November, 1923

Long worn, now cast aside : red robe, lie there—
  Not, when the organ throbs the nave along,
    By chests of kingly dust,
      And chantries old,
Shall I, with measured step, and quickening heart,
  Pass to the Judge's place ; and, bowed, implore
    Myself be not condemned
    Nor less than right decree.

Not with resounding trumpets, may I come
  To sit in judgment on the regal bench ;
    Dividing false from true,
    With sword and even scale.
Mantle and stole laid by, and cap of doom ;
  Bereft, alone, I wear no ermine more ;
    Nor judge—yet one Assize
    I, fearful, must attend.

The Right Hon.
T. P. O'Connor, M.P.

The Right Hon. T. P. O'Connor, M.P.

THE series of sketches which I have attempted in these articles—now nearing their close—was never, of course, intended to record, like a school list, relevant intellectual valuations. I chose a certain number of subjects who happened to interest me, and of whom I hoped it might be possible to write something that would interest the public.

Any such series would be incomplete which did not include the name of Mr. Thomas Power O'Connor —better known to almost countless generations of politicians as " T. P." He is the Father of the House of Commons ; he was elected member for Galway as long ago as the year 1880. In 1885 he was returned both for Galway and for the Scotland Division of Liverpool. He chose to represent the latter constituency : and from this stronghold he has laughed at all opposition ever since. He has thus represented this very Irish constituency in England for very nearly forty years.

He has known, and observed with keen eyes, a larger number of distinguished men than anyone still in public life, with the exception of Arthur Balfour. And all the time he has been taking notes. He has been too busy in a crowded life to make it at all likely that he will ever even attempt to write his autobiography. And yet nothing is more certain than that his peculiar gifts and his immense and varied experience would enable him to produce a more interesting book, extending over a period of fifty years, than probably any living man to-day could write. And upon its purely commercial side —though of this he is a better judge than I am— I recommend the matter to his consideration.

Mr. O'Connor has lived a very varied life. But all the time he has been primarily a journalist. This is not to say that he has not been deeply interested in politics and in politicians. He has. But none the less, there is something about the man which irresistibly recalls an earlier century. If Mr. O'Connor was not born with a silver spoon in his mouth, its place ought certainly to have been taken by a fountain pen. Pope said :

I lisped in numbers, for the numbers came,

and I think that O'Connor must always have written for the same simple reason. He represents the very spirit of Fleet Street; but it is an older Fleet Street. He would have been quite at home with those who wrote for a living a hundred and fifty years ago. Dr. Johnson said, in one of his more questionable generalisations : " No one but a fool ever wrote except for money." I suspect, without knowing, that Mr. O'Connor must share this view. He has supported himself and others during a long and anxious life by his pen, and by his pen alone. His material stock in trade or capital has been very slight. Put him in an empty room, with a dozen sheets of paper and a pen and ink : leave him for three hours : and it is quite certain that he will have produced something which will keep the wolf from the door for a week. And he will also have produced something which thousands of people will read with interest.

Right Hon. T. P. O'Connor, M.P.

The briefest statement of his various occupations as a journalist will show how diversified and how constant has been the toil which has produced so consummate a craftsman. He graduated at Queen's College, Galway, in his eighteenth year, obtaining the Senior Scholarship of History and Modern Languages. A year later, in 1867, he entered journalism as a junior reporter on *Saunders' Newsletter*, a Dublin Conservative journal. If it be true, as is often stated, that his distinguished though younger contemporary, Mr. Garvin, began his journalistic career as a contributor to a Fenian newspaper, it is a matter of some paradoxical interest that, about twenty years earlier, young O'Connor began to wield a vivacious pen upon the Conservative side.

Three years later he journeyed to London, as so many brilliant and ambitious young Irishmen had done before him, to better his fortunes. He had at that time neither recommendations nor reputation. Indeed, his only, but sufficient, capital consisted of hope and self-confidence. But the managers of the *Daily Telegraph*, then, as always, swift to appreciate ability, appointed him a sub-editor of that journal in the same year. His connection with this great newspaper, honourable and profitable to both parties, has been maintained ever since. It must indeed be long since any writer has ever, for more than half a century, interested so many readers in the same organ of the Press.

Soon afterwards he obtained employment in the London office of the *New York Herald*, and thereafter came a long and eventful succession of journalistic enterprises. He founded, and was first editor of the *Star*, the *Sun*, the *Weekly Sun*, *M.A.P.*, and *T.P.'s Weekly*. It is probable that he is a far more capable journalist than man of business. He has always possessed resource and initiative. But while he has established papers which have ultimately become extremely lucrative, it is believed that he himself never derived the pecuniary advantages to which he was fairly entitled from these ventures. More than once he has founded a paper, and sold it for ten or twenty thousand pounds, which in more patient commercial and calculating ownership has proved to be worth hundreds of thousands.

Mr. O'Connor's more ambitious efforts in authorship include a " Biography of Lord Beaconsfield," a " History of the Parnell Movement," a sketch entitled " Gladstone's House of Commons," and an effort in romance, which he called " Some Old-World Love Stories."

His study of Lord Beaconsfield is, perhaps, the only ill-natured thing that he ever wrote ; the circumstances, it may be, under which it was produced account for its malignity. I am told that it was written in a garret at a time when the fortunes of the author were so reduced that he could barely afford to pay for the paper upon which it was written. This picture recalls memories of Steele, Savage, Goldsmith, and Johnson ; and is perhaps one of the reasons which lead one to associate O'Connor with a school of writers which has long since passed away. The essay on Lord Beaconsfield, indeed, is little more than a bitter party pamphlet. Of this I am sure, that if Mr. O'Connor found leisure to re-edit this study, he would soon find that it was necessary also to rewrite it.

Right Hon. T. P. O'Connor, M.P.

I cannot write here of his relations with Charles Stewart Parnell; for the study would take too long. He has himself written much of a decision and a breach which undoubtedly caused him genuine anguish. An adequate study of Parnell's life has not yet been written. No one, again, could write this book more vividly, or with greater knowledge, than O'Connor.

He possesses a very remarkable gift for writing obituary notices. This sounds rather a gloomy attribute. But even if one cannot read an obituary notice of oneself, it is on the whole comfortable to reflect that it may be written by a pen at once so kindly and so lively as that of Mr. O'Connor. And therefore I express quite frankly the hope that Mr. O'Connor will outlive me; in virtue, I mean, rather of a remarkable prolongation of his span of life than by a curtailment of my own. It was said of Lord Chancellor Campbell that his biographical activities had added a new terror to judicial death. Of Mr. O'Connor such an imputation could never be made. It is a genuine pleasure to his kindly nature to note what is good and creditable in his fellow creatures, rather than that which is bad and discreditable. And when they are dead, he finds the tendency irresistible. But he contrives in some clever way, and in virtue of a journalistic gift altogether his own, to avoid the cloying effect of excessive and unbroken laudation. He writes with extreme picturesqueness; creating an atmosphere with a phrase, and indicating a type by a happy adjective. There is no one living who possesses quite Mr. O'Connor's gifts as a journalist. He can make even uninteresting people interesting without a sacrifice of good faith. And when he addresses himself, as he so often does, to people who are vital, and to incidents which are dramatic, he exhibits a Dumas-like quality of brilliant narrative. His account, for instance, of the life of Mrs. O'Shea and of its results upon the career of Parnell, furnished, within four columns of the *Daily Telegraph*, one of the most fascinating studies of this period which has ever appeared in the English language.

The position of Chief Obituary Writer to a great newspaper is perhaps a trifle ghoulish. It is, of course, notorious that Mr. O'Connor has neatly pigeon-holed and ready for immediate production a notice of every really distinguished man in this country above the age of sixty—and above the age of fifty, if the managers of the *Daily Telegraph* have been indulged with unfavourable accounts of the health of the patient. But occasionally Death the Avenger is too surprising even for Mr. O'Connor. And he has told me that it has frequently been his lot to sit up till four or five o'clock in the morning, elaborating his tribute to the prematurely dead.

I have spoken little of Mr. T. P. O'Connor as a politician, although he is, as I have said, the Father of the House of Commons. For it seems to me that politics have always played a secondary part in his life. He was, and is, in the first order of platform speakers, more especially when letting himself loose upon the historic grievances of Ireland, which he handles in a fashion of pleasurable lachrymosity. In the House of Commons he was, on the whole, less effective; not particularly adroit in the arts of extempory debate, and very lacking

in the quality of concinnity. But I do not really
see in O'Connor primarily the politician. Always
and all the time I see the journalist. Even in his
75th year his mind is teeming with new literary
and newspaper enterprises. No sooner is one
scheme abandoned than another is swiftly and
restlessly undertaken.

It has frequently been said of Mr. T. P. O'Connor
that he is insincere. I do not in the least share
this view. I think that he is so good-natured that
in conversation he always finds it easier to agree
than to disagree; and this tendency, innocent in
origin as it is, has sometimes misled those who
have founded themselves upon verbal arrangements
with him; but of insincerity in any real sense I find
no trace in a very consistent career.

He never varied in his support of the Nationalist
Party. Although he has been for fifty years, in
his residence, in his employments, and in his
habits, an Englishman, he never adopted the
simple and profitable course of saying " I have
become an English Liberal, and intend to take a
part in politics as a member of this rich and powerful
party." Had he been willing to do so, he could
have occupied some of the highest offices in the
State. Great distinctions and honours would have
been within his reach. I doubt whether he ever
considered this temptation; if he did, he never
yielded to it. He remains to-day plain Mr. T. P.
O'Connor, and his only titular distinction is that
he is the oldest, and one of the most respected,
members of the House of Commons.

An Englishman must add that he never wavered
in his warm-hearted support of the War. None was

more effective at recruiting meetings; none did more to keep that vast community—the Irish in England—in line with the national effort. And now over seventy he voyaged over the submarine-infested Atlantic in the attempt to place the true facts before the Irish American population. We have long known him as an Irish patriot; he responded to the compelling stimulus of a supreme moral appeal and broadened into a British patriot; not because he was disloyal to a primary loyalty; but because Great Britain had proved the principal bulwark of humanity as he understood humanity.

As we take leave of him we may recall almost with affection the confidential conversational manner, which is so attractive, if only because it holds out the promise of indiscretion; the Dublin brogue; the slight garrulousness of anecdote; and the snuff-soiled waistcoat, of this Veteran of the Pen, and we place—as we ought to place—the tribute upon record, that the instrument by which he lived was never steeped in venom; that it was ever, on the contrary, employed in emphasising what was good—in mitigating what was bad—in that human nature which has been the subject of a long life study.

The Viscount Burnham

The Viscount Burnham

LORD BURNHAM, though a live, able, and patriotic man, is not, on the whole, a spectacular man. But if I fail, as fail for this reason I may, to produce a lively article about him, I shall indeed be a bad literary artist if I do not present the impression of a great English citizen.

He was born on December 18, 1862. In his sixty-second year, he may look back with pride on a long period of work in the press, in the House of Commons, and in the country. His home labours have been both civic and national. Since 1916 his many activities have been coloured by membership of the House of Lords. This fact is a reminder that Lord Burnham's father was created a peer by King Edward the Seventh, who by that act expressed a personal esteem, and, as monarch, declared his gratitude for the achievements of a public man— described by a great contemporary as " great-hearted; full of benevolence; a human, dramatic, cheering force." Such was Sir Edward Lawson, the transmitter of some quite considerable gifts to his successors.

His eldest son, the subject of this brief commentary, may therefore be called with truth a child of fortune. Indeed, to be born in the purple of the proprietary press (I refuse the capital letters) is to be furnished with a valuable birth-certificate. Such a thing may become in due time security for great advances. Or it may provide a safe conduct through disputed territory.

In young Harry Lawson's case the boon of prosperity was certainly increased by the advantages of Eton and Balliol. I fancy that Lord Burnham is now, and always has been, a shade more cosmopolitan than most Etonians; and as to Balliol, I have no doubt whatever that he outdistances the late Dr. Jowett himself in his understanding of the ways of the world. But both Eton and Oxford found him equal to the necessary—if tedious—task of taking pains; and from both he acquired social graces which have never left him. By nature friendly, and of open, generous habit (eupeptic, in a word, physically and mentally), it is as a working and managing journalist that he has for a whole lifetime been engaged. What John Murray is in the world of publishing Harry Burnham is in the world of newspapers. His record, in fact, covers some forty years of increasing distinction. So that to-day, whilst I see in Lord Burnham the holder of honours almost numerous enough to be embarrassing, I cannot but marvel at the ingenious use which he has made of his opportunities. Whilst much has been done by tact, more still has been accomplished by strict attention to business. But something has been due to remote as well as to immediate antecedents, the associations of which, again, are not untouched by romance.

Enterprise and energy, alike in grandfather and father, introduced the young man to a sphere of indefinite scope. When the name of Levy was discarded for that of Lawson it is interesting (and indeed only fair) to notice that the exchange was due to an uncle's benevolence. " I myself," Lord Burnham has observed, " am not one to disparage

the advantages of Jewish origin." It is freely
admitted that from such origin ability often springs,
and that racial character may prove stronger than
any adventitious aids to success. The same thing
can be said of racial pride. And for my part I find
that symbolism rather attractive, which has added
to the heraldic equipment of a rising family the
motto " Of old I hold." These words comport
themselves sympathetically with the modern device
of " a globe, winged," for a crest ; and again, with
the figures of Clio and Mercury ; for these last are
the supporters of the Burnham arms. They indicate a claim to universalism which has actually
been justified. But while I salute the candid courage
of the attitude, I have never believed that Daniel
Deronda was a convincing figure in literature.

There is something very remarkable in all the
adaptability of which I have spoken. The thing
itself is often exhibited in that absorbent power
which English public life frequently illustrates. As
I think of Lawson the man, and of Burnham the
place, I pass back, in a flash of thought, to Disraeli
and Beaconsfield. The metropolis, in spite of de-
nunciations like those of William Cobbett, must
always draw men of parts to itself if they are to
make any mark on their age. More and more does
the nearer countryside respond, and Buckingham-
shire, with its memories of Hampden and Milton,
Burke and Waller, intensifies from century to century its connection with politics and literature, so
that it has scarcely a rival even in the famed
Home Counties. Burnham itself, sheltering under
the very wing of Beaconsfield, testifies by this
same conjunction to the opening of careers to

talent ; and proves by achievement the advantage of free competition.

Thus, then, as the story of Hall Barn, Lord Burnham's estate, connects itself with the activity of a veritable human hive, so does the fulfilment of a dream emerge from the realities of a business. And when I remember how Lord Morley spoke of the *Daily Telegraph* as " Disraeli's own organ "; or when I dwell on local associations, I am satisfied of the importance of links, and struck by the persistence of parallels.

But I pass on to the individual. I see how education, culture, intermarriage, have played a special part, with honourable results ; for, fittingly enough, Lord Burnham's name is enrolled in the " Companionship of Honour." Here is fresh testimony to adaptability and absorption, each appealing among us in turn to those vital principles by which stability is renewed from generation to generation. And stability becomes daily more precious to us, to England, as daily it seems to be more insanely risked and threatened.

Here, advantageously, a Burnham interposes his own individuality. Lord Burnham possesses many striking personal characteristics. He is persuasive, polished, urbane, and he can be very amusing. On committees, in assemblies, he has shown himself moderate, conciliatory, yet with a positive, and slightly obstinate, view entirely his own. I am not dealing with a character which shows no differences from its earlier self, but with one which has developed. Youthful political flights were taken, as far as oratory is concerned, when, as a contemporary of several others who are now members of the House of Lords

—Archbishop Lang, Lord Salisbury, Lord Cecil, Lord Sumner—Lawson's views were aired, between 1880 and 1886, in the interesting arena of the Oxford Union Society.

The Government of that era was Mr. Gladstone's, which then found in Lawson of Balliol an apparently convinced defender. The policies then at issue, like Mr. Gladstone's own character, were of bewilderment and complexity all compact. Passions were roused. This ensured a great keenness over politics. It meant a splendid introduction to political life for many men. Cleavages ensued. Whether from force of conviction or change of circumstance, it fell out, through the wear and tear of time, that this enthusiasm underwent certain transformations. It veered in Harry Lawson from the narrowness of conceptions which have turned out to be parochial, to find its eventual and permanent home in a broad and elevating Imperialism. I am dealing, it will be seen, with a genial expansiveness, the natural development of a receptive mind, not, above all, with one blown about by every wind of doctrine.

It is to be noted, however, that in the case of Lord Burnham a gradual expansion of view has been further enlarged by European sympathies, beginning with France. Take, as an interesting symptom of his mental attitude in relation to a very vexed question, his support of the Channel Tunnel scheme. Lord Burnham has raised his voice as resolutely in this cause, if not as hopefully, in the palpitating days of King George the Fifth as he did in the remote, the sanguine time of Queen Victoria. The vision is one that may or may not be consummated. The issue is still a lively one. Its implications verge, indeed, on regions of risk. But they exemplify the workings of a mind which attacks problems in its own original way.

And one thing is certain. In good seasons or bad, Lord Burnham has steadily worked for friendship with our nearest Continental neighbour. These efforts have taken many forms. They have found their happiest employment in social, intellectual, and literary fields. They have acted as a leaven in pleasant reunions. Herein Lord Burnham may well have drawn a moral from Montesquieu, or an instruction from Taine, for the benefit of a cause which is very real to him. For the same cause, with ease, lightness, and a sociable unpretentiousness, he will lift a special glass to the Entente, or introduce a French Ambassador to a festive gathering in London. In the same spirit he will be found delivering an oration himself; all with the object of lessening that insularity which in matters intellectual is still our bane. For Lord Burnham, France is still right at the heart of European civilisation, and since at her best she extends her refinements he does not stop at France.

His foreign interests range wider and deeper. The recent celebrations of the Byron centenary in Athens brought him forward to expound, on behalf of his countrymen, some of those ideas—their roots Hellenic, their branches universal—which still have inexhaustible powers of bearing fruit. High appreciation was his reward in fulfilling this mission, for the simple reason that he had mastered what he himself happily termed " the *lingua franca* of understanding."

Though often diversified by excursions such as

these, and even by wider travel, the direction of a great newspaper has largely occupied Lord Burnham's time. The pace of ordinary life, meanwhile, has grown faster. But sureness of movement, rapidity of decision, these also have grown in the man himself, with their frequent exercise. These decades have shown Fleet Street, in new and fascinating lights, as a place of adventure. The *Daily Telegraph* may have yielded its supremacy in circulation—that feature of which " the young lions of Peterborough Court " were once so proud. But the famous sheet, with its lavish information and comprehensive outlook, has changed outwardly but little. Inwardly, it has moved rather with than against the times. One day I hope that it will improve the paper upon which it is printed.

Its influence has not waned. In peace as in war, that influence has always been conspicuously sane. There was a time when the paper was ridiculed for its flamboyancy ; its occasional sensationalism ; its acceptance of the commercial necessity of what are now known as " stunts " ; a feature which seems destined, not only in journalism, to be for ever undergoing some novel metamorphosis. But even here the *Telegraph* can claim to have been a pioneer of the past. The roaring of the lions, of course, became a proverb through Matthew Arnold's vivid phraseology : but if " Matt " was poles asunder from that other Arnold whose orientalism was so long an asset of the paper, he himself nevertheless came to write for it in time ; and the list of eminent men enrolled in that service cannot be numbered ; for it is innumerable. Apart from style, there is, in fact, embedded in the old files of the *Daily Telegraph* enough material to furnish forth a faithful picture of facts, manners, thoughts, the very soil and origin of the vicissitudes through which we are passing to-day.

The same thing is happening even now before our eyes. The paper is very much alive ; and it will prove a rich asset to historians in the future. It seizes the contemporary idea. It holds to moderation. Lord Burnham himself has long stood for an increase of comprehensiveness ; just as he has stood for the higher interests of journalism. Into every corner of the craft, and its manifold workings, he penetrates with unfailing consideration for the human element. He has done much for the mechanical side ; whilst he has given special attention to the requirements of those who more strictly represent the professional side. The result is that by common consent he takes his place where there is naturally a place reserved for him : I mean, of course, at the top. From that altitude he exercises a gentle sway, a benevolent rule ; one which is always directed by kindness, and in matters of charity rises to munificence.

Lord Burnham is now President of the Institute of Journalists, and he also presides over the Empire Press Union, and many other kindred bodies. It was the late Lord Northcliffe, the godfather, if not the parent, of many a journalistic innovation, who hailed him, in 1919, with a compliment worthy of record. The occasion was the presentation of a portrait. The compliment took a quadruple form. Lord Burnham was eminent, the speaker pointed out, as a commander of men, as a legislator, as a philanthropic worker, and as " the chief orator of the newspaper world." I think this enumeration could be enlarged; for what I have said already is enough to reach the quintuple or sextuple point; but there is something to be added under the headings to which I have just alluded, before I take leave of an admired political associate and valued friend.

Leadership of the Press involved, when the Great War of 1914 broke out, consummate discretion. It was largely due to Lord Burnham that difficulties were overcome; concessions granted; grievances eliminated. The command of men includes, of course, a great variety of patriotic service, in one who has touched life at so many points, one who is as much himself in dispensing good-fellowship through hospitality, as in improving by competence in the practical affairs of life the lot of those who look up to, and rely upon, him. He has often proved that patriotism is the keynote of his aims, and of all his interests; he has worn the King's uniform with intelligence and zeal; yet all the while with the consciousness that his own larger rights are in the command of an army scattered indeed, but under his direction cohesive.

I have had not a few opportunities of observing Lord Burnham as a legislator. His speeches are cogent, thoughtfully expressed, and sufficiently outspoken. He is performing, at the present time, certain duties in the House of Lords, which lend a piquant interest to some of his declarations on the subject of that Chamber, alive as he is to its greatness and yet to its cumbrousness; to its outstanding claims, which are supreme, and to its chances of solid usefulness, which have been so gravely, and so unnecessarily, compromised. It is not only here that Lord Burnham, in his quiet way, has exhibited the instinct of the reformer. In all political matters his view is coloured by a deep conviction of the far-flung importance of the British Empire as a whole. Not long since, he returned from a tour in the West Indies. His tale of the lack of intercommunication was a sorrowful one : but the bond he was striving to strengthen, he found, possessed a peculiar and even a sanguine spell. As an emissary of good-will he had set out. As a missionary of Empire (but still unpretentious) he returned.

The philanthropist in Lord Burnham gives him a special place in our midst. He has the knack of being generous himself, and, by setting an example, he induces the same tendency in others. And with his lavish benevolence towards deserving objects he combines a personal thoughtfulness, which sheds, liks his own ingratiating smile, a light on those around. In those speeches for which he is more specially noted, he comes forward, always full of his subject, which is never himself. I am sure that the world and age in which we live will long concede an enduring niche for the kindly memory of Harry Burnham.

The Viscount Leverhulme

The Viscount Leverhulme

ABOUT fifty-five years ago a fresh-faced, stocky, Lancashire boy stood behind the counter of a small grocer's shop in Bolton. There was nothing about him to attract special notice except his eyes. These were of a brilliant, gleaming, arresting blue. No one could be quite ordinary who had such eyes. No artist could have caught all their various lights. That boy was one day to be the Viscount Leverhulme. I had this description twenty years ago from a very old Bolton man who knew William Lever and his father well. The boy is now a merchant prince, and one of the richest and most adventurous men in the British Empire.

Enterprise has always been the peculiar quality which has made England ; and enterprise must, in ever-changing forms, remain the hope of the Empire. In Lord Leverhulme, long known to the commercial world as William Hesketh Lever, we make the acquaintance of a merchant-prince who is true to a fundamental type. He has created a vast business out of very simple material. This fact might range him, at first sight, with many who have gone before him. But he has done the most original things. He has done the most startling things. So much has he enlarged the principles of business ; so much use has he made of opportunity, that we see in him one of the most unconventional beings who have ever imposed their character upon trade, or their influence upon an age. In Venice he would have been a great Prince and Doge.

But I cannot think of time in connection with Lord Leverhulme. Nor can I speak of influence without noting that—the greatest of human gifts being his—the gift of vision—he possesses a power, of which he is quite conscious, which is defiant alike of analysis and of imitation. Born at Bolton on September 19, 1851, and therefore a veteran in his seventy-third year, Lord Leverhulme's spirit is not in the slightest degree changed from that which upheld him in his earliest days. Those eyes of which I have already spoken are still the eyes of confident and constructive youth. This is perhaps why, despite his devotion to art, Lord Leverhulme has not always found it easy to approve the ways, or perhaps I should say the technique, of painters. This prejudice apart, the quality of prescience is very natural in a Lancashire man. For Lancashire has enriched our proverbs; and the implications of vital truth, commercial, if not economic, have spread from Lancashire outwards.

The Levers of Bolton, like the Hulmes of Manchester, who come into the story of Lord Leverhulme's life only indirectly, have concentrated their special foresight upon education. I should be romancing if I forced the note of heredity or ancestry in this case. Lord Leverhulme is a Lancashire man, and that is enough of ancestry for any man. But there are some achievements and associations which do touch him at this point; and he is justly proud of his remoter kin.

He is apt to look rather severely on anything that savours of pretentiousness. " The Oxford graduate," he has recently observed, " is not a patch on the ' hard knocks ' graduate." Logically, this might almost imply a disbelief in anything beyond the rudiments of instruction. The phrase was really egotistic, for this same critic looks gratefully back to the education he himself received at the Church Institute of Bolton ; and, after all, he sent his boy to Eton and Trinity. He has, indeed, remained a devoted adherent of the Congregational Church which provided his own education. He has furthered the aims of that body by splendid benefactions. And in education he has long since become a leader, because he has so often supplied bountiful help.

It is still to Mr. W. T. Mason, who was responsible for the training he received at Bolton, that Lord Leverhulme attributes something essential to his own constructive methods ; and he will point to Mr. Mason's eminent pupils still living in Lancashire with great satisfaction, for it was no mean roll. And the names of his contemporaries are linked with certain landmarks in his life which I now propose to follow.

I look back more than fifty years. The young Lever's short period of education was soon to be exchanged for a busy life. If anything could add a charm to each stage of progression, those mystically inclined (and I do not exclude his lordship) may note that each of these stages has had some apparent connection with the number "four." The year 1864 had seen him hard at work learning from Mason. The year 1874 found him ready for a marriage in which he found great happiness. Then it was that he launched out recklessly on a home, decorating the first mantelpiece with two precious examples of porcelain, specimens of Derby *bisque*. The year 1884 saw " the registration of Sunlight." In the year 1894 Lever Brothers floated themselves as a company. The year 1904 was a time of un-exampled progress. The year 1914 was conspicuous for a record royal visit ; soon after which every business, large or small, had to take stock of a new world because of the Great War. And now, in 1924, Lord Leverhulme looks around him, more keenly bent than ever on new campaigns ; looking forward with all the fuller zest because a fresh and mighty spurt seems always possible, in every year that has a " four " in it.

Much, indeed, has happened to bring Lord Leverhulme into prominence in this period—this long, eventful period which cannot for any mystical or other reason be fitted to the sacred number "four." He is actually in the sixth decade of his most strenuous activity. I hope that he and I may forgather in his eighth decade ; and even then I do not expect to see him on crutches.

Let me now pursue, with circumspection, and yet, I hope, with introspection, the windings of this long life. I am sure there was a time when Lord Leverhulme did not dream of a peerage. And yet he has always been something of a dreamer. His dreams, I think, always had a humanitarian tinge. His temperament has always been one open to artistic claims. He speaks of such influences as being his inspiration and his stimulus. Certainly many of his dreams have taken visible shape. In considering the development of his own ideas, he will readily confess that these have greatly expanded. But he declares that since he was twenty-one, engaged as a grocer in his father's warehouse at Bolton, he has changed little as a man. Very early in life he took up the idea of co-partnership. For more than a generation he has been a pioneer in town-planning and model-housing. Embedded in his theories and in his practice all this time have been high hopes for the welfare of the community. On these lines he has developed ; and if pressed for reasons, he will gently set aside any far-reaching sociological explanation of his efforts. Ask " why he delights in constructing houses "—" Ask a bird why it sings " is the reply.

Nevertheless the contact of sociology with his benevolence is direct; and to call co-partnership " prosperity-sharing " is to join its sensibility to its security. To think of it at all, indeed, means rendering honour to men like Robert Owen, who ruined himself for the sake of an ideal. For he and his friends had to encounter the most desperate antagonism. But development is naturally many-sided. In this connection, Lord Leverhulme, as we know him, stands out to a later generation as a man who has accomplished many incredible things. But it is just here that he himself is apt to interpose a questioning note.

Recently, when celebrating the division of a sum of £206,000, a year's dividends in co-partner-ship, Lord Leverhulme, amidst congratulations, held out new and magnificent insurance prospects to a gratified, if not wholly disinterested, band of workers. He then made some retrospective com-ments on things in general. He threw the whole work of his life into bold relief against the back-

ground of things as they were and as they ought
to be. He drew a picture of the past. He recalled
the Lancashire that had no Southport, no More-
cambe ; he envisaged the time when Liverpool
itself knew little, and thought less, of Birkenhead.
In those days it took a week to go by water from
London to Edinburgh. Our railroads, as we know
them, the telephone, the gramophone, the wireless,
or the aeroplane—these were unthought of. Great,
then, had been our material advances. But the
question was : Had we progressed ? His answer
was in the negative. For it is only humanitarianism
that counts. And in human relationships, he said,
we had progressed but little. He proved himself, in
fact, an unconscious supporter of my Rectorial
Address at Glasgow.

I think that it is this attitude, often translated
into action, which differentiates Lord Leverhulme
from the average commercial magnate, and from
the commercial type as a whole. The idea of success
is one which cannot be escaped. In our days, it is
regarded as both a talisman and as a magnet. But
to Lord Leverhulme the term is anathema. Nothing
alarms him so much as that very word Success,
and yet we all know that Lord Leverhulme is no
coward. Mention this thing only, he says, when
the roll is finished, the story done. For looking at
it squarely, with honest Lancashire eyes, he must
needs dwell on the terrific chances—the abnormal
risks—of the world of business. He will enlarge
on the hourly chances of bankruptcy which business
men must encounter, whilst stoutly denying that
a figure of eight hundred or a thousand millions,
incurred for a nation's indebtedness, need cause

any qualms in a country which has the power, as he believes we have, to see any mighty trial through. Lord Leverhulme perhaps faces personal trials with a little less certainty. And yet most men know that this confidence in country and race has been tolerably well reflected in the man himself, since the old humble days.

It was a small beginning, but that grocer's business was carried on by Lord Leverhulme himself till he was over thirty. It was then transferred, after five years under his own direction, to other hands, for the fairly solid consideration of £60,000. He did not join the Socialist Party. He trusted the existing basis of economic life, preferring to improve it rather than to destroy it.

There followed a diversion into Cheshire.

And then came soap.

I pause reverently on the subject of soap, for it is undoubtedly a very great subject. I know that Lord Leverhulme has dabbled in other commodities. But, as he says, fresh from adventures in Hampstead or the Outer Hebrides—it may be amongst tiresome borough councillors or amongst recalcitrant fishermen—*everything comes back to soap.*

There is something almost awe-inspiring in the continuous progress of those undertakings which have made the name of Lever familiar to the whole world.

The triumph of soap which bears the Lever brand is a theme which might be extended to epical dimensions. I have not forgotten the absorption of Hudson ; nor many a Homeric struggle over other combinations and interests. These struggles are still thrilling to think of, as they emerge from the heyday of the past. There have been times when Lord Leverhulme has had to fight with his back to the wall for his saponaceous life. He in his prime fought Lord Northcliffe in his prime; and Lord Leverhulme was the victor. In this contest Lord Northcliffe sustained the greatest humiliation of his career, and his collision with a man not less great than himself, who happened to be right, and was strong enough to fight, cost him a quarter of a million.

Lord Leverhulme has enjoyed all this, just as he enjoyed many a political contest which kept him out of Parliament; or sent him into it. He cared very little which. He filled, however, an ample place in the House of Commons between 1906 and 1910. And he has always been a whirlwind of a man.

I suppose that from A to Z there is no artificer who has not something to do with the manufacture of soap. Soap has, I hope, an attraction for us all. We should hardly dare to walk about the world but for the effectual operation of soapsuds. To the higher flights of fancy what could be more suggestive than the iridescence of a soap-bubble? The ramifications of a great soapmaker please the architect as they please the shipbuilder. His efforts are important in the public arena. They are indispensable within the domestic hearth. The soap interest adds a new glory to the advertiser's conception of the universe. A man who makes soap must be familiar with the organisation of the animal, vegetable, and mineral kingdoms. If Sunlight Village had not sprung into being rather after the time when William Morris achieved his fame, surely that poet might have taken Port Sunlight for the setting of his Earthly Paradise.

Lord Leverhulme's generosity has always been astounding. I myself know of one case in which he gave £30,000 to a deserving charity on the condition that his gift should remain anonymous. He will not, I suspect, thank me for this addition to his postbag. But he, like others, must sustain the consequences of his qualities.

The simple materials upon which Lord Leverhulme started have grown, from principles and from their application, into a network of applied usefulness. He is able to contrast in a favourable sense the Bolton of to-day with the Bolton of his youth. And so, in his own despite, he must admit some progress achieved. He has seen with delight the resultant benefits which can be affiliated upon his favourite aphorisms. At one moment he is quoting Emerson, who teaches that "only that comes out of business which we put in, and that cant and lying, or the attempt to secure a good which does not belong to us, are once for all baulked and vain." And he can turn, too, in case of need, to Shakespeare, whose philosophy he has deeply studied. His quotations, if severely practical, are always classical.

The rewards of caution, as of courage, have been equally analysed by him. But the root of all progress, he has always believed, has been, for himself, a simple energy and probity. "I have not evolved any schemes with consciousness beforehand," he says. "I have always done the day's work not regretting yesterday, and not being afraid of to-morrow."

But all this enterprise and all this confidence have always come back, in the end, to soap. The tables by which Lord Leverhulme is surrounded in his London office are crowded with samples of this fluctuating commodity, which is always being evolved afresh and anew, in countless variegated forms. It is a simple material, like the musical scale, which out of seven original notes will bring an infinity of music. But here the musical note which strikes, or can be struck, most melodiously, is that esoteric harmony which sets its aspirations toward the future. For I do not doubt that round the Leverhulme name, in the course of time, will grow those fine traditions which will continue to increase the importance of a family and of a home.

And so the honours which already accrue to a name which in itself consecrates what is happily in England an everyday romance, will always help to maintain those ideas of stability which England still cherishes and needs.

General John Bernard Seely

General John Bernard Seely

GENERAL JOHN BERNARD SEELY, D.S.O., C.B., P.C., was educated at Harrow—a circumstance which has always recommended that school to him, for General Seely is a man of such fundamental loyalty that anything with which he has ever been associated, his country, his county, his yeomanry, his horses, or his yacht, are always the best in the world. His claim to be included in this series of articles is that he is undoubtedly what, according to Mr. Arnold Bennett, is known in the Five Towns as "A Card." His career has been one of great interest and great adventure. The fact that neither lose in the telling is one of the most lovable traits in a very unusual character. His achievements have been extremely remarkable. In fields of great and critical danger he has constantly, over a long period of years, displayed a quality of cool valour which everyone in the world who knows the facts freely recognises.

And yet he is of a Latin rather than of an Anglo-Saxon type. D'Artagnan would have clasped hands with him in friendship. Athos would have understood and understanding have been indulgent to him. Aramis, while not overrating his subtlety, would have placed a just valuation upon his sword; and Porthos would have loved him. The tribute is great, but not excessive; and of Seely it may be said (and on the whole fairly) that he would have thought himself in quite adequate company.

That he is conscious of this circumstance himself is a wholly delightful characteristic which his friends value, and it is quite unimportant to ask what his enemies think; for he has none. I do not know whether the story is true that he recommended his chauffeur for the Victoria Cross in the early days of the war; and when asked what in particular he had done, replied, with bland surprise: "He has driven me everywhere I have been in the last three months!" If the story is untrue, it is at least *ben trovato*, for Jack Seely, who has always been utterly indifferent to physical risk, counting his life nothing if a worthy object were on the other side of the scale, capable of exceptional courage, at once cool and spiritual in its highest manifestation, has always frankly enjoyed discussing and describing what he has achieved. The trait is, as I have said, Latin rather than Anglo-Saxon, and the true ancestor of our General was Brigadier Étienne Gerard.

General Seely was brought up to the Bar, and it is reported of him that on a memorable occasion he unsuccessfully defended a person accused of murder. As his client was leaving the dock after the sombre allocution from the Bench, his counsel intercepted his exit and observed: "It will at least be a satisfaction to you to know before you face your Maker that everything which forensic ability could contribute has been done on your behalf."

But the Bar was not destined to shackle its manacles on a spirit so ebullient, and when the South African War broke out Seely gained leave from the War Office to raise a squadron of the Hampshire Yeomanry, in which he was a Captain. The congestion of the moment rendered it impossible to obtain shipping. Quite undaunted by this obstacle, he immediately chartered a ship at his own risk from one of his uncles, Sir Francis Evans, the chairman of the Union-Castle Line, and offered it to the War Office. The offer was accepted, and he sailed from Southampton with one other squadron of Yeomanry in January, 1900.

Thereafter commenced a career of adventure and daring which was not surpassed by any officer of equal rank in South Africa. His force was attached to the 8th Division, and took part in all the operations leading up to Prinsloo's surrender in July, 1900. On one occasion the subject of our observations was reported killed. At this particular moment (although he was unaware of the fact) he was the Conservative candidate for the Isle of Wight at a bye-election. Many who voted for him (and many who abstained) were, according to the current report, of opinion that he was dead. However this may be (and such calculations are very disputable), he was elected by a majority of 1,000.

And all the time in South Africa he and his men were playing their part in the difficult guerilla warfare in which the Boers excelled. On one occasion, which became notorious, when in command of a rearguard, Seely was ordered to leave the kopje in the centre of the position from which he was directing operations with two troops, leaving two others to hold it. He sent back the two troops, but refused to retire himself, in the belief that he could be of more use there to the rearguard than by riding away. After hard fighting he completely frustrated the attempt of the Boers to encircle him, and extricated his command at a trifling cost in wounded. On rejoining his column he was placed under arrest for disobedience to orders by an intelligent General, whose name is now mercifully forgotten, and remained under arrest for the remainder of the trek. A Court of Enquiry was held under General Rundle, and he was restored to his command.

Early in the following year he was given command of a mixed force in Natal, which operated from Utrecht, to which district, after the abortive peace negotiations, General Botha had removed the greater part of his forces. The object of the operations was to hem in General Botha; but after personally reconnoitring the whole front encircling him, he broke through a portion of Smith-Dorrien's column and got clear away. Two nights before he broke through, at a place called One Tree Hill, Seely was in the outpost line at 1 o'clock on a misty moonlight night, and saw a horseman approaching through the haze. He shot, but missed him. General Botha has since told him that he was certainly the man at whom he fired, for he had ridden up to this One Tree Hill to see if it was occupied, at that very time, and had been aimed at by a single shot.

In May, 1901, Seely's squadron was ordered home. The Squadron Leader had been twice mentioned in despatches, and had received the D.S.O.

And from this point his political career began. Between 1902 and 1906 he acted with Hugh Cecil and Winston Churchill in a successful attempt to defeat Mr. Brodrick's Army Corps scheme. More and more he drifted into disagreement from the Conservative party. He became known as " Chinese Seely," from the impeccable rectitude with which he denounced the employment of coolies on the Rand.

His sincerity was never impugned, but the vehemence of his advocacy in a cause so dishonest was not, perhaps, the sanest or the most ingenuous of his political career. He believed himself to be, and for all I know may be, a Free Trader, though in one comparatively so intelligent this seems difficult to believe. However this may be, Mr. Chamberlain's Tariff Reform proposals gave him, as they gave Mr. Churchill, a fairly decent pretext for leaving the Conservative Party altogether.

And so it happened that in 1906 Seely became Liberal Member for the Abercrombie Division of Liverpool. In 1908, when Mr. Asquith formed his Government, he became Under-Secretary of State for the Colonies, and he carried through the House of Commons the South Africa Union Bill.

His progress was now rapid. When Lord Haldane became Lord Chancellor he was made Secretary of State for War. It is undoubtedly true that he contributed much to the mobility of the Expeditionary Force which Lord Haldane had brought into being. The only failure in Haldane's calculation was to make shipping arrangements by which it was certain that the Expeditionary Force would arrive in time to co-operate effectively with the French, if the Germans attacked in force through Belgium. The Admiralty refused to guarantee a sufficient number of ships to transport the force unless they were permitted to hold an immense amount of tonnage idle for an indefinite period. Seely invited four of the ablest shipowners in the world to advise him in his dilemma. They were, Sir Thomas Royden, of the Cunard; Sir Lionel Fletcher, of the White Star; Sir Richard Holt, of the Blue Funnel Line; and

Sir Owen Philipps, of the Royal Mail and many other companies. Sir Thomas Royden and Sir Lionel Fletcher took up the task, and, in order fully to discharge it, gave up all their private work for many months. It is hardly too much to say that the labours of Sir Thomas Royden and his colleagues saved the situation in France in the first two critical months. Probably Paris would have fallen if the shipping arrangements had been less intelligently conceived and prepared.

The set-back in General Seely's career caused by his resignation over the Ulster crisis need not detain us long. The Government had set him and others an impossible task by including Ulster within the scope of their Home Rule proposals. All the world knows now that half the Cabinet, including Mr. Lloyd George and Mr. Churchill, never believed that it would be possible to force Home Rule upon an unwilling Ulster. Yet they made the mad attempt, whether for purposes of bluff, or for purposes of negotiation, it is impossible to say. The true criticism which can be made, and must be made, against General Seely and Mr. Churchill is that they should have attempted to give orders so grave in a quarrel, in which they did not believe, to General Paget, and should not even have thought it necessary to reduce these orders to writing.

The comment upon General Paget is, of course, at least as grave. A subaltern would have had more sense than to take such orders after lunch and without a written voucher. But Generals in private talk always damn politicians, and in public matters are invariably chloroformed by them.

Even graver incidents than Ulster (and that

was grave enough) were to supervene. The curtain
opened upon the scene of the Great War. Our
South African soldier of fortune immediately applied
for and obtained military employment at the Front.
He was in it from the start; took part in the whole
retreat, and in the glorious recovery on the Marne.
When the Allied counter-offensive was brought to a
stop on the Aisne, he was sent by Sir John French
to Antwerp to report on the situation, and for services, the principal of which was the contribution
of a gay and personal gallantry, he was mentioned
in despatches, and was made a Commander of the
Crown of Belgium. He was in Dixmude the night
before it fell. Admiral Rolland's sailors, with whom
he fought, who had advanced on the town in one of
the epic episodes of the war, refused to surrender,
and were killed to a man. No more valiant defence
was made in the war.

In January, 1915, Lord Kitchener gave Seely
command of the Canadian Cavalry Brigade, consisting of the two Canadian permanent cavalry
regiments, Lord Strathcona's Horse and the Royal
Canadian Dragoons, the two permanent batteries
of the Canadian Royal Horse Artillery, and the
Second King Edward's Horse—a yeomanry regiment
mostly composed of Englishmen and Scotchmen
from the Dominions. The aggregate force was about
4,000 men. The Brigade left England early in May.
It was attached to the 1st Canadian Division, and
took part in the Battle of Festubert.

Towards the end of the battle Seely found himself in command of all the Canadian units. He
was mentioned in despatches, and received the
C.B. There followed a long period of trench warfare,

lasting till January, 1916, during which the Brigade occupied many sectors of the line from Ploegsteert and the Ypres salient. Thereafter this Brigade, together with all available cavalry, was engaged in training with a view to that break-through on the Somme which the dreamers at the G.H.Q. (but no one else) believed to offer a fruitful field for cavalry activity. This folly was soon corrected ¡by the experience of the battle, and in its later phases the Brigade was employed as infantry.

In March, 1917, the Germans retired to the Hindenburg Line, and the Brigade was ordered forward, with instructions to occupy a long front of about fourteen miles with the infantry just beyond Peronne. Seely, characteristically enough, galloped along the whole front, and perceived that the Germans were delaying the Allied advance with very small forces. He concentrated his Brigade by night (omitting by an oversight to inform his superior officers) and arranged to attack and capture Equancourt, then apparently the centre of resistance. The operation was entirely successful, and after capturing the place he sent word back to the infantry commanders some miles behind, suggesting that they should occupy the captured position. This they did, and the same night he received a telegram from Sir Douglas Haig, congratulating his Brigade on a brilliant feat of arms. Early the next morning he was awakened in bed by the infantry corps commander, demanding in a furious rage to know what he meant by ordering his men about without reference to him. Seely's explanations left him unmollified, and he informed his insubordinate officer that he intended immediately to summon a Court of Inquiry. By a brilliant after-thought, the Commander-in-Chief's telegram was produced, and the enraged warrior was immediately appeased.

On the next day the Brigade attacked and took Guyencourt Ridge. It was on this occasion that Lieut. Harvey, of Lord Strathcona's Horse, an International Rugby football player, won the V.C. for an astonishing act of gallantry. Commanding the leading troop, he found at Guyencourt hidden wire and a trench with forty Germans in it and one machine gun. He galloped up to the wire, slipped off his horse as he approached it, jumped the wire on foot, and, with a revolver in his hand, shot the machine gunner ; then turned the machine gun on the trench, killing twelve of the enemy in less time than it takes to tell.

From Guyencourt Seely advanced to Athis, where he was plunged into extreme sorrow, for his eldest and very gallant son Frank had been killed leading his company of the Hampshire Regiment at the Battle of Arras. He was profoundly shaken by this tragic bereavement, but received it with the same Spartan spirit with which he would have met his own disablement or death.

Space does not allow me to recount all the achievements of this brilliant Brigade. It led the first big tank attack at Cambrai on November 20th. One of his Squadron Leaders received the V.C., having captured a German battery and sabred the gunners himself. Later still, when the great German assault came, General Seely, under the orders of General Pellé, commanding the 5th French Corps, fought a rearguard action covering Noyen, and gave time to the French Corps to withdraw all their artillery as well as their infantry corps across the river. General Pellé issued the following order on the 26th March :—

Au moment où la 2me Division de Cavalerie anglais et la Brigade de Cavalerie canadien quittent le 5me Corps d'Armée français, je viens à leur exprimer ma reconnaissance. La conduite de ces belles troupes pendant la journée de 26 mars a forcé l'admiration de tous.

One more incident must be narrated in the history of this remarkable Brigade. On the morning of March 30th it was at Boves, the retreat still continuing, and the Germans being within eight miles of Amiens. General Pitman told Seely that the situation was wellnigh desperate, and instructed him to go forward, in the hope of co-operating, without engaging his force too completely. The Brigade started off from the east, threaded its way by two bridges over the small stream which runs through Boves, passed into the open country, and went over successive ridges towards Moreuil. Seely galloped forward with his signal troop to the village of Castel, where he found a French Divisional Commander, who told him that part of his Division still occupied the village of Moreuil; but that the ridge and wood were in possession of the Germans. It seemed to Seely that unless they could be dislodged Amiens must fall; the division between the French and English armies would be complete; and all would be lost. He told the incredulous French General that he would recapture Moreuil Wood. The General hopefully but incredulously replied : " I have given orders for the evacuation of Moreuil, but I will hold on while you try to do it."

Few more gallant feats of arms were performed during the war. Indeed a miracle happened. There were more than 700 Germans in the wood at the critical moment; and casualties among the horses rapidly reduced the charging Brigade to an infantry battalion. The hero of the assault was Captain Flowerdew, commanding the leading squadron, which was Strathcona's. He was mortally wounded, but cried out, " Carry on. We've won." He received—and nobly earned—a posthumous V.C.

On April 3rd General Rawlinson, just appointed to command the 4th Army, addressed the Brigade and thanked them for their brilliant services. On April 4th the official communiqué contained this sentence : " In the recent heavy fighting on the River Loos the Canadian Cavalry Brigade repeatedly distinguished itself by successful attack both mounted and dismounted." Seely himself was gassed on April 1st, but carried on for ten days, when he was ordered to hospital. His work in France was done, for shortly afterwards he was ordered home to take up the duties of Vice-President of the Munitions Council. He carried from the War a trophy which I think he will value more than all his decorations, in the shape of a cigarette case which Marshal Foch sent him in memory of the Moreuil day, inscribed : "*Au Ministre de* 1912 : *au Vaillant de la Grand Guerre.*"

And he took with him to Canada in 1920 this message from the same Field-Marshal to the men who had faced death so often by his side :

I hope you will tell the men of your fine Brigade that I rejoice to send them a message. In the great German attack of March, 1918, at the most agonising moment of the battle of the 30th March, your Brigade, by its incomparable dash and valour, recaptured the Morcuil ridge, and thus contributed in the highest degree to saving the whole Allied position.

General Seely was mentioned in the course of the War five times in Military Despatches and once in Naval Despatches. He lost his eldest son on the field of battle, was himself gassed, and had as many hairbreadth escapes as any man in the British Army who survives. He was the National Liberal candidate in a Derbyshire constituency, which he would undoubtedly have retained against his Socialist opponent if Mr. Bonar Law had not been advised by Colonel Leslie Wilson to write a letter of encouragement to a farcical Conservative candidate, whose intervention, trivial as it was, was just sufficient to hand over the seat to the Bolshevist. Such was the man who was defeated: such were the men who defeated him.

Lord Bearsted

Lord Bearsted

VERY few people realise it, but Lord Bearsted is one of the great men of our day. He has counted for more, and done far more, than many eloquent gentlemen who fill a conspicuous place in our popular Press.

It was only in 1921, a little more than three years ago, that Sir Marcus Samuel was raised to the Peerage. He had long been a leader in commercial life, so that this bestowal may have seemed a belated recognition. But his knighthood, which recalled a great service to the Navy, dated from 1898. His baronetcy, of civic origin, went back to 1903. The highest honour was appropriately timed. For it was stamped with the eventfulness of a period of history not yet closed—a period which still fires the mind with thoughts of the strange accidents, the stranger deliverances, of a great world-war. And to some of these deliverances, Sir Marcus Samuel, now Lord Bearsted of Maidstone, contributed as much as many men whose names are better known.

His promotion, in the face of some evident disadvantages, was the fruit of many triumphs. It pointed to the originality, the vigilance, the perennial resourcefulness of a highly vitalised career.

He was welcomed to the red benches of the House of Lords by peers both spiritual and temporal. Nor was the Press unkind even if it was not specially well informed. Lord Bearsted of " The Mote " now holds in Kent a possession which recalls the ancient *môt*, the assemblage of olden time, with all its associations of immemorial freedom. The amenities of his home, where he entertains all sorts and conditions of men, chime admirably with his leadership in the City of London, where, having added lustre to the Lord Mayor's seat, he is now the Senior Alderman.

Nor can it be forgotten what obstacles have beset the pathway of the pioneer.

It was in East London, on November 5, 1853, that Marcus Samuel, his father's second son, was born. The region is one which answers to special calls, and in many ways is quite unlike the picture traditional contempt has tried to draw. There belongs to it a peculiar spell; because it is an outlet to the sea. Other influences were strong for the boy. His father held an established place in the Jewish community. Both to the racial and paternal factor the son has often paid loyal tribute, and the somewhat remote world of Whitechapel has been a considerable gainer thereby.

Thus, if the beginnings of life were relatively small, the antecedents were honourable. And the prospects were wide. Some early tuition was received at Edmonton; but an imaginative nature chiefly educates itself. The East London of Lord Bearsted's youth has expanded greatly. The Port of London itself, which owes much to him, has vastly expanded too. Here the daily life of the streets has perpetually surged with inflow and outflow of men and merchandise, which exert a compelling power where the intercourse of nations is constantly vibrating. In this vibration there is nothing more insistent than " the call of the East."

Away from home a fresh chance of development was given in Brussels. The Gallic tongue will yield up its mysteries if resolutely attacked. There was tremendous resolution in the youthful Samuel. It was perhaps in his case to the good that he preferred to acquire, what for most Englishmen is difficult, a serviceable knowledge of French, rather than to cultivate the rudiments of a conventional Latinity. His course lay clearly planned. At the early age of nineteen he made a definite start on a business career in the Far East.

The Samuel interests were solid enough, with a father's influence in the background and an elder brother near at hand. But the self-reliance of the young man quickly asserted itself. He soon swung into a busy life of vast operations. Famine stretched its tentacles over India. Organisation was desperately needed. If food was a necessity, effective supplies from outside, especially of rice, were more urgent still. Marcus Samuel explored every conceivable channel of relief, and achieved, young as he was, more than one conspicuous personal triumph by his energy, perseverance, originality, and practical resourcefulness. At this point romance, at any rate that of travel, touched his prospects and drove him forward.

I do not know precisely at what stage our adventurer foresaw that he would wear the mantle of Whittington, or stretch the bow of Ulysses, or acquire the immense purse of Fortunatus. But I do know that his natural prevision was always remarkable. Sir Forrest Fulton, presenting him to the Lord Chancellor in 1902, laid special stress on " sagacity and foresight " as characteristic of the new Lord

Mayor. But the high possibilities, which in this and other ways had been turned into realities, were largely derived from the experience which had ripened into abundant knowledge. From China or Malacca, from Formosa or Sumatra, from Sarawak or Borneo, from Siam or Egypt, with diligence and determination, the most precious trade secrets were gradually wrested in days now remote. But all this was not possible of accomplishment without a struggle; nor, again, without corresponding advances into territories wider than those of trade.

Trade, as such, is seldom the sole object of a great personality. In this particular case, Nature herself was lavish to redundancy of her greatest gifts, though few knew where to look for them or what to do with them when found.

But the many-sided man looks out for chances. Trade on any advanced scale implies finance. Finance soon involves politics. International politics, to effect anything at all, must ripen into statesmanship. The individual who travels widely considers these things because he is forced to think outside himself. Marcus Samuel took particular stock, so it happened, of Japan·

There was a time when to most people the Land of the Rising Sun was sufficiently represented by that poetic emblem, when ideas about Japan seemed to have little substance. By study and observation the stability, character, and ultimate destiny of the island-state of the East became practical certainties, though many, in this island-state at home, feared and misunderstood the new orientation. Nevertheless, Japan came, financially, into a reasoned esteem. The first City commitment, in the shape of a loan subscribed in London, was a Samuel commitment.

From that success Lord Bearsted has never turned back. But it is even more important to remember that Japan is still an object-lesson cogent enough to modify current or preconceived views of the world's history. Years ago, when Japan was at war with Russia, the many were in favour of backing the wrong horse. Lord Bearsted declared that Japan was the right horse, and he backed his fancy with all his resources.

So much for the fiscal, political, patriotic effort. It speaks for itself. But it possesses an interesting corollary for the world of business also. Lord Bearsted's belief in petroleum was drawn from the same well of conviction, his own mind ; and frequently it met with the same sort of questioning. Yet the greatness of Japan as a nation now appears as a natural fact. And when a commodity, such as petroleum, is given to man by Nature, there is no more limit to its development, under scientific control, than there is to the advance which a gifted people can make by the aid of the sea.

This parallel gives point to many things that Lord Bearsted has succeeded in doing during the last thirty years. Many of his enterprises have brought great advantage to this country. He has added something more than a footnote to the history of his times : he has succeeded in supplying a most interesting chapter, from which future generations will continue to learn.

The first petroleum wells had been rendered commercially potent in the 'sixties. For a long time the nearest approaches to success were Americans and Britain entered the field at some disadvantage. But whether American, Dutch, or British, many were the fortunes sunk in fruitless developments. Lord Bearsted himself will testify that it might almost become a misfortune to "strike oil," if no outlet could be found for the crude substance, and no assurance that the world was ready for any quantity of this dynamic product. That uncertainty long prevailed, so much so, that a little time before the year 1914 petroleum actually became a drug in the market. Nevertheless, concurrent with this uncertainty, a conviction gained ground that a new driving-power, a challenge above all things to the waste and wastefulness of coal, must soon effect a metamorphosis everywhere. And inventiveness advanced every effort to make this promise good.

Figures are sometimes fallacious, and percentages misleading; but an indication of the change that has taken place, in one direction alone, is given in the fact that the use of liquid fuel at sea has in the last ten years increased tenfold. Our own eyes tell us what petrol is doing on land. Its possibilities in the air are infinite. Those who believed when days were dark are as confident now that to whatever heights the demand may rise the teeming supplies of the earth will respond : more, that the economic difficulties connected with the supply will be adjusted. These anticipations I share ; but still one must realise how they ever came within the realm of probability. They did so because one man rose to every opportunity, shrinking from no audacious experiment, giving support to every reasonable undertaking, however perilous. Appropriately enough, Lord Bearsted was the moving spirit all through, and of his eventful career in this respect I must now speak as fully as I can within my limits, regarding him in the triple capacity of trader, financier, and researcher. Inspiring all has been the singlehearted-ness of a forty years' faith.

The trader, in early days, had to consider such problems as the cupidity of packers; the tainting of cargoes; the clearing of jungles; the provision of equipment; the supply of men and their main-tenance; the construction of ships; and the rivalry of men and magnates.

In relation to the last point, here are the words of Lord Bearsted himself:

> When I started I was convinced that only a world-wide system which would prevent my opponents from annihil-ating me was necessary, and so, contrary to the opinion of many of my associates, I established depots simul-taneously throughout the Far East. Had I not done so, the Standard Oil Company could have made a dead set against me, and so have brought about my ruin.

These words betray the man. Other words throw a yet more penetrating light:

> I had to fight another enemy: this was the Royal Dutch Company, afterwards destined to become my business associates.

There is something more in this than the episodic clash of commercial warfare, for the strategy was as fine as the battlefield was unusual. The daring of the resolute campaigner is seen at one point; the astuteness of the wise diplomatist at another. He goes forward with Trojan zeal: he takes a rebuff or bides a later time with Spartan patience. When he came really to an issue with the Standard Company, he swiftly made it plain that he had forestalled them. When he made terms with the Dutch, they could have cut his trading throat, and yet it was to a new Dutch field that he was able to look when other supplies had failed. It was to such concessions as these that fresh developments were due. And there was more in the Dutch alliance than I can record here; it was a conjunction not to be despised; it remains an object-lesson in international co-operation.

I turn to the researcher. Lord Bearsted is a researcher of no mean order whose research has been conducted away from a laboratory, with his own eyes, and by the exercise of a kind of sublimated common sense. But he has been an inventor as well. For one problem he devised a new fan for exhausting petroleum gas rapidly from the holds of steamers. For other problems he devised plans which were gladly adopted by marine engineers as soon as they comprehended his original idea of using oil-fuel beneath the boilers of ships. The utilising of the double bottoms of ships for the carriage of oil in bulk is one of his achievements; and of the movement which gave us the internal combustion engine he was a champion—a pioneer, indeed, in applying its lessons to marine engines. He it was when petrol to the value of half a million sterling could not be utilised, who recommended with success the return of the substance to the earth, so justifying once more, in a complicated situation, the simplest and most obvious of remedies. *Pari passu* with this progressive ingenuity came the discovery of toluol, a thing which our Government regarded coldly, but the French were ready, even with enthusiasm, to grasp. For the piping days of peace external treatment might suffice. Our later necessity was for an internal lubricant. When we entered that great struggle we were almost in extremity. Our affairs were seriously disturbed within ; it was anything but easy for innovators to get a hearing.

It seems providential now that persistence gained the day. It is lucky that Mr. Winston Churchill was in charge of the Admiralty on the outbreak of hostilities, and that for some twenty years from the year 1892 the name of Admiral Fisher had guaranteed efficiency and far-sightedness in the Navy. It was, in fact, Lord Fisher who became Chairman of the Royal Commission on Oil Fuel in 1912. Meanwhile Sir Marcus Samuel, as another admiral, long after the war was over, declared, never left the authorities alone until all his points were practically conceded.

The support of Lord Fisher was a great gain. But in season and out of season the pioneer himself had to be continually hammering at the Admiralty doors. Yet that was not enough. There came a time when our own material resources were quite inadequate to carry out plans for making high explosives in England. A refinery was imported from Holland, England as a whole little dreaming that such an undertaking had even been contemplated. The German menace was at its height. Many another experiment had to be carried out with similar contempt for the risks that must be run. But these things were accomplished in such a way that Lord Bearsted is entitled to be regarded as one of the deliverers of his country.

Research, too, exerted here and in many another field its penetrating activity, and in the end reaped its overwhelming reward. The Samuel interests have been for many years most liberal to the

University of Cambridge. Lord Bearsted's name is one to conjure with in Birmingham and in Sheffield. He has lavished gifts on London and Maidstone. To recite his benefactions, devoted as they have been to art and to science, to education and to philanthropy, is scarcely necessary ; but the breadth of his sympathies is one of the most attractive features of his character, and whilst in the trader, the researcher, the financier I observe a practical application of straightforward business principle which pursues an object relentlessly ; I see also in Lord Bearsted one who has bestowed many favours both in private and in public, which prove him to be by nature considerate, patriotic, and genuinely benevolent.

As an ally of Nature—which does more splendid things for us than we can do for ourselves, though graciously disposed to accept, if not to require, some degree of human encouragement—Lord Bearsted has played a part in our times which is at once vital and instructive. He is not by any means played out. History, I think, will do justice to one who did much to rescue this country from dangers and disasters which were but vaguely understood ; to aid him it is fortunate that there were some whose understanding availed, against great odds, to win through. An ingenious writer once counted the decisive battles of the world as in number fifteen. I do not know how many of the victories of this last great war should be counted as decisive : I think that there were at least five ; but if there were only three, Lord Bearsted must in virtue of toluol be counted as the winner of one of them. And he would, I think, be willing that I should associate with his the brilliant and learned name of the late Lord Moulton.

Sir Harold Smith, K.C., M.P.

Photo: Beresford.

Sir Harold Smith, K.C., M.P.

RECORDER OF BLACKBURN. BENCHER OF GRAY'S INN

[*No one would have ridiculed more mercilessly than my brother Harold, at the time of his death, the idea that in the span of years allotted to him he had made good his claim to be included in a series of contemporary personalities. But something must be conceded to fraternal piety. The article which follows will, I hope, make it plain, upon evidence less partial than mine, that he possessed many varied qualities. His life, though happy and full of zest, was marked at every stage by anxieties. I cannot doubt that, with the maturing and strengthening of great natural parts, he would have risen to eminence in his own profession ; and possibly to a position of considerable importance in the world of politics, which he very well understood.*]

FOR a brother to write of a brother must always be a task of delicacy, and yet I think, at least with the aid of death, that it may be surmounted.

So much that was kind and thoughtful has been written about my late brother since his premature death, that I should have thought it unnecessary to add anything but a sincere and grateful message of thanks but for one single circumstance.

Many of the notices of his career have spoken of him as if he were some paler phantom of myself, reflecting my views, and my personality, rather than possessing his own.

To the family, and to those who knew us both well, such a conception is simply absurd. Perhaps I can illustrate that absurdity best by stating a few circumstances in his own career.

He was one of five children left fatherless by the death, at the age of forty-three, of the late Frederick Smith, Barrister-at-Law, of Birkenhead. Our mother was left with about £500 a year with which to educate, clothe and support five children—three boys and two girls. All the boys were educated—I hardly know how—at the Birkenhead School, a school far too good to be inexpensive. Evidently no University education was conceivable, except for a boy who could win a scholarship. Harold's mind did not run upon these lines. He reached, indeed, considerable distinction in English Literature, and in History; and if the Birkenhead School of that day had specialised, in suitable cases, in Modern History, he would unquestionably have reached scholarship form, either in that subject or in literature. But in pure scholarship he proved no apt or very interested pupil. And so it happened that at the age of seventeen it became necessary for him to choose a career, at an age when his own judgment was even more immature than mine. Little suitable guidance was forthcoming. In an unhappy moment he was apprenticed to a firm of Cotton Brokers in Liverpool, which accepted his services, such as they were, for five years, and taught him, though he was intelligent and receptive, nothing of the slightest value upon the technical side of the business. He was used simply to carry messages from one Liverpool firm of brokers to another. These years were absolutely wasted.

I cannot help contrasting the way in which I myself was able to spend those years. I was a scholar of Wadham College. The whole of the cultivation of Oxford was open to me. I was placed at once in competition with, and was able to measure the capacity of, all those who were to be my rivals at the Bar and in politics. Whether I was reading for the schools or not, I was all the time being educated. The most brilliant young men in England were my companions, my friends, my rivals; and during this period Harold was running uninformed errands from one broker's office to another.

He then went into the frozen meat business under the friendly guidance of his life-long friend, Mr. William Byrne. Here he became immediately successful; and he would undoubtedly have attained a very considerable measure of material prosperity had he adhered to an occupation which he completely mastered; and which every year became of greater national importance. But a family business, nearly one hundred years old, in Birkenhead—a Valuing and Estate Agency—claimed, for family reasons, his support; and thereafter, with very great success, he devoted himself to the study of a third and entirely different branch of business activity. Upon this subject he became an authority.

I must not omit from this summary of his life at this time, other sides of a very various personality. He was an absolutely first-class Rugby football player. He played for Birkenhead Park, for Cheshire, for the North of England; for the Barbarians; and in a misapprehension of his qualification, he was selected to play for Ireland. He became a very fine lawn tennis player; not attaining of course to the very first rank—he never in his busy life had the leisure—but playing for the County of Northamptonshire and able to hold his own in any company. Thorough at this game, as at everything which he undertook, he became a consummate master of court craft: indeed, in the knowledge of a game to which I have given much time, but in which I have acquired little proficiency, he was second to none. In later years he organised the Parliamentary team; and played in the first pair with his devoted friend Leo Lyle.

In another and very different pursuit he possessed talents altogether extraordinary. He was an amateur actor of very great brilliancy. By a strange chance Beerbohm Tree happened to be in the North of England when Harold was playing, in an amateur society, the part of Svengali in " Trilby." Generous as always, Tree wrote to him :—

" You are the first amateur actor whom in the whole of my life I have urged to take up the stage as a profession. I am confident that, if you do so, you will meet with brilliant success."

By this time I had acquired a degree of authority and influence, partly, I think, founded upon my own success; but more upon affection; which made it certain that my brother would at least carefully consider any advice which I offered him. I threw the whole weight of that influence in the attempt to persuade him to give up business; to abandon all thought of the stage; and to adopt the Bar and politics. He had satisfied me that he possessed the qualities required for success in both pursuits. And

I knew well (none better) how exacting were the standards of both.

In the end I prevailed, and he fought a gallant though a notoriously hopeless fight in Huddersfield, almost at the same moment that he entered as a student the Society of Gray's Inn, of which he was one day to become a Bencher, and one of the most influential members. There are many in Huddersfield who still recall his campaign.

He was thirty-three years old when he entered Gray's Inn. He had not been specially trained for the Bar. I was able to give him little help; for at the Bar nearly every one, unless closely connected with an important firm of Solicitors, must depend upon his own powers. But he had some evident assets. He had business experience; he had limitless courage and energy; at that time of his life he seemed to have exuberant health; and he possessed a very distinguished appearance. Six feet high, with the lithe and muscular frame of an athlete, he combined an extremely dark colouring with very vivid blue eyes.

His career was one of more than ordinary success; and after twelve years he found himself in a position to take silk without either grave risk or excessive self-confidence.

As a Silk he made great and almost unexpected progress; and indeed his income at the time of his death placed his professional prospects beyond reasonable doubt. The present Master of the Rolls, shortly before his promotion, was engaged against him in a long and troublesome case, which involved arguments on many difficult points of law. He told me with generous warmth that Harold was master of them all; and that on every point he proved himself a formidable and fully-equipped opponent. Mr. Justice Horridge, one of the most learned of our King's Bench judges, wrote to me, with the knowledge of one before whom he often appeared :—" He was both a brilliant advocate and a very fully-equipped lawyer." Mr. Justice Rigby Swift wrote of him in a touching letter :—" He was my dearest friend ; and I do not think that I was much less to him." And now that he has gone, it is possible to say that he had so definitely stamped his influence and personality upon the Society of Gray's Inn as to make it plain that, if a long life had been conceded to him, he must have become one of that responsible few who keep burning brightly from generation to generation the torch of our famous Inns of Court.

In the midst of all this legal advancement he wrested from the Liberal Party the constituency of Warrington. Warrington politically is a curious place ; and I believe that in the whole history of this ancient borough, no one has ever represented it before without local interest. The Socialists are very strong there. He defeated the Socialists and, in my judgment, would have continued to defeat them, by using their own weapons. In the market-place at Warrington there is a spot suitable for public disputation. The Socialists appropriated it, as they appropriate all such places in every industrial centre. But they were driven from it. Night after night, in winter and summer, Harold Smith was to be found there addressing all who cared to hear him, in the open air ; and meeting and beating the Socialists at their own game ; and with their own weapons. He was always ready to debate on their platform, or on his, with their most redoubtable champion. He won the seat at one election, he held it at another ; I cannot believe that he would have lost it. But he was a strong supporter of the Coalition ; and " Die-hard " influences in the constituency rendered his position intolerable to a proud man. He exchanged it for the Wavertree Division of Liverpool. Warrington has since been lost to the Socialists ; it will not be regained except by a candidate possessing my brother's gifts and courage. No " Die-hard " will ever win that seat.

When the War came, he was, indeed, a man whose health was affected, though neither he, nor those who loved him, realised any incurability in the ailments of which even then he complained. In the case of an athletic man they merely occasioned anxiety. He offered himself at once for military service, and was rejected. He carried the matter himself to the highest court of medical appeal ; and was told that he was wholly unfit—he was then thirty-nine years of age—for service in the field. He thereupon obtained a commission in the R.N.R. and sacrificed his profession (a month after he was married) to the task of carrying naval despatches. This duty he discharged to the end of the War ; narrowly on more than one occasion escaping hostile torpedoes.

I must add a word of his work at the Press Bureau. That Bureau was universally admitted to be necessary ; it was universally abused and resented by the Press. He, and he alone, organised it upon its business side, in the first fortnight of the War. No such institution was known, or had hitherto been conceived of, in this country. If the greatest genius in the world had organised it, its unpopularity would have been no less. For what he did I received alike the credit and the discredit. But the edifice which he, by a rare effort of imaginative originality, created, was never, in its main features, departed from until the date of the Armistice. Lord Buckmaster and his successors maintained it almost as he left it. A moment's reflection will not be wasted upon the gigantic task of those who conceived the necessary nature of this office; and in a month determined and defined its permanent course. When Lord Buckmaster left the Directorship in order to become Lord Chancellor he wrote to him : " It is impossible to exaggerate the services which you rendered by the original and able work which you did when the Bureau was first set up."

He was most mercifully spared the knowledge of the nature of his ailment and of the certainty of his death until the night before he died. He had little suffering except that which must always follow upon an operation so deep-seated. The day before that operation he put all his affairs in order with cool composure. An accumulation of terrible physical symptoms told at the end their plain tale to a mind so acute.

But for at least a fortnight after his removal to the country, cheating hopes deluded him and us. Sitting in his beautiful country garden, amid the flowers which he loved so much, it seemed to all of us that he was gaining strength. But one by one those hopes were chilled; though at first for each unfavourable symptom an explanation could be honestly given which did not exclude hope. But there came a day when he was no longer strong enough to leave his bed for the garden. Nor did he ever leave it again.

And the night before his death he had a complete realisation of his cruel and imminent fate. He sent first for his doctor and thanked him for kindly and friendly services, adding : " I see now that from the first you were set a hopeless task." He then asked to see me, and talked to me for twenty minutes with complete calmness and fortitude. I do not, for reasons which are plain, set out that talk here ; but I would add that he said to me : " I feel nothing of the Dr. Johnson terror of death ; I am completely happy and comfortable ; but I would like to have played a longer hand in the game."

He then asked to see his wife ; and with her he spoke for half an hour, forgetting nothing of which it behoved him at such a moment to speak to her.

Ten minutes after she left him he became unconscious ; and was never to speak again.

To me it has happened in the short period of six months to stand at the graveside of two dear and strong brothers, both younger than myself. Of my brother Captain Sydney Smith I say nothing in this place ; but I have written this of Harold because it grieves me that such an injustice should be done to his memory as to suppose that he was some faint re-echo of myself. He was, on the contrary, a man who gave strength himself ; and had need to derive it from no other. My own life is indefinably weakened by his death. I am a poorer man in virtue of it.

Index

Index

Index

Index

Index

Index

Scotland, Scotsmen, 55, 75, 134, 139, 143, 166
Scott, Sir Walter, 105
Scrope, Lord, 225
Seager, Bishop, 229
Sedan, 4
Seely, Frank, 295
Seely, General John, 287–98
Selborne, Earl of, 181
Shakespeare, 101 ; (quoted), 85
Shaughnessy, Lord, 206
Sheffield, 308
Sherbrooke, Viscount (Robert Lowe), 67
Siam, 84, 99
Simon, Right Hon. Sir John, 15, 154
Sinn Feiners, 196
Smith, Frederick, 310
Smith, Capt. Sydney, 317
Smith, Sir Harold, K.C., M.P., 309
Snowden, Mrs., 235
Snowden, Rt. Hon. Philip, 43, 153, 231–8
Soap, 283–5
Social Reform, 18
Socialism, Socialist, Socialists, 10, 41, 49, 72, 173, 182, 185, 192, 231–8, 283, 298, 314
" Soldiers' Friend," the, 151
Somerset House, 87
Somme, battle of the, 147, 200
South African War, the, 18
Southampton, 289
Southport, 282
South Wales, 188
Soviet murders, 121
Standard Oil Company, 305
Stanley, family of, 125–6, 223, 225
Star Chamber, 157
Star, The, 261
" Stedfast," 127
Steele, Richard, 262
Stevenson, R. L., 139, 163
Stewards' Cup, Henley, 215
Stock Exchange, 105
Strachan, Sir Richard, 89
Strand, the, 253
Strathcona's Horse, 295
Sumatra, 302
Sumner, Lord, 271
Sun, The, 261
Sunday Times, The, 33
Sunlight Soap, 283–5
Surtees, John, 101
Sutton, Mr., of Manchester, 241
Swift, Mr. Justice Rigby, 314
Swindon, 187

TAINE, 272
Tait, Archbishop, 55, 57, 60
Tanks, 120, 121
Tariff Reform, 2, 117, 291
Tea-parties, International, 77
Temple, Archbishop, 57
Thackeray's " Book of Snobs," 130
Thomas, Rt. Hon. J. H., 185, 193, 235
Times, The, 89, 172, 211
Toluol, 306
Tories, 5, 13, 116, 156, 216, 221
T.P.'s Weekly, 262
Trade, Board of, 4
Transvaal, the, 40
Treasury, the, 66, 109
Tree, Sir H. Beerbohm, 313
Trinity College, Cambridge, 65, 279
Trinity College, Dublin, 195
Trinity College, Oxford, 55
Trinity Hall, Cambridge, 215
Trotsky, M., 49
Turkey, 90, 170

UGANDA, 98
Ullswater, Viscount, 224
Ulster, 8, 17, 29, 168, 173, 200
Ulysses, 301
Union-Castle Line, 289
Union of Railwaymen, the National, 187
Unionist Party, 4, 66, 83
United States, the, 50, 108–9
University College, Oxford, 239
Ursa Major, 175
Utrecht, 290

VALERA, EAMON DE, 207
Venice, 278
Verdun, 147
Vereeniging, Peace of, 145
Versailles, Treaty of, 38
Via Dolorosa, 150
Viceroyalty of India, the, 110
Victoria, Queen, 271

WADHAM COLLEGE, OXFORD, 311
" Wait and See " phrase, 30
Walpole, Sir Robert, 193
War Cabinet, 9, 70, 202, 245
War Office, the, 77
Warrington, 314
Washington, 170
Waterloo, 141
Wavertree Division, Liverpool, 315
Webb, Sidney, 49, 52
Weekly Sun, The, 261

Index